SADLIER

Grammar Workshop

Common Core Enriched Edition

Grades 3–5

Common Core Connection

Sadlier

GrammarWorkshop.com

- **NEW** lessons and practice to meet the Common Core State Standards
- **NEW** online, interactive quizzes for each lesson that are automatically scored
- Simple, systematic three-step lessons that make learning and teaching quick and easy

Aligned to Common Core

BUILDING A FOUNDATION IN LANGUAGE

In full alignment with the Common Core State Standards, *Grammar Workshop*'s explicit instruction in grammar, usage, and mechanics—**the conventions of standard English**—helps students meet the new standards.

- Standards-based program that explicitly teaches the conventions of standard English
- Systematic three-step lessons that make learning and teaching quick and easy
- Flexibility for use with any English Language Arts program

Through **explicit instruction**, ample practice, and immediate application of skills, students will master grade-appropriate conventions of standard English.

- Each Level is divided into six units focused on teaching:
  - Sentences
  - Nouns
  - Verbs
  - Adjectives, Adverbs, and Prepositions*
  - Pronouns
  - Capitalization, Punctuation, and Spelling

Correlations to the CCSS are also available within the teacher's edition, or online at **GrammarWorkshop.com**

Beverly Ann Chin, Ph.D., Senior Series Consultant and Professor of English and Director of the English Teaching Program at the University of Montana

*Only in grades 4 and 5.

FOCUSING ON CONVENTIONS OF STANDARD ENGLISH

Explicit instruction focused on communication of written ideas clearly and correctly helps students understand the conventions of standard English.

With *Grammar Workshop*, Common Core Enriched Edition:

- Lessons provide direct instruction and model the rules of grammar, usage, and mechanics
- Scaffolded exercises include an integrated array of online components
- Lessons and reviews present a variety of contexts and applications
- Students write or revise sentences by expanding and combining them

Teacher's Edition

- **Common Core State Standards correlation** is noted on the lesson pages.
- Clear, concise lesson plans offer three easy steps including writing prompts for independent writing
- The flexible design of the program enables teachers to use it with any English Language Arts program
- Informal Assessments monitor students' progress through their reading, writing, and speaking

Level Orange (4) Teacher's Edition

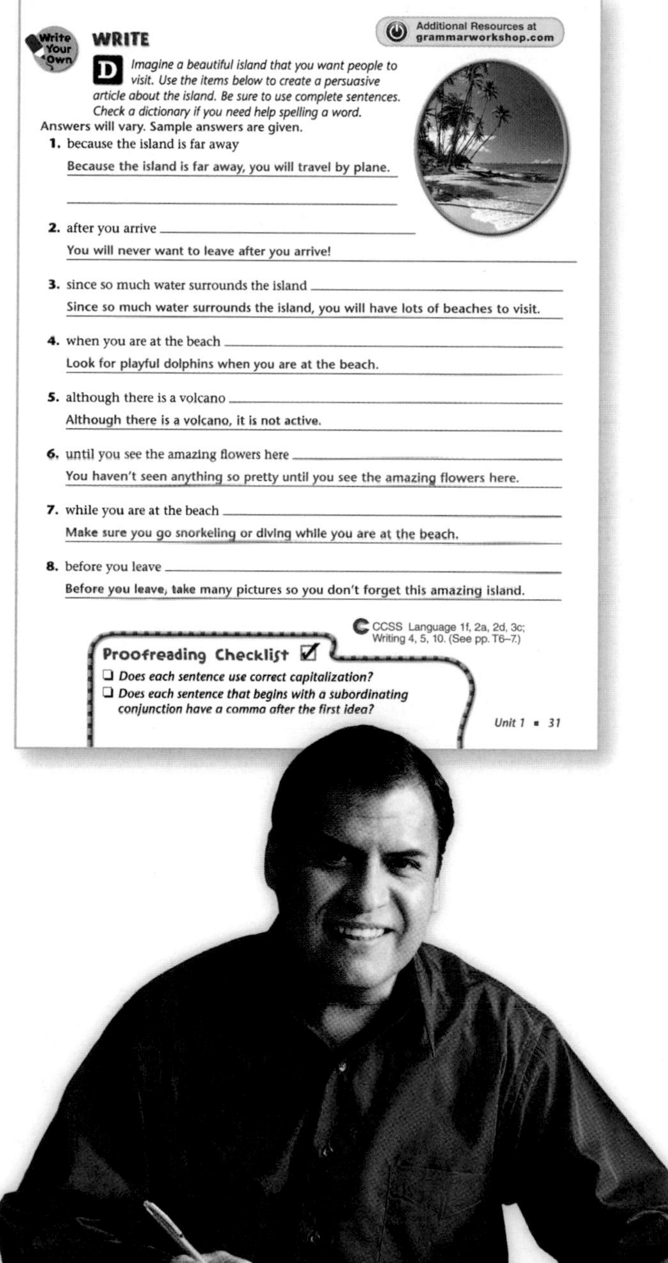

Write Your Own **WRITE**

Additional Resources at grammarworkshop.com

D *Imagine a beautiful island that you want people to visit. Use the items below to create a persuasive article about the island. Be sure to use complete sentences. Check a dictionary if you need help spelling a word.*

Answers will vary. Sample answers are given.

1. because the island is far away
   Because the island is far away, you will travel by plane.
2. after you arrive
   You will never want to leave after you arrive!
3. since so much water surrounds the island
   Since so much water surrounds the island, you will have lots of beaches to visit.
4. when you are at the beach
   Look for playful dolphins when you are at the beach.
5. although there is a volcano
   Although there is a volcano, it is not active.
6. until you see the amazing flowers here
   You haven't seen anything so pretty until you see the amazing flowers here.
7. while you are at the beach
   Make sure you go snorkeling or diving while you are at the beach.
8. before you leave
   Before you leave, take many pictures so you don't forget this amazing island.

CCSS Language 1f, 2a, 2d, 3c; Writing 4, 5, 10. (See pp. T6–7.)

Proofreading Checklist ☑

- ❑ *Does each sentence use correct capitalization?*
- ❑ *Does each sentence that begins with a subordinating conjunction have a comma after the first idea?*

Unit 1 ▪ 31

Aligned to Common Core

GRAMMAR SUCCESS IN THREE STEPS

Each lesson has the same easy-to-follow, three-step instructional sequence:

1. **Learn** features succinct and bite-sized skill instruction with clear explanations and modeling.
2. **Practice** includes three scaffolded activities, each building on the prior and increasing in difficulty.
3. **Write** encourages students to apply what they learned with three types of writing activities: Revising Sentences, Combining Sentences, and Write Your Own.

Step 1: Learn explains and models the **conventions of Standard English**.

Lesson 6: Complex Sentences

LEARN

- You have learned about compound sentences. Compound sentences combine related ideas using a connecting word such as *and, but,* or *or.*

  A **complex sentence** also combines related ideas. The ideas are joined by a **subordinating conjunction**. Look at the sentence below.

  The subordinating conjunction *because* joins the two related ideas.

The following **subordinating conjunctions** are often used to connect related ideas.

Subordinating Conjunctions			
after	although	because	before
since	until	when	while

- The subordinating conjunction may come in the middle of the sentence.
- The subordinating conjunction may come at the beginning of the sentence.

  Notice that when the first idea in the sentence begins with a subordinating conjunction, a comma follows that idea.

PRACTICE

A *Read each sentence. Write **complex** if the sentence is made up of two related ideas joined by a subordinating conjunction. Write **not complex** if it is not a complex sentence.*

1. After a long drive, we finally reached the mountain. ______
2. We wanted to see the mountain because it is so majestic. ______
3. A mountain is higher than the area around it. ______

PRACTICE A *continued*

4. The taller mountains reach into the colder layers of the atmosphere. ______
5. Since the mountain slope is gentle, it is perfect for skiing. ______
6. Mountains take millions of years to form. ______
7. A mountain can form when Earth's crust bends. ______
8. Unlike mountains, the plains are low and flat. ______
9. Because they are low-lying areas, plains can flood easily. ______
10. Plains may be surrounded by small hills or mountains. ______

B *Read each complex sentence. Write the subordinating conjunction that joins the two related ideas. The first one is done for you.*

1. When an earthquake happens, you can take steps to be safe. When
2. You should take cover until the ground stops shaking. ______
3. Since earthquakes sometimes happen under the ocean, you may see waves on the surface. ______
4. A tsunami can take place after an earthquake strikes. ______
5. Some cities are prepared for an earthquake because they have had so many. ______
6. Although some earthquakes are dangerous, most are not. ______
7. Scientists could study an earthquake better when they had the latest tools. ______
8. Before an earthquake hits, some animals seem nervous! ______
9. We saw a wide crack in the ground while we were hiking. ______
10. The ground cracked because parts of the earth had split apart. ______

Level Orange (4) Student Edition

Step 2: Practice lets students put what they've learned to work with three exercise sets of **increasing complexity**.

Step 3: Write gives students an opportunity to further apply grammar skills to their writing.

C *Write a subordinating conjunction to complete each sentence. Choose a subordinating conjunction from the box, or use a subordinating conjunction of your own.*

Remember
A **complex sentence** is formed by joining two related ideas with a subordinating conjunction.

after	although	because	before
since	until	when	while

1. Thomas went to Costa Rica ______ he wanted to see a volcano.
2. ______ I have read about volcanoes, I haven't seen one.
3. Thomas showed us his photographs ______ he returned from his trip.
4. ______ she is a park ranger at Denali National Park, Aunt Mary can tell us about glaciers.
5. Glaciers leave rocks behind ______ they move across the land.
6. ______ we traveled to Alaska last spring, I had never seen a glacier.
7. I read books about glaciers ______ we took our trip.
8. I saw one of these large sheets of ice ______ our plane landed.
9. I put on a heavy coat ______ it is cold on top of a glacier.
10. ______ there once were many glaciers in America, there are few today.
11. ______ some glaciers contain a lot of air, they can look blue.
12. We heard loud noises ______ pieces of a glacier broke off.

Write Your Own

WRITE

Additional Resources at grammarworkshop.com

D *Imagine a beautiful island that you want people to visit. Use the items below to create a persuasive article about the island. Be sure to use complete sentences. Check a dictionary if you need help spelling a word.*

1. because the island is far away ______
2. after you arrive ______
3. since so much water surrounds the island ______
4. when you are at the beach ______
5. although there is a volcano ______
6. until you see the amazing flowers here ______
7. while you are at the beach ______
8. before you leave ______

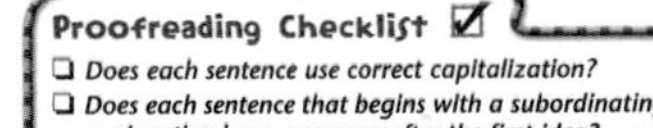

Proofreading Checklist
- ❑ *Does each sentence use correct capitalization?*
- ❑ *Does each sentence that begins with a subordinating conjunction have a comma after the first idea?*

Level Orange (4) Student Edition

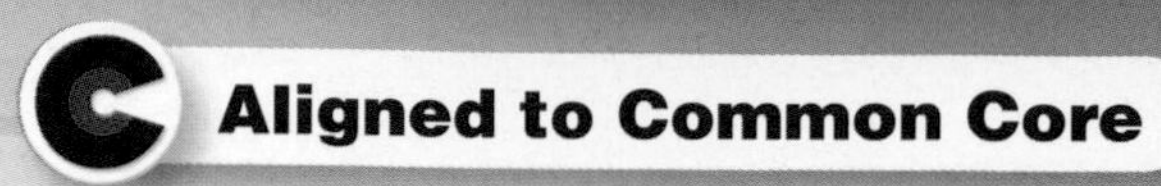

SUPPORT FOR STUDENTS

Featured In the Student Edition

Remember	Reinforces the concept introduced in the lesson
	GrammarWorkshop.com, a fully integrated array of online components supports, reinforces, and enriches lessons
	Spirals back to earlier work, building on prior knowledge and adding to a student's sense of skill mastery
Proofreading Marks	Featured with editing activities, allowing students to practice the skills and concepts taught

∧	Add	ⅇ	Take out	/	Small letter
⊙	Period	≡	Capital letter		

online connections

GrammarWorkshop.com

Each unit includes the following free resources for additional practice:

- Additional Practice worksheets
- Proofreading Passages
- Interactive Games and puzzles

Supports English Language Learners

A variety of suggestions are offered within the Teacher's Edition on teaching English Language Learners (ELL) in their acquisition of vocabulary and language. Check out pages T12 and T13 for more information and ideas!

ASSESSMENT OPTIONS

Student Edition

- Each **Unit Review** includes exercises for each lesson in the Unit. It can serve as reinforcement or as a review of the Unit's skills and concepts.
- Each **Unit Test** assesses students' understanding of the skills and concepts presented in the unit. To provide test-taking practice, each Unit Test utilizes two standardized-test formats.

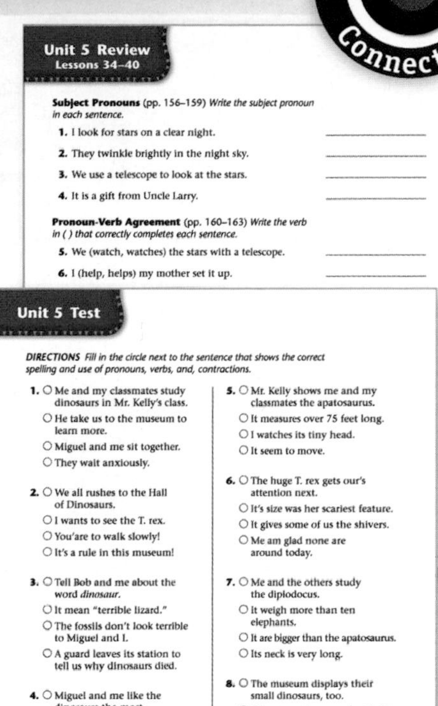

Common Core Connection

Unit 5 Review
Lessons 34–40

Subject Pronouns (pp. 156–159) *Write the subject pronoun in each sentence.*

1. I look for stars on a clear night. ________
2. They twinkle brightly in the night sky. ________
3. We use a telescope to look at the stars. ________
4. It is a gift from Uncle Larry. ________

Pronoun-Verb Agreement (pp. 160–163) *Write the verb in ( ) that correctly completes each sentence.*

5. We (watch, watches) the stars with a telescope. ________
6. I (help, helps) my mother set it up. ________

Unit 5 Test

DIRECTIONS Fill in the circle next to the sentence that shows the correct spelling and use of pronouns, verbs, and contractions.

1. ○ Me and my classmates study dinosaurs in Mr. Kelly's class.
   ○ He take us to the museum to learn more.
   ○ Miguel and me sit together.
   ○ They wait anxiously.
2. ○ We all rushes to the Hall of Dinosaurs.
   ○ I wants to see the T. rex.
   ○ You'are to walk slowly!
   ○ It's a rule in this museum!
3. ○ Tell Bob and me about the word *dinosaur*.
   ○ It mean "terrible lizard."
   ○ The fossils don't look terrible to Miguel and I.
   ○ A guard leaves its station to tell us why dinosaurs died.
4. ○ Miguel and me like the dinosaurs the most.
   ○ They're putting up many new displays in the museum.
   ○ We reads about one display.
   ○ "The Age of Reptiles" is her name.
5. ○ Mr. Kelly shows me and my classmates the apatosaurus.
   ○ It measures over 75 feet long.
   ○ I watches its tiny head.
   ○ It seem to move.
6. ○ The huge T. rex gets our's attention next.
   ○ It's size was her scariest feature.
   ○ It gives some of us the shivers.
   ○ Me am glad none are around today.
7. ○ Me and the others study the diplodocus.
   ○ It weigh more than ten elephants.
   ○ It are bigger than the apatosaurus.
   ○ Its neck is very long.
8. ○ The museum displays their small dinosaurs, too.
   ○ We see one dinosaur that is the size of a chicken.
   ○ Us also saw a fossil of a dinosaur with feathers.
   ○ Well never see anything like that in a zoo.

186 • Unit 5

Online at GrammarWorkshop.com

William H. Sadlier

Name: ________

Grammar Workshop, Level Green, Lesson 39 Quiz

Look at the underlined pronoun. Enter the noun that is its antecedent.

1. A fifteen-year-old boy invented earmuffs to keep his ears warm.
2. This is the first vehicle with wheels. It was pulled by a donkey.
3. Beverly read three stories. She read them in the library.
4. Alice in Wonderland liked strawberry tarts. Do you like them too?
5. A gorilla that is angry will stick out its tongue.

Interactive Quizzes, one for each lesson, assess students' understanding of the content taught in the lessons. The automatic scoring of these self-assessments informs students of the skills and concepts they have mastered.

Test Booklet

For each grade level, a 48-page Test Booklet supplies:

- **Unit Tests**, 2–4 pages for every unit, varying in format depending on the skill (e.g., sentence completion or circling the correct word/phrase)
- **Mastery Tests**, 4 pages for every 2 units, in standardized-test format
- **Final Mastery Test**, 4 pages, serving as a summative assessment of the program

CREATING THE RIGHT BLEND FOR YOU

Grammar Workshop seamlessly combines print and online resources, personalizing a blended approach for students and teachers.

TEACHER'S ANNOTATED EDITION

Grammar Workshop

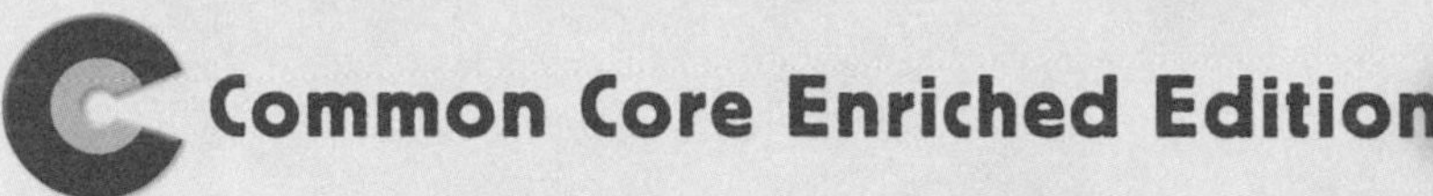

Level Orange

Beverly Ann Chin, Ph.D.
Senior Series Consultant
Professor of English
University of Montana
Missoula, MT

Photo Credits
Getty Images/Digital Vision/Jack Hollingsworth: iii; iStockphoto.com/Randy Plett Photographs: v; Photodisc/Amos Morgan: viii center, Punchstock/Image Source: viii right.

For additional online resources, go to grammarworkshop.com and enter the Teacher Access Code: GW13TUR82JLK

Printed in the United States of America.

ISBN: 978-1-4217-1064-8
3456789 RRDH 16 15 14

CONTENTS

Introduction

Grammar Workshop prepares students with systematic lessons and effective grammar practice that will improve their ability to communicate clearly and correctly in their writing and help prepare them for standardized tests. This program, which is aligned with the **Common Core State Standards (CCSS) for English Language Arts** for all grammar and some writing standards, will help teachers to focus instruction in the conventions of Standard English.

Proven Instructional Approach

Direct Instruction Each lesson clearly explains and models the rules and principles of grammar, usage, and mechanics—the conventions of Standard English—and then supports the instruction with scaffolded exercise sets that give students practice both in the skills themselves and in the application of those skills to writing.

Each lesson begins with a Learn section, in which a grammar principle or rule is explained and clearly illustrated. Following the Learn section are three sets of Practice exercises, each one more challenging than the previous one. In the Write section that concludes each lesson, students put grammar into practice with exercises that ask them to write their own sentences or to improve sentences by revising or combining them. When writing, they are made aware of the importance of text type and audience when making decisions about using formal or informal language, as well as the need to consult a dictionary for help with spelling or clarification of word meaning.

Deliberate Pacing The lessons are carefully developed and paced, and the amount of instruction in each lesson is manageable for students who are new to the grammar principle or rule. The measured pacing is ideal for all students, especially striving learners and English Language Learners. In addition, the lessons are self-contained, allowing teachers to present individual lessons as needed.

Print Components

Student Edition—Print and eBook

Through explicit instruction, ample practice, and immediate application of skills, students will master grade-appropriate conventions of Standard English.

- Levels Green, Orange, and Blue (Grades 3, 4, and 5) are divided into six units focused on teaching:
  - Sentences
  - Nouns
  - Verbs
  - Adjectives, Adverbs, and Prepositions**
  - Pronouns
  - Capitalization, Punctuation, and Spelling

- Each lesson has the same easy-to-follow, three-step instructional sequence:
  1. **Learn** features succinct and bite-sized skill instruction with clear explanations and modeling.
  2. **Practice** includes three scaffolded activities, each building on the prior and increasing in difficulty.
  3. **Write** encourages students to apply what they learned with three types of writing activities: Revising Sentences, Combining Sentences, and Write Your Own.
- Lessons are followed by a Unit Review to reinforce learning, and a Unit Test in standardized test format to monitor progress.

** Per CCSS, prepositions only taught in grades 4 and 5.

Annotated Teacher's Edition

In the Annotated Teacher's Edition:

- Common Core State Standards correlation is noted on the lesson pages.
- Clear, concise lesson plans offer three easy steps that include writing prompts for independent writing and activities to meet the needs of English Language Learners.
- The flexible design of the program enables teachers to use it with any reading or language arts program. A Pacing Chart clearly shows how various components might be scheduled over an academic year.
- Use the included Informal Assessments to monitor students' progress through their daily speaking, reading, and writing.

Student Test Booklet

For each grade level, a 48-page Test Booklet supplies:

- **Unit Tests**, 4–8 pages for every unit, varying in format depending on the skill (e.g., sentence completion or circling the correct word/phrase)
- **Mastery Tests**, 4 pages for every 2 units, in standardized-test format
- **Final Mastery Test**, 4 pages, serving as a summative assessment of the program

Digital Components

Support and extend instruction with online resources.

- ***NEW!*** Online Quiz for each lesson—automatically scored
- Additional Practice worksheets
- Proofreading passages
- Interactive Games
- Professional Development Videos

See page T11 for additional information about the Digital Components.

Common Core State Standards

Grammar Workshop, Common Core Enriched Edition, Level Orange aligns with the Common Core State Standards (CCSS) for English Language Arts for grammar and writing. This correlation is also available at **grammarworkshop.com**.

Language Standards K–5	
Common Core State Standards (Grade 4)	**Level Orange (Grade 4) Lessons**
Conventions of Standard English	
1. Demonstrate command of the conventions of standard English grammar and usage when writing or speaking.	
a. Use relative pronouns (*who, whose, whom, which, that*) and relative adverbs (*where, when, why*).	Lesson 40
b. Form and use the progressive (e.g., *I was walking; I am walking; I will be walking*) verb tenses.	Lesson 20
c. Use modal auxiliaries (e.g., *can, may, must*) to convey various conditions.	Lesson 18
d. Order adjectives within sentences according to conventional patterns (e.g., *a small red bag* rather than *a red small bag*).	Lessons 24, 25
e. Form and use prepositional phrases.	Lesson 34
f. Produce complete sentences, recognizing and correcting inappropriate fragments and run-ons.	Lessons 1, 2, 6, 7, 11, 12, 16, 25, 26, 27, 28, 29, 31, 32, 36, 39, 41, 42, 43, 44, 46, 47, 48
g. Correctly use frequently confused words (e.g., *to, too, two; there, there*).	Lessons 50, 51
2. Demonstrate command of the conventions of standard English capitalization, punctuation, and spelling when writing.	
a. Use correct capitalization.	Lessons 1, 2, 6, 8, 42, 43, 44, 45, 48, 49
b. Use commas and quotation marks to mark direct speech and quotations from a text.	Lesson 49
c. Use a comma before a coordinating conjunction in a compound sentence.	Lessons 5, 7
d. Spell grade-appropriate words correctly, consulting references as needed.	Lessons 2, 6, 9, 10, 11, 19, 21, 22, 23, 29, 50, 51

Knowledge of Language	
3. Use knowledge of language and its conventions when writing, speaking, reading, or listening.	
a. Choose words and phrases to convey ideas precisely.	Lessons 8, 13, 26, 30, 33, 34, 42
b. Choose punctuation for effect.	Lessons 1, 42
c. Differentiate between contexts that call for formal English (e.g., presenting ideas) and situations where informal discourse is appropriate (e.g., small-group discussion).	Lessons 6, 32, 41, 47, 49

Writing Standards K–5

Common Core State Standards (Grade 4)	Level Orange (Grade 4) Lessons
Text Types and Purposes	
1. Write opinion pieces on topics or texts, supporting a point of view with reasons and information.	Lesson 50
2. Write informative/explanatory texts to examine a topic and convey ideas and information clearly.	Lessons 43, 51
3. Write narratives to develop real or imagined experiences or events using effective technique, descriptive details, and clear event sequences.	Lessons 19, 20, 21, 22, 29
Production and Distribution of Writing	
4. Produce clear and coherent writing in which the development and organization are appropriate to task, purpose, and audience. (Grade-specific expectations for writing types are defined in standards 1–3 above.)	Lessons 6, 10, 21, 22, 29, 43, 46, 47, 48, 50
5. With guidance and support from peers and adults, develop and strengthen writing as needed by planning, revising, and editing.	Lessons 6, 20, 29, 47
Range of Writing	
10. Write routinely over extended time frames (time for research, reflection, and revision) and shorter time frames (a single sitting or a day or two) for a range of discipline-specific tasks, purposes, and audiences.	Lessons 6, 10, 20, 21, 22, 29, 46, 47, 48, 50

RESEARCH BASE

Current research, including that which underlies the Common Core State Standards, shows that explicit grammar instruction plays a critical role in learning to write well and, therefore, in children's success in school and on standardized assessments. Instruction in grammar that focuses on teaching students to communicate their written ideas with clarity and correctness helps them to understand the conventions of Standard English. They can then make appropriate choices about grammar, usage, and mechanics to improve their writing. GRAMMAR WORKSHOP, COMMON CORE ENRICHED EDITION, is designed to promote grammar acquisition with instructional strategies supported by research.

THE RESEARCH

How Do Students Learn Grammar?

■ *Researchers agree that although extensive reading and writing is important to grammar acquisition, explicit instruction is crucial to mastering the conventions of written English. Three effective strategies recommended for improving students' grammar acquisition include sentence combining, sentence expansion, and sentence imitation (Haussamen et al., 2003).*

Grammar Workshop

The lessons in GRAMMAR WORKSHOP, COMMON CORE ENRICHED EDITION, provide direct instruction by clearly explaining and modeling the rules of grammar, usage, and mechanics. Instruction is supported with exercise sets that employ scaffolding and that include skills such as combining and expanding kernel sentences, correcting common errors, and using grammatical terminology.

THE RESEARCH

What Principles Should Guide Grammar Instruction?

■ *If students are truly to internalize the standards of written English, teachers first need to introduce the basic parts of speech so there is a context within which to begin a discussion of grammar concepts (Shepherd, 2005). Following this, it is important to place grammar instruction within the framework of students' own writing (Angelillo, 2002).*

Grammar Workshop

GRAMMAR WORKSHOP, COMMON CORE ENRICHED EDITION, provides students with ample opportunities to learn and put into practice the principles of English grammar. Furthermore, these opportunities appear in a variety of contexts, assuring that students are exposed to a variety of applications. Students demonstrate what they have learned in the Practice sections and then apply their knowledge in editing or sentence-completion activities. At the conclusion of each lesson, students write their own sentences or revise sentences by expanding and combining them.

Research References

A more comprehensive discussion of current research in grammar instruction and suggestions for classroom practices that reflect that research can be found in the Sadlier Professional Development Papers at **grammarworkshop.com**. The references that follow, some of which are cited on the foregoing page, represent a sampling of the works consulted in the preparation of the GRAMMAR WORKSHOP program and the Professional Development Paper.

Angelillo, J. (2002). *A fresh approach to teaching punctuation: Helping young writers use conventions with precision and purpose.* New York: Scholastic.

Calkins, L. (1980). When children want to punctuate. *Language Arts*, 57, 567-573.

Dyson, A. H., & Freedman, S. W. (2003). Writing. In J. Flood, D. Lapp, J. Squire, & J. Jensen (Eds.). *Handbook of research on teaching the English language arts.* Mahwah, NJ: Lawrence Erlbaum, 967–992.

Farnan, N., & Dahl, K. (2003). Children's writing: Research and practice. In J. Flood, D. Lapp, J. Squire, & J. Jensen (Eds.). *Handbook of research on teaching the English language arts.* Mahwah, NJ: Lawrence Erlbaum, 993–1007.

Graham, S., & Perin, D. (2007). *Writing next: Effective strategies to improve the writing of adolescents in middle and high schools—A report to Carnegie Corporation of New York.* Washington, DC: Alliance for Excellent Education.

Haussamen, B., with Benjamin, A., Kolln, M., & Wheeler, R. S. (2003). *Grammar alive! A guide for teachers.* Urbana, IL: National Council of Teachers of English.

Hillocks, G., & Smith, M. (2003). Grammars and literacy learning. In J. Flood, D. Lapp, J. Squire, & J. Jensen (Eds.). *Handbook of research on teaching the English language arts.* Mahwah, NJ: Lawrence Erlbaum, 721–737.

Holdzkom, D., Porter, E. J., Reed, L., & Rubin, D. (1984). *Research within reach: Oral and written communication.* St. Louis, MO: Mid-Continent Regional Educational Laboratory.

Killgallon, D. (1997). *Sentence composing for middle school.* Portsmouth, NH: Boynton/Cook.

National Assessment Governing Board. (2007). *Writing framework and specifications for the 2007 National Assessment of Educational Progress.* Washington, DC: National Assessment Governing Board.

National Council of Teachers of English & International Reading Association. (1996). *Standards for English language arts.* Urbana, IL: National Council of Teachers of English.

National Governors Association Center for Best Practices, Council of Chief State School Officers. (2010) *Common Core State Standards.* Washington, DC: National Governors Association Center for Best Practices, Council of Chief State School Officers

Noguchi, R. R. (1991). *Grammar and the teaching of writing: Limits and possibilities.* Urbana, IL: National Council of Teachers of English.

Strickland, D., & Feeley, J. (2003). Development in the elementary school years. In J. Flood, D. Lapp, J. Squire, & J. Jensen (Eds.). *Handbook of research on teaching the English language arts.* Mahwah, NJ: Lawrence Erlbaum, 339–356.

Strong, W. (2001). *Coaching writing: The power of guided practice.* Portsmouth, NH: Heinemann.

Weaver, C. (1996). *Teaching grammar in context.* Portsmouth, NH: Boynton/Cook.

Best Practices For Teaching Grammar

Grammar Workshop, Common Core Enriched Edition, is based on the following best practices for the teaching of grammar in the context of students' writing.

1. Read your students' writing to identify the conventions (grammar, usage, and mechanics) that students are using correctly and consistently as well as those conventions that students need to learn and/or review. By looking for patterns in students' writing, you can decide which conventions are most important to teach. You can prioritize your instruction by asking, "Which convention problems most seriously hinder the reader's understanding of the message?"

2. Focus and scaffold your instruction through the writing workshop model of "I do, We do, You do." In the "I do" part of the workshop, present direct instruction so that students **learn** a specific editing strategy or grammar concept. In the "We do" part of the workshop, guide students as they **practice** the strategy/concept you have just modeled. As students do these exercises, monitor their understanding of the strategy/concept. In the "You do" part of the workshop, have students independently **apply** the editing strategy/grammar concept to their own writing, with assistance from you and/or their classmates. At the end of the writing workshop, ask students how the workshop improved their written message.

3. Use texts from different content areas and genres to connect reading and writing. Create a display of examples of effective and creative uses of grammar, usage, and mechanics from diverse sources, such as advertisements, newspapers, literature, and Websites. Help students identify the conventions that are followed—or not followed. With students, explore how the language and conventions enhance or impede meaning.

4. Analyze the differences between formal and informal writing. You might encourage students to write informally to a close friend and then write the same message formally to a different audience. Then reverse the process by having students write formally first, then rewrite informally. By encouraging students to "code-switch," you help them understand how purpose, audience, and genre influence a writer's decisions about language and conventions. You can also help students explore the relationship between oral and written language.

Digital Components

A fully integrated array of digital components has been developed to support, reinforce, and enrich the instruction and practice of the grammar skills and concepts in Level Orange. These components can be found at **grammarworkshop.com**.

Practice Worksheets The Practice Worksheets, one for each lesson, provide additional practice. They can also be used for lesson review or reteaching.

Proofreading Passages The Proofreading Passages, one for each unit, allow teachers to assess students' understanding of the grammar skills and concepts taught in the unit. After completing a unit, students are challenged to apply their knowledge of the skills and concepts just learned by finding and correcting errors in grammar, usage, or mechanics in a passage.

Interactive Games and Activities The Interactive Games and Activities help to strengthen students' understanding of the grammar skills and concepts taught in each lesson. These games and activities are presented in a fun and engaging format.

Interactive Quizzes The Interactive Quizzes, one for each lesson, are self-assessments that are automatically scored. They provide immediate feedback to students on their understanding of the grammar skills and concepts presented in the lessons.

Professional Development Videos Two videos are available to help teachers more effectively implement the *Grammar Workshop* program in light of the Common Core State Standards and in the context of student writing.

Correlation to the Common Core State Standards (CCSS) The correlation gives a listing of the lessons in Level Orange that align with the Common Core State Standards for grammar and writing.

Pacing Guide The Pacing Guide provides a roadmap for delivering instruction. It can also be used as a reference to help teachers build effective lessons.

Proofreading Checklist and Test-Taking Strategies The Proofreading Checklist and Test-Taking Strategies are useful references for students when they complete writing assignments or prepare for tests.

Supporting English Language Learners

In some of today's classrooms, students come from diverse backgrounds and have varying degrees of English proficiency. Following are suggestions that will support English Language Learners (ELL) in their acquisition of vocabulary and language.

■ Use real objects, pictures, gestures, and facial expressions to teach words and clarify meaning.

■ Teach words that are essential for understanding a paragraph or story, but also focus on basic words—words that a native English speaker in the elementary grades would not necessarily need to learn.

■ Provide scaffolding by having students choose from a list of words to complete partially finished sentences and paragraphs. Ask students who have a better command of English to define words, use words in sentences, and answer questions that involve those words.

■ Encourage active participation, repeating directions and modeling how to perform tasks so students understand what to do. Be patient. Remember that because of cultural differences, students may be reluctant to participate.

■ Use Standard English to model the language that students read and write. Use corrections to positively reinforce students' use of English, and provide students with ample opportunities for listening and speaking.

■ Focus on vocabulary and language development throughout the day, integrating instruction in those areas in other lessons. Encourage students to use English as much as possible to gain confidence over time.

It is important to remember that cultural differences can affect how students learn and behave in the classroom. To provide the best possible learning environment for these students, teachers need to be culturally sensitive and aware of the implications of these differences.

The following table identifies some of the difficulties English Language Learners may have with English. It lists lessons in **GRAMMAR WORKSHOP, COMMON CORE ENRICHED EDITION**, to which you can direct these students.

GRAMMAR WORKSHOP and English Language Learners		
Target Area in English	**Comment**	**Treatment in GRAMMAR WORKSHOP, Levels Green (Gr. 3), Orange (Gr. 4), Blue (Gr. 5)**
Articles	English Language Learners often leave out the article before a singular count noun.	Gr. 3: Lesson 27 Gr. 4: Lesson 25 Gr. 5: Lesson 30
Capitalization	Arabic, Chinese, and Hebrew do not use capital letters; Dutch and German capitalize some forms of the second-person pronoun; German capitalizes all nouns.	Gr. 3: Lessons 1–3, 8, 10, 34, 37, 41–44, 46–47 Gr. 4: Lessons 1, 8, 42–45, 48–49 Gr. 5: Lessons 1, 10, 29, 46–49, 52–53
Homophones	Speakers of Asian languages in particular may be confused by the concept of words sounding alike but having different meanings.	Gr. 3: Lesson 49 Gr. 4: Lesson 50 Gr. 5: Lesson 54
Negatives	Multiple negations are common in French and Russian, among other languages.	Gr. 3: Lesson 33 Gr. 4: Lesson 33 Gr. 5: Lesson 36
Plural Nouns	Some Asian languages have no plural forms for nouns.	Gr. 3: Lessons 12–14, 16–17, 20, 22, 27 Gr. 4: Lessons 9–11, 13–14, 17, 19 Gr. 5: Lessons 11–13, 17, 30
Subjects, Double	Some languages add personal pronouns to the noun subject, leading English Language Learners to say, "Maria she is pretty."	Gr. 3: Lessons 4, 11, 34 Gr. 4: Lessons 2–3, 35 Gr. 5: Lessons 2–5, 40
Verb Tenses	In some languages, time is not signaled by word endings but rather by words that native English speakers would call adverbs.	Gr. 3: Lessons 16–20, 23–24, 35 Gr. 4: Lessons 13–17, 19–22, 36 Gr. 5: Lessons 17–20, 24–26, 40
Word Order	• In some languages, word order determines the part of speech. For example, the verb is the last word in sentences in Turkish, Korean, and Japanese. • In Russian, subject and object may switch places without affecting meaning.	Gr. 3: Lessons 4–5, 11, 34, 36 Gr. 4: Lessons 2–4, 7, 35, 37 Gr. 5: Lessons 2–6, 9, 40–41

Assessment Options

There are many ways to assess students' understanding of the skills and concepts in Grammar Workshop, Common Core Enriched Edition. The assessment suggestions below can provide insight into students' progress.

Informal Assessment

■ **Speaking** Observe whether students use the taught grammar and usage skills in classroom discussions and when speaking in other formal settings.

■ **Reading** Observe whether students recognize and appreciate the kind of English used in the nonfiction materials they read.

■ **Writing** Observe whether students use the taught grammar, usage, and mechanics skills in their writing.

Formal Assessment

Student Edition

■ **Unit Review** Each Unit Review includes exercises for each lesson in the Unit. It can serve as reinforcement or as a review of the Unit's skills and concepts.

■ **Unit Test** Each Unit Test assesses students' understanding of the skills and concepts presented in the unit. To provide test-taking practice, each Unit Test utilizes two standardized-test formats.

Interactive Quizzes

The Interactive Quizzes, one for each lesson, assess students' understanding of the content taught in the lessons. The automatic scoring of these self-assessments inform students of the skills and concepts they have mastered. The Interactive Quizzes are available at **grammarworkshop.com**.

Test Booklet (optional purchase)

The Test Booklet consists of six Unit Tests, three Mastery Tests, and one Final Mastery Test. Each Unit Test includes test items for each lesson in the corresponding unit. Each Mastery Test covers the grammar, usage, and mechanics skills in the preceding two units. These tests are in a standardized-test format. The Final Mastery Test covers the skills of all six units. Like the Mastery Test, it is in a standardized-test format. The Mastery and Final Mastery Tests will show how much progress students have made to date. Answers to the test booklet items are available at **grammarworkshop.com**.

Pacing Chart (with online practice and quizzes)

The **Grammar Workshop** program is designed to be used with any Reading and Language Arts program. Its format is simple and allows for great flexibility. Activity assignments can be adjusted to conform to the special needs of any class. The chart below shows how various components of Level Orange might be scheduled over an academic year.

Week	Student Text	Follow-Up Activities
1	**Unit 1** Lessons 1–2, pp. 8–15	Activities on p. T18 Online practice and quizzes
2	Lessons 3–5, pp. 16–27	Activities on pp. T19–T20 Online practice and quizzes
3	Lessons 6–7, pp. 28–35	Activities on pp. T20–T21 Online practice and quizzes
4	Unit 1 Review, pp. 36–37 Unit 1 Test, pp. 38–39	Activities on p. T21 Unit 1 online editing activity Unit 1 Test*
5	**Unit 2** Lessons 8–9, pp. 40–47	Activities on p. T22 Online practice and quizzes
6	Lessons 10–11, pp. 48–55	Activities on p. T23 Online practice and quizzes
7	Unit 2 Review, pp. 56–57 Unit 2 Test, pp. 58–59	Activities on p. T24 Unit 2 online editing activity Unit 2 Test* Units 1 and 2 Mastery Test*

*Available in the Test Booklet (optional purchase)

Week	Student Text	Follow-Up Activities
8	**Unit 3** Lessons 12–13, pp. 60–67	Activities on pp. T24–T25 Online practice and quizzes
9	Lessons 14–15, pp. 68–75	Activities on pp. T25–T26 Online practice and quizzes
10	Lessons 16–17, pp. 76–83	Activities on pp. T26–T27 Online practice and quizzes
11	Lessons 18–19, pp. 84–91	Activities on pp. T27–T28 Online practice and quizzes
12	Lessons 20–21, pp. 92–99	Activities on pp. T28–T29 Online practice and quizzes
13	Lessons 22–23, pp. 100–107	Activities on pp. T29–T30 Online practice and quizzes
14	Unit 3 Review, pp. 108–109 Unit 3 Test, pp. 110–111	Activities on p. T30 Unit 3 online editing activity Unit 3 Test*
15	**Unit 4** Lessons 24–25, pp. 112–119	Activities on p. T31 Online practice and quizzes
16	Lessons 26–27, pp. 120–127	Activities on p. T32 Online practice and quizzes
17	Lessons 28–29, pp. 128–135	Activities on p. T33 Online practice and quizzes
18	Lessons 30–32, pp. 136–147	Activities on pp. T34–T35 Online practice and quizzes
19	Lessons 33–34, pp. 148–155	Activities on pp. T35–T36 Online practice and quizzes
20	Unit 4 Review, pp. 156–157 Unit 4 Test, pp. 158–159	Activities on p. T36 Unit 4 online editing activity Unit 4 Test* Units 3 and 4 Mastery Test*

*Available in the Test Booklet (optional purchase)

Week	Student Text	Follow-Up Activities
21	**Unit 5** Lessons 35–36, pp. 160–167	Activities on p. T37 Online practice and quizzes
22	Lessons 37–39, pp. 168–179	Activities on pp. T38–T39 Online practice and quizzes
23	Lessons 40–41, pp. 180–187	Activities on pp. T39–T40 Online practice and quizzes
24	Unit 5 Review, pp. 188–189 Unit 5 Test, pp. 190–191	Activities on p. T40 Unit 5 online editing activity Unit 5 Test*
25	**Unit 6** Lessons 42–44, pp. 192–203	Activities on pp. T41–T42 Online practice and quizzes
26	Lessons 45–47, pp. 204–215	Activities on pp. T42–T43 Online practice and quizzes
27	Lessons 48–49, pp. 216–223	Activities on p. T44 Online practice and quizzes
28	Lessons 50–51, pp. 224–231	Activities on p. T45 Online practice and quizzes
29	Unit 6 Review, pp. 232–233 Unit 6 Test, pp. 234–235	Activities on p. T46 Unit 6 online editing activity Unit 6 Test* Units 5 and 6 Mastery Test*
30		Final Mastery Test*

*Available in the Test Booklet (optional purchase)

An editing activity for the unit is available at **grammarworkshop.com**.

Lesson 1 (pp. 8–11)

Kinds of Sentences

OBJECTIVES

- Punctuate sentences
- Correct capitalization and punctuation of sentences
- Write four kinds of sentences

TEACH/MODEL

■ **Learn** Review the definitions and sentences at the top of page 8. Have students say more examples of each kind of sentence.

PRACTICE/APPLY

Connecting Speaking and Writing

■ Assign **Practices A** and **B**. Model how to use the proofreading marks before assigning **C**. Before assigning the **Write** activity in **D**, ask students to say aloud to themselves each sentence they plan to write before writing it. Review responses to **A–D** orally.

FOLLOW-UP

■ **ELL** Using lesson sentences, ask students to emphasize the different way each kind of sentence should sound.

CCSS Language 1f, 2a, 3b. (See pp. T6–7.)

Additional practice, quizzes, and activities for each lesson are available at **grammarworkshop.com.**

Lesson 2 (pp. 12–15)

Complete Subjects and Predicates

OBJECTIVES

- Identify complete subjects and complete predicates in simple sentences
- Write complete subjects or predicates to complete sentences

TEACH/MODEL

■ **Learn** Using books, magazines, and other classroom materials, work with students to read aloud sentences and identify complete subjects and predicates.

PRACTICE/APPLY

Connecting Speaking and Writing

■ Assign **Practices A** and **B**. Before assigning **C**, tell students that the answers they choose must make sense in the sentences. In the **Write** activity in **D**, ask students to say aloud to themselves each sentence they plan to write before writing it. Review responses to **A–D** orally.

FOLLOW-UP

■ **ELL** Have students read aloud the whole sentence in each row of the chart on page 12. Ask them to create and say new sentences by replacing first the complete subject and then the complete predicate in each row.

■ **Writing** Have students write two sentences about a musical instrument they like. Then have them rewrite each sentence twice, changing first the subject and then the predicate in the original sentence.

CCSS Language 1f, 2a, 2d. (See pp. T6–7.)

Additional practice, quizzes, and activities for each lesson are available at **grammarworkshop.com**.

Lesson 3 (pp. 16–19)

Simple Subjects

OBJECTIVES

- Identify simple subjects
- Write subjects to complete sentences
- Combine related sentences by joining subjects

TEACH/MODEL

■ **Learn** Discuss the example sentences in the chart on page 16. Ask volunteers to replace the complete subject in each and say the new sentence. Work with the class to identify the simple subject in each complete subject students say.

PRACTICE/APPLY

Connecting Speaking and Writing

■ Assign **Practices A–C**. Before assigning the **Write** activity in **D**, ask students to say aloud to themselves each sentence they plan to write before writing it.

■ Review responses orally. In **A** and **B**, discuss the simple subjects that contain more than one word. In **C**, ask students to identify the simple subject of each sentence. In **D**, have them read aloud the two sentences in each item and then read the combined sentence. Point out how much less repetitive the new sentence sounds.

FOLLOW-UP

■ **ELL** Read aloud the first sentence in **B**. Ask, "*Whom* or *what* is this sentence about?" Have students read aloud the remaining sentences, asking after each, "*Whom* or *what*?" Help students to use this question to identify subjects.

Lesson 4 (pp. 20–23)

Simple Predicates

OBJECTIVES

- Identify simple predicates
- Write predicates to complete sentences
- Combine related sentences by joining predicates

TEACH/MODEL

■ **Learn** Discuss the example sentences in the chart on page 20. Ask volunteers to replace the complete predicate in each and say the new sentence. Work with the class to identify the simple predicate in each complete predicate students say.

PRACTICE/APPLY

Connecting Speaking and Writing

■ Assign **Practices A–C**. Before assigning the **Write** activity in **D**, ask students to say aloud to themselves each sentence they plan to write before writing it.

■ Review responses orally. As students share answers in **C**, have them identify the simple predicate in each sentence. In **D**, have them read aloud the two sentences in each item and then read the combined sentence. Point out how much less repetitive the new sentence sounds.

FOLLOW-UP

■ **Writing** Have students write two sentences about a person they consider to be a hero. Ask them to circle the simple predicate in each sentence.

Additional practice, quizzes, and activities for each lesson are available at **grammarworkshop.com**.

Lesson 5 (pp. 24–27)

Compound Sentences

OBJECTIVES

- Identify simple and compound sentences
- Correct punctuation in compound sentences
- Combine sentences to form compound sentences

TEACH/MODEL

■ **Learn** Say aloud pairs of short, related simple sentences about animals. (*Snakes are cold-blooded. They lie in the sun to get warm.*) With the class, join each pair of related sentences using *and*, *but*, or *or*. Discuss why each coordinating conjunction that was used makes sense.

PRACTICE/APPLY

Connecting Speaking and Writing

■ Assign **Practices A–C**. Before assigning the **Write** activity in **D**, ask students to say aloud to themselves each sentence they plan to write before writing it. Review responses to **A–D** orally.

FOLLOW-UP

■ **ELL** Have students read aloud each pair of related sentences at the top of page 24. Point out that the compound sentences do not change the meaning of the sentence pairs.

■ **Writing** Write and display three pairs of related simple sentences. Ask the class to join each pair with a comma and *and*, *but*, or *or* to make a compound sentence.

CCSS Language 2c. (See pp. T6–7.)

Lesson 6 (pp. 28–31)

Complex Sentences

OBJECTIVES

- Identify complex sentences and their subordinating conjunctions
- Write subordinating conjunctions to complete complex sentences
- Write complex sentences

TEACH/MODEL

■ **Learn** Have students brainstorm other complex sentences, using the subordinating conjunctions on page 28. Use the lesson sentences and the new sentences to explain that in a complex sentence, the two related ideas are connected by a subordinating conjunction.

PRACTICE/APPLY

Connecting Speaking and Writing

■ Assign **Practices A–C**. Before assigning the **Write** activity in **D**, ask students to say aloud to themselves each sentence they plan to write before writing it. Review responses to **A–D** orally.

FOLLOW-UP

■ **ELL** With students, substitute the different conjunctions in the sentences in **C**. Point out that the subordinating conjunctions give the sentences different meanings.

■ **Writing** Have students write five complex sentences about a favorite outdoor experience. As sentences are shared, have others use a different subordinating conjunction in each sentence.

CCSS Language 1f, 2a, 2d, 3c. Writing 4, 5, 10. (See pp. T6–7.)

Additional practice, quizzes, and activities for each lesson are available at **grammarworkshop.com**.

Lesson 7 (pp. 32–35)

Correct Fragments and Run-ons

OBJECTIVES

- Identify fragments and run-ons
- Rewrite run-on sentences
- Correct fragments and run-ons
- Write subjects or predicates to make fragments complete sentences

TEACH/MODEL

■ **Learn** Write and display a run-on sentence. (*I loved this book, you will like it, too.*) With the class, separate it into two short sentences. Then add *and* to form a compound sentence. Next, say a fragment that is missing a predicate. With students, make a complete sentence by adding a predicate. Repeat with a fragment that needs a subject.

PRACTICE/APPLY

Connecting Speaking and Writing

■ Assign **Practices A** and **B**. Review how to use the proofreading marks before assigning **C**. Before assigning the **Write** activity in **D**, ask students to say aloud to themselves each sentence they plan to write before writing it.

■ Review responses orally. In **D**, point out the action verbs that begin **2** and **3**. Explain that depending on the intonation used, **2** and **3** can also be read as imperatives. Read each as an imperative.

FOLLOW-UP

■ **ELL** Have students read aloud the run-on sentences in **A**. Point out the difficulty in reading the sentences with correct intonation without punctuation and capitalization as cues.

CCSS Language 1f, 2c. (See pp. T6–7.)

Unit 1 Review (pp. 36–37)

Lessons 1–7

OBJECTIVE

- Review skills and concepts from Unit 1, Lessons 1–7

USING THE UNIT REVIEW

■ To review the skills and concepts taught in the unit, have students complete the Unit 1 Review on pages 36–37. If they need more help with a skill or concept, have them turn to the appropriate pages for a lesson review.

FOLLOWING THE UNIT REVIEW

■ Have students write six sentences about something that happens in a park. Ask students to include one question and one command or exclamation. After they finish, have them revise and edit their writing to apply what they learned in the unit. For example, they might combine two related sentences into a compound sentence or complex sentence, or they might add a subject or predicate to correct a fragment. Have students proofread their sentences for correct capitalization and end punctuation.

Unit 1 Test (pp. 38–39)

OBJECTIVE

- Assess students' understanding of the skills and concepts from Unit 1

USING THE UNIT TEST

■ Discuss the standardized-test format of the Unit Test. Show how to fill in a circle to indicate an answer choice. You may also want to review the **Test-Taking Strategies** available at **grammarworkshop.com**.

■ Have students complete the test on pages 38–39. Be sure they understand the directions before beginning.

An editing activity for the unit is available at **grammarworkshop.com**.

Lesson 8 (pp. 40–43)

Common and Proper Nouns

OBJECTIVES

- Identify common nouns, proper nouns, and abstract nouns
- Correct errors in capitalization
- Revise sentences by using more descriptive nouns

TEACH/MODEL

■ **Learn** Have students identify three proper nouns at the top of page 40 that are more than one word. Then work with students to brainstorm more common and proper nouns. Prompt responses that include proper nouns consisting of more than one word.

PRACTICE/APPLY

Connecting Speaking and Writing

■ Assign **Practices A–C**. Before assigning the **Write** activity in **D**, ask students to say aloud to themselves each sentence they plan to write before writing it. Review responses to **A–D** orally.

FOLLOW-UP

■ **ELL** Work with students to read each sentence in **B**. Point out that the words beginning with capital letters help them to identify proper nouns as they read.

■ **Writing** Have students write four sentences about a class trip, using common and proper nouns in each.

CCSS Language 2a, 3a. (See pp. T6–7.)

Additional practice, quizzes, and activities for each lesson are available at **grammarworkshop.com**.

Lesson 9 (pp. 44–47)

Singular and Plural Nouns

OBJECTIVES

- Write the plural form of nouns
- Correct the use and spelling of singular and plural nouns
- Combine sentences by joining nouns in the subject or predicate

TEACH/MODEL

■ **Learn** With students, brainstorm singular nouns that end with the spelling patterns shown at the top of page 44. Have students identify which rule applies to each new noun and then use the rule to form the plural of each.

PRACTICE/APPLY

Connecting Speaking and Writing

■ Assign **Practices A–C**. Before assigning the **Write** activity in **D**, ask students to say aloud to themselves each sentence they plan to write before writing it. Review responses to **A–D** orally.

FOLLOW-UP

■ **ELL** Work with students to use a variety of plural nouns in sentences. Point out that the *–s* at the end of a plural noun can have a soft sound like /s/ in *weeks* or a hard sound like /z/ in *days*.

■ **Writing** Have students write four sentences about a family meal, using plural nouns in each. Ask students to include at least one plural noun that follows each spelling rule at the top of page 44.

CCSS Language 2d. (See pp. T6–7.)

Additional practice, quizzes, and activities for each lesson are available at **grammarworkshop.com**.

Lesson 10 (pp. 48–51)

Irregular Plural Nouns

OBJECTIVES

- Identify nouns as singular or plural
- Write the irregular plurals of nouns
- Correct the spelling of irregular plural nouns
- Write rhymes using irregular plural nouns

TEACH/MODEL

■ **Learn** Say sentences that include singular nouns from the top of page 48. (*They have a child.*) Work with the class to change each sentence so that the correctly spelled plural of that noun is used. (*They have children.*)

PRACTICE/APPLY

Connecting Speaking and Writing

■ Assign **Practices A–C**. Before assigning the **Write** activity in **D**, ask students to say aloud to themselves each sentence they plan to write before writing it.

■ Review responses orally. In **D**, ask volunteers to read aloud their rhymes. Have the class spell aloud each irregular plural noun.

FOLLOW-UP

■ **ELL** Have students make up new oral sentences with the boldface nouns from **A**. Then repeat, but if the noun is singular, have students make it plural; and if the noun is plural, have them make it singular before using it in a new sentence.

■ **Writing** Have students write five sentences about their neighbors, using a plural noun from the lesson in each sentence.

CCSS Language 2d; Writing 4, 10. (See pp. T6–7.)

Lesson 11 (pp. 52–55)

Possessive Nouns

OBJECTIVES

- Write the possessive form of singular and plural nouns
- Correct the spelling of possessive nouns
- Write sentences using possessive nouns

TEACH/MODEL

■ **Learn** Discuss that the first example sentence on page 52 means, "The mother of Janet teaches quilting." With students, list other singular and plural nouns. For each, ask a volunteer to spell aloud the possessive form of the noun and use it in a sentence.

PRACTICE/APPLY

Connecting Speaking and Writing

■ Assign **Practices A–C**. Before assigning the **Write** activity in **D**, ask students to say aloud to themselves each sentence they plan to write before writing it. Review responses to **A–D** orally.

FOLLOW-UP

■ **ELL** Point out that the plural and plural possessive forms of nouns ending in *-s* sound identical. Say aloud sentences that include each kind of noun, and have students use context clues to determine whether the noun in each is possessive.

■ **Writing** Have students write five sentences about sharing games or books with friends. Two sentences should include singular possessive nouns, and three should use plural possessive nouns.

CCSS Language 1f, 2d. (See pp. T6–7.)

Unit 2 Review (pp. 56–57)

Lessons 8–11

OBJECTIVE

- Review skills and concepts from Unit 2, Lessons 8–11

USING THE UNIT REVIEW

■ To review the skills and concepts taught in the unit, have students complete the Unit 2 Review on pages 56 and 57. If they need more help with a skill or concept, have them turn to the appropriate pages for a review of the lesson.

FOLLOWING THE UNIT REVIEW

■ Ask students to write six sentences that give facts about their school for visitors. Ask students to include a variety of nouns: common, proper, and abstract, singular and plural, and possessive. Have students revise and edit their writing to apply what they learned in the unit. For example, they might correct the spelling of plural or possessive nouns. Have students proofread their sentences for correct spelling, capitalization, and punctuation.

Unit 2 Test (pp. 58–59)

OBJECTIVE

- Assess students' understanding of the skills and concepts from Unit 2

USING THE UNIT TEST

■ Discuss the standardized-test format of the Unit Test. Review how to fill in the circle to indicate an answer choice. You may also want to review the **Test-Taking Strategies** available at **grammarworkshop.com**.

■ Have students complete the test on pages 58 and 59. Be sure they understand the directions before beginning.

An editing activity for the unit is available at **grammarworkshop.com**.

Unit 3

Verbs

Lesson 12 (pp. 60–63)

Action Verbs

OBJECTIVES

- Identify action verbs
- Write action verbs to complete sentences
- Write predicates with action verbs to complete sentences

TEACH/MODEL

■ **Learn** Read aloud each subject and predicate pair at the top of page 60. For each subject, invite volunteers to add new predicates that contain other action verbs. Work with the class to identify the action verb in each new predicate.

PRACTICE/APPLY

Connecting Speaking and Writing

■ Assign **Practices A–C**. Before assigning the **Write** activity in **D**, ask students to say aloud to themselves each sentence they plan to write before writing it.

■ Review responses orally. In **D**, watch for students who use a linking verb instead of an action verb.

FOLLOW-UP

■ **Writing** Have students write five sentences about a summer sports festival that includes activities such as biking and swimming. Tell students to use action verbs in their sentences. Suggest that they use the sentences in **C** or **D** as models.

CCSS Language 1f. (See pp. T6–7.)

Lesson 13 (pp. 64–67)

Present-Tense Verbs

OBJECTIVES

- Write present-tense verbs that agree with the subjects
- Correct errors in subject-verb agreement
- Revise sentences by using more descriptive verbs

TEACH/MODEL

■ **Learn** Use examples of past, present, and future tenses (*I painted, I paint, I will paint*) to help students understand the concept of tense. Discuss how to make subjects and present-tense verbs agree. Then say a variety of singular and plural subjects. Invite students to offer several present-tense verbs that agree with each subject.

PRACTICE/APPLY

Connecting Speaking and Writing

■ Assign **Practices A–C**. Before assigning the **Write** activity in **D**, ask students to say aloud to themselves each sentence they plan to write before writing it. Review responses to **A–D** orally.

FOLLOW-UP

■ **ELL** Look through illustrated books and magazines with students. Invite them to say sentences about the images they find, using present-tense verbs to tell what is happening.

■ **Writing** Have students choose five photos in Unit 3 and write a sentence about each one, using present-tense verbs. Ask students to use at least two subjects that are singular nouns and two that are plural nouns.

CCSS Language 3a. (See pp. T6–7.)

Lesson 14 (pp. 68–71)

More Present-Tense Verbs

OBJECTIVES

- Write present-tense verbs that agree with the subjects
- Correct errors in subject-verb agreement
- Combine sentences by joining present-tense verbs

TEACH/MODEL

■ **Learn** Review subject-verb agreement. Then write and display these verbs: *hiss, touch, crush, fizz, mix, hurry*. For each, ask students to change each verb so that it agrees with a subject that is a singular noun.

PRACTICE/APPLY

Connecting Speaking and Writing

■ Assign **Practices A–C**. Before assigning the **Write** activity in **D**, ask students to say aloud to themselves each sentence they plan to write before writing it. Review responses to **A–D** orally.

FOLLOW-UP

■ **ELL** Say verbs that fit the lesson spelling patterns (*dress, itch, push, buzz, fax, fly*). Have students say sentences using each with singular-noun and plural-noun subjects. Have other students check subject-verb agreement in each sentence.

■ **Writing** Have students choose three verbs from **B** and use each to write two new sentences: one with a subject that is a singular noun and one that is a plural noun.

Additional practice, quizzes, and activities for each lesson are available at **grammarworkshop.com**.

Lesson 15 (pp. 72–75)

Past-Tense Verbs

OBJECTIVES

- Write the past tense of verbs
- Correct the spelling of past-tense verbs
- Revise sentences to make verb tenses consistent

TEACH/MODEL

■ **Learn** Discuss each rule for forming past-tense verbs at the top of page 72. Help students brainstorm two or three more verbs that fit each rule. Invite volunteers to say sentences using the past-tense forms of these verbs.

PRACTICE/APPLY

Connecting Speaking and Writing

■ Assign **Practices A–C**. Before assigning the **Write** activity in **D**, ask students to say aloud to themselves each sentence they plan to write before writing it.

■ Review responses orally. In **C**, have students identify the mistakes and tell how to fix them. In **D**, invite students to read aloud their sentence pairs. Have the class check the verbs in each pair for agreement.

FOLLOW-UP

■ **ELL** In **A** and **B**, have students identify the rule from the top of page 72 that applies to each past-tense verb. Then for each verb, call on a volunteer to say a sentence using it.

■ **Writing** Have students write eight sentences, using two new past-tense verbs that fit each spelling rule in the lesson.

Lesson 16 (pp. 76–79)

Future-Tense Verbs

OBJECTIVES

- Recognize that present, past, and future-tense verbs are verbs in the simple tense
- Write future-tense verbs
- Correct errors in the use of future-tense verbs
- Write sentences with future-tense verbs

TEACH/MODEL

■ **Learn** One at a time, say the following verbs: *like*, *display*, and *share*. Have students use the past-, present-, and future-tense forms of each to replace the forms of *study* in the example sentences on page 76. Ask others for new sentences using the future-tense form of each verb.

PRACTICE/APPLY

Connecting Speaking and Writing

■ Assign **Practices A–C**. Before assigning the **Write** activity in **D**, ask students to say aloud to themselves each sentence they plan to write before writing it. Review responses to **A–D** orally.

FOLLOW-UP

■ **ELL** Say several regular verbs, varying between past-, present-, and future-tense forms. Have students use each in a sentence with details that indicate time. (*I played last week.*) Then have them change the tense and say a new sentence with new time details. (*I will play tomorrow.*)

■ **Writing** Have students choose five photos from classroom books or magazines and write a sentence telling about each, using a future-tense verb.

CCSS Language 1f. (See pp. T6–7.)

Additional practice, quizzes, and activities for each lesson are available at **grammarworkshop.com**.

Lesson 17 (pp. 80–83)

Linking Verbs

OBJECTIVES

- Write the present tense or past tense of the linking verb *be*
- Correct errors in the use of linking verbs
- Write sentences with linking verbs

TEACH/MODEL

■ **Learn** Work with students to identify the subject of each example sentence under the chart on page 80. Discuss how the linking verb and the subject in each sentence agree. Then make the subject of each sentence plural if singular, and make it singular if plural. Have students change the verb to agree.

PRACTICE/APPLY

Connecting Speaking and Writing

■ Assign **Practices A–C**. Before assigning the **Write** activity in **D**, ask students to say aloud to themselves each sentence they plan to write before writing it.

■ Review responses orally. In **D**, have students read aloud their sentences. Ask the class to identify the linking verb in each sentence.

FOLLOW-UP

■ **ELL** Ask students to cover the present-tense column of the chart on page 80, say the present-tense forms of *be*, and use each in a sentence. Ask them to cover the past-tense column and repeat.

■ **Writing** Have students write six sentences about ways in which they have changed. Have them use both present- and past-tense forms of the linking verb *be*.

Lesson 18 (pp. 84–87)

Main Verbs and Helping Verbs

OBJECTIVES

- Identify main verbs and two kinds of helping verbs, including modals
- Write main verbs and helping verbs to complete sentences
- Write sentences with main verbs and helping verbs

TEACH/MODEL

■ **Learn** Discuss why the main verb in each example sentence on page 84 is more important than the helping verb. Work with students to identify the tense of each helping verb in the list on page 84. Have them say one or two main verbs that work with each helping verb. Explain that modals are used with other verbs to express ability (*can*), possibility (*may*), obligation (*must*), and to give advice (*should*).

PRACTICE/APPLY

Connecting Speaking and Writing

■ Assign **Practices A–C**. Before assigning the **Write** activity in **D**, ask students to say aloud to themselves each sentence they plan to write before writing it. Tell them to underline all movie titles. Review responses to **A–D** orally.

FOLLOW-UP

■ **ELL** Have students say their own sentences using each verb from the box in **C**.

■ **Writing** Have students rewrite five sentences they wrote for previous class assignments. Have them add a helping verb if there isn't one.

C CCSS Language 1c. (See pp. T6–7.)

Additional practice, quizzes, and activities for each lesson are available at **grammarworkshop.com.**

Lesson 19 (pp. 88–91)

Using Helping Verbs

OBJECTIVES

- **Identify helping verbs that agree with the subject of sentences**
- **Correct errors in the use of helping verbs**
- **Write sentences with main verbs and helping verbs**

TEACH/MODEL

■ **Learn** Provide other sentences with the helping verbs *has, have,* and *had*. Point out that in each sentence, the helping verb agrees with the subject.

PRACTICE/APPLY

Connecting Speaking and Writing

■ Assign **Practices A–C**. Before assigning the **Write** activity in **D**, ask students to say aloud to themselves each sentence they plan to write before writing it.

■ Review responses orally. In **C**, have students identify the mistakes and tell how to fix them. In **D**, ask students to read aloud their sentences. Have the class identify each helping/main verb pair they hear.

FOLLOW-UP

■ **ELL** Begin a story such as the following: *Juan and I have started an art project. He has gathered the supplies. I have cleared the table.* Invite each student to add a sentence to the story, using a helping verb in the sentence.

■ **Writing** Have students write six sentences about making friends, using helping verbs in their sentences.

CCSS Language 2d; Writing 3. (See pp. T6–7.)

Lesson 20 (pp. 92–95)

Progressive Forms of Verbs

OBJECTIVES

- **Identify the present, past, and future progressive forms of verbs**
- **Write the present, past, and future progressive forms of verbs correctly**
- **Write a story using the progressive forms of verbs**

TEACH/MODEL

■ **Learn** Say the following sentences: 1. I was getting on the bus when I saw my friend. 2. I am waving to him now. 3. I will be calling her tomorrow.

■ Have students identify the sentence that shows ongoing action, ongoing action until another action occurred, and ongoing action in the future. (*sentence 2, sentence 1, sentence 3*)

PRACTICE/APPLY

Connecting Speaking and Writing

■ Assign **Practices A–C**. Before assigning the **Write** activity in **D**, ask students to say aloud to themselves each sentence they plan to write before writing it. Review responses to **A–D** orally.

FOLLOW-UP

■ **ELL** Say, *"Last week, we went on a class trip. We were waiting for the bus when . . ."* One at a time, have students add to the story. Guide the progression of the narrative so that different progressive forms can be used.

■ **Writing** Ask students to write about a game they watched. They should use at least five progressive verbs.

CCSS Language 1b; Writing 3, 5, 10. (See pp. T6–7.)

Additional practice, quizzes, and activities for each lesson are available at **grammarworkshop.com**.

Lesson 21 (pp. 96–99)

Irregular Verbs

OBJECTIVES

- Identify the past forms of irregular verbs
- Correct errors in the use of irregular verbs
- Write sentences with irregular verbs

TEACH/MODEL

■ **Learn** Choose irregular verbs from the chart on page 96, and model how to use them in sentences. Then give each student both past forms of one of the verbs, and have the student say a sentence with each past form. (*grew/have grown*: *I grew an inch/I have grown a lot this year.*) With the class, check subject-verb agreement in each sentence.

PRACTICE/APPLY

Connecting Speaking and Writing

■ Assign **Practices A–C**. Before assigning the **Write** activity in **D**, ask students to say aloud to themselves each sentence they plan to write before writing it.

■ Review responses orally. In **D**, have volunteers read aloud their completed stories.

FOLLOW-UP

■ **ELL** Have students say sentences with verbs from the chart on page 96. Work together to check subject-verb agreement in each oral sentence.

■ **Writing** Have students write five sentences about a picnic. In each, they should use the past forms of the irregular verbs from the chart on page 96. Two or three sentences should use *has*, *have*, or *had* with an irregular verb.

CCSS Language 2d; Writing 3, 4, 10. (See pp. T6–7.)

Lesson 22 (pp. 100–103)

More Irregular Verbs

OBJECTIVES

- Identify the past forms of irregular verbs
- Correct errors in the use of irregular verbs
- Write sentences with irregular verbs

TEACH/MODEL

■ **Learn** Have students say sentences with the past forms of the verbs in the chart on page 100. Then ask them to close their books. Say irregular verbs from the chart. Ask volunteers to give the past-tense form and the past form used with *have*. Have others say sentences with each verb.

PRACTICE/APPLY

Connecting Speaking and Writing

■ Assign **Practices A–C**. Before assigning the **Write** activity in **D**, ask students to say aloud to themselves each sentence they plan to write before writing it.

■ Review responses orally. In **C**, have students identify the mistakes and tell how to fix them. In **D**, invite students to read aloud their stories about Paul Bunyan.

FOLLOW-UP

■ **ELL** Say past forms of the irregular verbs on page 100, one at a time. Have students use the verbs in sentences.

■ **Writing** Have students write six sentences about two cousins who met at a park and what they did once they arrived there. Have them use a different past form from the chart on page 100 in each sentence.

CCSS Language 2d; Writing 3, 4, 10. (See pp. T6–7.)

LESSON PLANS

Lesson 23 (pp. 104–107)

Contractions with *Not*

OBJECTIVES

- Write contractions with *not*
- Correct the spelling of contractions
- Write sentences with contractions

TEACH/MODEL

■ **Learn** Write and display contractions from page 104 with *no* punctuation. Have volunteers add apostrophes to each and tell what letter(s) they replace. Then say sentences with the verbs and *not*. Have students repeat each sentence, using a contraction instead of the verb with *not*.

PRACTICE/APPLY

Connecting Speaking and Writing

■ Assign **Practices A–C**. Before assigning the **Write** activity in **D**, ask students to say aloud to themselves each sentence they plan to write before writing it. Review responses to **A–D** orally.

FOLLOW-UP

■ **ELL** Ask students to say sentences using each contraction on page 104. Review that apostrophes replace letters such as the *o* in *not*. Point out and discuss that *won't* has an unusual form.

■ **Writing** Have students write five sentences that give home safety rules; students should use a lesson contraction in each.

CCSS Language 2d. (See pp. T6–7.)

Unit 3 Review (pp. 108–109) Lessons 12–23

OBJECTIVE

- Review skills and concepts from Unit 3, Lessons 12–23

USING THE UNIT REVIEW

■ To review the skills and concepts taught in the unit, have students complete the Unit 3 Review on pages 108 and 109. If they need more help with a skill or concept, have them turn to the appropriate pages for a review of the lesson.

FOLLOWING THE UNIT REVIEW

■ Have students write five sentences describing what it would be like to live in a different era. Ask them to include regular and irregular past-tense verbs as well as progressive-tense verbs, linking verbs, and contractions in their descriptions. Then have them revise and edit their writing to apply what they learned in the unit. Have students proofread for correct capitalization and punctuation.

Unit 3 Test (pp. 110–111)

OBJECTIVE

- Assess students' understanding of the skills and concepts from Unit 3

USING THE UNIT TEST

■ Discuss the standardized-test format of the Unit Test. Review how to fill in the circle to indicate an answer choice. You may also want to review the **Test-Taking Strategies** available at **grammarworkshop.com**.

■ Have students complete the test on pages 110 and 111. Before beginning, make sure that they understand the directions.

Unit 4

An editing activity for the unit is available at **grammarworkshop.com**.

Adjectives, Adverbs, and Prepositions

Lesson 24 (pp. 112–115)

Adjectives

OBJECTIVES

- Identify adjectives and the nouns they describe
- Write adjectives in the correct order
- Write adjectives to complete sentences
- Combine related sentences by moving adjectives

TEACH/MODEL

■ **Learn** Discuss the example sentences at the top of page 112. Ask students to identify the nouns that *large, several, two, white, many*, and *dry* describe, and then have them name other adjectives that describe those nouns.

PRACTICE/APPLY

Connecting Speaking and Writing

■ Assign **Practices A–C**. Before assigning the **Write** activity in **D**, ask students to say aloud to themselves each sentence they plan to write before writing it. Review responses to **A–D** orally.

FOLLOW-UP

■ **ELL** Ask students to read aloud sentences from **A** and **B**. Challenge students to try to use adjectives that have meanings similar to those of adjectives in the lesson sentences.

■ **Writing** Have students choose five adjectives from the box in **C** and use each in a new sentence about a garden.

CCSS Language 1d. (See pp. T6–7.)

Additional practice, quizzes, and activities for each lesson are available at **grammarworkshop.com**.

Lesson 25 (pp. 116–119)

A, An, The

OBJECTIVES

- Identify articles
- Write articles to complete sentences
- Correct errors in the use of articles
- Write sentences with articles

TEACH/MODEL

■ **Learn** After discussing each rule, say a list of nouns. Have volunteers add an article that would work with each. (*giraffe, otter, tails, ape, fly, alligators*)

PRACTICE/APPLY

Connecting Speaking and Writing

■ Assign **Practices A–C**. Before assigning the **Write** activity in **D**, ask students to say aloud to themselves each sentence they plan to write before writing it.

■ Review responses orally. In **C**, have students identify mistakes and tell how to fix them. In **D**, have students read aloud their sentences with and without adjectives. Discuss how adding an adjective that begins with a consonant or vowel sound affects the use of *a* or *an* in the original sentence. (*an opossum, a lazy opossum, an odd opossum*)

FOLLOW-UP

■ **ELL** Say *a alligator, an alligator*. Ask which is correct, and explain that *an* is used before nouns that begin with vowel sounds. Have students give other examples using *an* correctly with nouns.

■ **Writing** Have students write five sentences about food shopping. Ask students to include *a, an,* or *the* and a singular or plural noun in each sentence.

CCSS Language 1d, 1f. (See pp. T6–7.)

Additional practice, quizzes, and activities for each lesson are available at **grammarworkshop.com**.

Lesson 26 (pp. 120–123)

Demonstrative Adjectives

OBJECTIVES

- Identify demonstrative adjectives
- Correct errors in the use of demonstrative adjectives
- Write sentences with demonstrative adjectives

TEACH/MODEL

■ **Learn** Discuss the rules and example sentences on page 120. Explain that since *this* and *these* tell about things that are close by, *here* is part of their meaning; and since *that* and *those* tell about things that are farther away, *there* is part of their meaning. *This here* or *those there* or the like is therefore unneeded repetition.

PRACTICE/APPLY

Connecting Speaking and Writing

■ Assign **Practices A–C**. Before assigning the **Write** activity in **D**, ask students to say aloud to themselves each sentence they plan to write before writing it. Review responses to **A–D** orally.

FOLLOW-UP

■ **ELL** Use the first paragraph in **C** to model using context clues to figure out whether to use *this, that, these,* or *those*. Have students do the same with other sentences with *this, that, these,* or *those*.

■ **Writing** Ask students to write four sentences about a place they know well. They should include *this, that, these,* and *those* once each in their sentences.

CCSS Language 1f, 3a. (See pp. T6–7.)

Lesson 27 (pp. 124–127)

Comparing with Adjectives

OBJECTIVES

- Use adjectives ending in *-er* and *-est* to compare
- Correct errors in adjectives that compare
- Write sentences using adjectives that compare

TEACH/MODEL

■ **Learn** Have students brainstorm one or two more adjectives that fit each spelling rule on page 124. Ask for one-syllable adjectives and two-syllable adjectives that end in *-y*. Have students add *-er* or *-est* to each adjective and tell whether and how its spelling changes when an ending is added.

PRACTICE/APPLY

Connecting Speaking and Writing

■ Assign **Practices A–C**. Before assigning the **Write** activity in **D**, ask students to say aloud to themselves each sentence they plan to write before writing it. Review responses to **A–D** orally.

FOLLOW-UP

■ **ELL** Say statements such as *I have three friends/I have two books*. After modeling the kinds of questions to ask, have students ask related questions using adjectives ending in *-er* or *-est*. (*Who is older? Who is funniest?*)

■ **Writing** Have students brainstorm two more adjectives that fit each lesson spelling pattern. Have students add *-er* or *-est*, write each adjective, and then choose six to use in sentences that compare two or three familiar stories.

CCSS Language 1f. (See pp. T6–7.)

Additional practice, quizzes, and activities for each lesson are available at **grammarworkshop.com**.

Lesson 28 (pp. 128–131)

Comparing with *More* and *Most*

OBJECTIVES

- Use *more* or *most* with adjectives to compare
- Correct errors in the use of *more* and *most* when comparing
- Write sentences using *more* and *most* to compare

TEACH/MODEL

■ **Learn** Say one-, two-, and three-syllable adjectives (*sensible, special, tall, regular, mean, tiring*). Have students add *more/most* or *-er/-est* to each. Use *silly* and *happy* to show that some two-syllable adjectives, such as most that end with *-y*, take *-er/-est* rather than *more/most*.

PRACTICE/APPLY

Connecting Speaking and Writing

■ Assign **Practices A–C**. Before assigning the **Write** activity in **D**, ask students to say aloud to themselves each sentence they plan to write before writing it. Review responses to **A–D** orally.

FOLLOW-UP

■ **ELL** With students, brainstorm adjectives that take *more/most* and those that take *-er/-est*. Have students say the correct forms of the adjectives and then use them in sentences.

■ **Writing** Have students write four sentences using *more* and *most* with adjectives to compare school to home.

CCSS Language 1f. (See pp. T6–7.)

Lesson 29 (pp. 132–135)

Comparing with *Good* and *Bad*

OBJECTIVES

- Use the comparative and superlative forms of *good* and *bad*
- Correct errors in the use of *good* and *bad*
- Write a description using *good* and *bad*

TEACH/MODEL

■ **Learn** After discussing the rules on page 132, help students brainstorm groups of two and three things (songs, pets, grades, foods) and compare items in each group by saying phrases that include *good, better, best, bad, worse,* and *worst.*

PRACTICE/APPLY

Connecting Speaking and Writing

■ Assign **Practices A–C**. Before assigning the **Write** activity in **D**, ask students to say aloud to themselves each sentence they plan to write before writing it. Review responses to **A–D** orally.

FOLLOW-UP

■ **ELL** Draw a horizontal line with hash marks labeled *sleet, rain, clouds, sunshine.* At the left side of the line, write *bad.* On the right side, write *good.* Have students use the diagram to make statements of comparison. (*Sleet is worse than rain. Sunshine is the best.*)

■ **Writing** Have students write four sentences using forms of *good* and *bad* to tell about kinds of fruit or snacks.

CCSS Language 1f, 2d; Writing 3, 4, 5, 10. (See pp. T6–7.)

Additional practice, quizzes, and activities for each lesson are available at **grammarworkshop.com**.

Lesson 30 (pp. 136–139)

Adverbs

OBJECTIVES

- Identify adverbs and the verbs they describe
- Write adverbs to complete sentences
- Revise sentences by adding adverbs

TEACH/MODEL

■ **Learn** Discuss the example sentences on page 136. Have students identify the verbs that the adverbs describe. Then have students identify the adverbs that tell *how*, *when*, and *where*, and call on volunteers to say a verb that each adverb could describe. Finally, have students use the adverb and verb in a sentence.

PRACTICE/APPLY

Connecting Speaking and Writing

■ Assign **Practices A–C**. Before assigning the **Write** activity in **D**, ask students to say aloud to themselves each sentence they plan to write before writing it. Review responses to **A–D** orally.

FOLLOW-UP

■ **ELL** Review that adverbs can come before *or* after the verbs they describe. Say aloud adverb/verb and verb/adverb pairs. For each, call on a student to tell which word is a verb and which is an adverb and to say a sentence using the pair.

■ **Writing** Have students write six sentences about jobs they would like to have as adults. Have students include two *how*, two *where*, and two *when* adverbs.

CCSS Language 3a. (See pp. T6–7.)

Lesson 31 (pp. 140–143)

Comparing with Adverbs

OBJECTIVES

- Use the correct forms of adverbs to compare
- Correct errors in adverbs that compare
- Write sentences using adverbs that compare

TEACH/MODEL

■ **Learn** Have students replace the comparative adverb in each example sentence on page 140 with another adverb that fits in the sentence. Have students use both *more/most* and *-er/-est*.

PRACTICE/APPLY

Connecting Speaking and Writing

■ Assign **Practices A–C**. Before assigning the **Write** activity in **D**, ask students to say aloud to themselves each sentence they plan to write before writing it. Review responses to **A–D** orally.

FOLLOW-UP

■ **ELL** With students, brainstorm other adverbs that use *more/most* or *-er/-est* to compare. Have students say the correct forms of the adverbs and then use them in sentences.

■ **Writing** Have students write six sentences that compare how different animals move. Students should include at least one sentence each using comparative adverbs with *more*, *most*, *-er*, and *-est*.

CCSS Language 1f. (See pp. T6–7.)

Additional practice, quizzes, and activities for each lesson are available at **grammarworkshop.com.**

Lesson 32 (pp. 144–147)

Using *Good* and *Well*

OBJECTIVES

- Write *good* or *well* to complete sentences
- Correct errors in the use of *good* and *well*
- Write sentences using *good* and *well*

TEACH/MODEL

■ **Learn** Discuss the rules and example sentences at the top of page 144. In each sentence, have students identify the noun or verb that *good* or *well* describes. When discussing *well* as an adjective, explain that *good* can also tell about a person's health: *Kim feels good* and *Kim feels well* are both correct.

PRACTICE/APPLY

Connecting Speaking and Writing

■ Assign **Practices A–C**. Before assigning the **Write** activity in **D**, ask students to say aloud to themselves each sentence they plan to write before writing it. Review responses to **A–D** orally.

FOLLOW-UP

■ **ELL** To reinforce when to use *good* and when to use *well*, have students draw an arrow from *good* or *well* to the noun or verb each describes in the sentences in **A–B**.

■ **Writing** Have students write five pairs of sentences, using *good* and *well*, to tell about a favorite activity, hobby, or interest. Have students use the sentences they wrote in **D** as a model.

CCSS Language 1f, 3c. (See pp. T6–7.)

Lesson 33 (pp. 148–151)

Negatives

OBJECTIVES

- Identify negative words
- Correct errors in the use of negatives
- Revise sentences by adding negative words

TEACH/MODEL

■ **Learn** Work with students to say sentences using these negatives: *no, not, nothing, none, never, nowhere, nobody, no one, don't, wasn't,* and *aren't*. Offer feedback as needed.

PRACTICE/APPLY

Connecting Speaking and Writing

■ Assign **Practices A–C**. Before assigning the **Write** activity in **D**, ask students to say aloud to themselves each sentence they plan to write before writing it. Review responses to **A–D** orally.

FOLLOW-UP

■ **ELL** Work with students to form and say contractions that combine *do, does, is, are, could,* and *should* with the negative *not*. Then explain that two negatives used together cancel the meanings of both negatives. Also, explain that adding *not* to *am, is,* and *are* sometimes results in *ain't*, which is considered to be an informal use and often not a proper substitute for *am not, is not,* and *are not.*

■ **Writing** Have students choose six sentences from earlier writing assignments that do *not* contain negatives. Have them rewrite each sentence, adding a negative.

CCSS Language 3a. (See pp. T6–7.)

Additional practice, quizzes, and activities for each lesson are available at **grammarworkshop.com.**

Lesson 34 (pp. 152–155)

Prepositions and Prepositional Phrases

OBJECTIVES

- Identify prepositions and prepositional phrases
- Write prepositional phrases to complete sentences
- Revise sentences by adding prepositional phrases

TEACH/MODEL

■ **Learn** Model how to create prepositional phrases with the common prepositions listed on page 152. Have students create and say prepositional phrases and use them in oral sentences. Point out that some of the prepositions tell *where* and some tell *when.* Identify these prepositions with the class.

PRACTICE/APPLY

Connecting Speaking and Writing

■ Assign **Practices A–C**. Before assigning the **Write** activity in **D**, ask students to say aloud to themselves each sentence before writing it. Review responses to **A–D** orally.

FOLLOW-UP

■ **ELL** With students, make a list of prepositions that tell *where* and a list of those that tell *when*. For *where* prepositions, have students hold objects and show *above, around, below,* and so on, and say sentences to tell what the prepositions show.

■ **Writing** Have students write six sentences about children in a playground, using a different preposition in each sentence. Ask students to include at least two *where* and two *when* prepositions.

CCSS Language 1e, 3a. (See pp. T6–7.)

Unit 4 Review (pp. 156–157)

Lessons 24–34

OBJECTIVE

- Review skills and concepts from Unit 4, Lessons 24–34

USING THE UNIT REVIEW

■ To review the skills and concepts taught in the unit, have students complete the Unit 4 Review on pages 156 and 157. If they need more help with a skill or concept, have them turn to the appropriate pages for a review of the lesson.

FOLLOWING THE UNIT REVIEW

■ Have students write six sentences about animal life in the forest. Then have students revise and edit their writing to apply what they learned in the unit. They might use adjectives to compare animals and adverbs to compare their actions. Or they might rewrite sentences to include demonstrative adjectives, negatives, or prepositional phrases. Have students proofread sentences for correct capitalization and punctuation.

Unit 4 Test (pp. 158–159)

OBJECTIVE

- Assess students' understanding of the skills and concepts from Unit 4

USING THE UNIT TEST

■ Discuss the standardized-test format of the Unit Test. Review how to fill in the circle to indicate an answer choice. You may also want to review the **Test-Taking Strategies** available at **grammarworkshop.com.**

■ Have students complete the test on pages 158 and 159. Be sure they understand the directions before beginning.

An editing activity for the unit is available at **grammarworkshop.com.**

Lesson 35 (pp. 160–163)

Subject Pronouns

OBJECTIVES

- Identify subject pronouns
- Write the subject pronouns that agree with their antecedents
- Revise sentences by replacing nouns with subject pronouns

TEACH/MODEL

■ **Learn** Have students replace the subjects in the example sentences with nouns that require different subject pronouns and then say the new pairs of sentences.

PRACTICE/APPLY

Connecting Speaking and Writing

■ Assign **Practices A–C**. Before assigning the **Write** activity in **D**, ask students to say aloud to themselves each sentence they plan to write before they write it. Review responses to **A–D** orally.

FOLLOW-UP

■ **ELL** Have students say questions and statements using subject pronouns from the chart on page 160. Point out that only two subject pronouns, *he* and *she*, show gender.

■ **Writing** Have students write seven sentences about an acting class, using a different subject pronoun in each sentence.

Additional practice, quizzes, and activities for each lesson are available at **grammarworkshop.com.**

Lesson 36 (pp. 164–167)

Pronoun-Verb Agreement

OBJECTIVES

- Write verbs that agree with subject pronouns
- Correct errors in pronoun-verb agreement
- Write sentences with pronoun-verb agreement

TEACH/MODEL

■ **Learn** For each example sentence on page 164, have students replace the verb with another verb that makes sense in the sentence. Encourage students to use verbs with the spelling patterns shown. Then have students replace the pronoun in each sentence with another that agrees with the verb.

PRACTICE/APPLY

Connecting Speaking and Writing

■ Assign **Practices A–C**. Before assigning the **Write** activity in **D**, ask students to say aloud to themselves each sentence they plan to write before they write it.

■ Review responses orally. In **D**, invite students to share their completed sentences.

FOLLOW-UP

■ **ELL** Have students read aloud each sentence in **A** and then repeat the sentence, changing the subject pronoun. Ask students to make sure the new subject pronoun and the verb agree.

■ **Writing** Have students write seven sentences about a parade. Each sentence should contain a different subject pronoun and a present-tense verb that agrees with it.

CCSS Language 1f. (See pp. T6–7.)

Additional practice, quizzes, and activities for each lesson are available at **grammarworkshop.com**.

Lesson 37 (pp. 168–171)

Object Pronouns

OBJECTIVES

- Identify object pronouns
- Write object pronouns to complete sentences
- Revise sentences by replacing nouns with object pronouns

TEACH/MODEL

■ **Learn** Provide sentence subjects and transitive verbs (*Luis takes, You watch, The machine washes, We race, The boat carries*, and the like). Have students add object pronouns to form and say complete sentences. Point out and discuss that both *you* and *it* are subject pronouns as well as object pronouns.

PRACTICE/APPLY

Connecting Speaking and Writing

■ Assign **Practices A–C**. Before assigning the **Write** activity in **D**, ask students to say aloud to themselves each sentence they plan to write before they write it.

■ Review responses orally. In **D**, have students read aloud the groups of sentences they wrote. Point out how much more interesting each group of sentences sounds when the overused nouns are replaced by object pronouns.

FOLLOW-UP

■ **Writing** Have students write six sentences about having fun with friends, using a different object pronoun in each.

Lesson 38 (pp. 172–175)

Using *I* and *Me*

OBJECTIVES

- Use *I* and *me* to complete sentences
- Correct errors in the use of *I* and *me*
- Combine sentences by joining a noun and a pronoun

TEACH/MODEL

■ **Learn** Tell students that when they perform the action, they should use *I*. (*I run fast.*) When they receive the action, they should use *me*. (*Jay invited me.*) When speaking about another person and themselves, they should follow the same rules: That is, they should use *I* when they and the other person perform the action, and they should use *me* when they and the other person receive the action. (*John and I play a game. Mom drove Ann and me.*)

PRACTICE/APPLY

Connecting Speaking and Writing

■ Assign **Practices A–C**. Before assigning the **Write** activity in **D**, ask students to say aloud to themselves each sentence they plan to write before they write it. Review responses to **A–D** orally.

FOLLOW-UP

■ **ELL** Ask second-person questions, and have students answer using *I* or *me* in each response. (*Do you see the sky? I see the sky. Who helped you? Ed helped me.*)

■ **Writing** Have students write six sentences about working with a friend to make something. Ask students to use *I* three times and *me* three times in their sentences.

Additional practice, quizzes, and activities for each lesson are available at **grammarworkshop.com**.

Lesson 39 (pp. 176–179)

Possessive Pronouns

OBJECTIVES

- Identify possessive pronouns
- Correct errors in the use of possessive pronouns
- Write sentences using possessive pronouns

TEACH/MODEL

■ **Learn** Write and display those possessive pronouns used before a noun (*my, your, her, his, our, its, their*), and those used alone (*mine, yours, hers, his, ours, theirs*). Have students say sentences using the pronouns in each list.

PRACTICE/APPLY

Connecting Speaking and Writing

■ Assign **Practices A–C**. Before assigning the **Write** activity in **D**, ask students to say aloud to themselves each sentence they plan to write before they write it. Review responses to **A–D** orally.

FOLLOW-UP

■ **ELL** Have students read aloud each completed sentence in **B**. Then challenge them to say the sentences again, changing each possessive pronoun to a different one. (*Our tabby cat. . . .*)

■ **Writing** Ask students to pretend they are kindergarten teachers. Have them write six sentences they might say in the classroom. Ask students to use a different possessive pronoun in each, including three possessive pronouns used before a noun and three used alone.

CCSS Language 1f. (See pp. T6–7.)

Lesson 40 (pp. 180–183)

Relative Pronouns and Relative Adverbs

OBJECTIVES

- Identify relative pronouns and relative adverbs
- Write relative pronouns and relative adverbs to complete sentences
- Use relative pronouns and relative adverbs to combine two sentences

TEACH/MODEL

■ **Learn** On the board, write three complex sentences from Lesson 6. In each sentence, point out the subordinating conjunction that joins the ideas. Then explain that in this lesson, the ideas in the complex sentences are joined by relative pronouns or relative adverbs.

PRACTICE/APPLY

Connecting Speaking and Writing

■ Assign **Practices A–C**. Before assigning the **Write** activity in **D**, ask students to say aloud to themselves each sentence they plan to write before writing it. Review responses to **A–D** orally.

FOLLOW-UP

■ **ELL** To reinforce the use of relative pronouns and relative adverbs, have students say the sentences in Learn, **A**, and **B** orally.

■ **Writing** Have students write four complex sentences about an exciting summertime experience. One sentence should use *who, whom*, or *that*; another should use *that* or *which*; and the last two should use *where, when*, or *why*. Ask peers to check each other's sentences.

CCSS Language 1a, 3c. (See pp. T6–7.)

Additional practice, quizzes, and activities for each lesson are available at **grammarworkshop.com**.

Lesson 41 (pp. 184–187)

Contractions with Pronouns

OBJECTIVES
- Write contractions for pronouns and verbs
- Correct the spelling of contractions
- Write sentences using contractions

TEACH/MODEL

■ **Learn** Review the contractions from the chart on page 184. Then call on students, giving each a pronoun and verb from the chart. Have students form a contraction, tell where the apostrophe goes and what letter(s) it replaces, and say a sentence with the contraction.

PRACTICE/APPLY

Connecting Speaking and Writing
■ Assign **Practices A–C**. Before assigning the **Write** activity in **D**, ask students to say aloud to themselves each sentence they plan to write before they write it. Review responses to **A–D** orally.

FOLLOW-UP

■ **ELL** In a column, write and display *I*, *you*, *he*, *she*, *it*, *we*, *they*. In a second column, write *am*, *is*, *are*. In a third column, write *has* and *have*. Have each student choose a pronoun and the verb in each column that agrees with the pronoun, form a contraction, and say a sentence using the contraction.

■ **Writing** Have students write five sentences about a class field trip. Have students use a different contraction from page 184 in each.

CCSS Language 1f, 3c. (See pp. T6–7.)

Unit 5 Review (pp. 188–189)

Lessons 35–41

OBJECTIVE
- Review skills and concepts from Unit 5, Lessons 35–41

USING THE UNIT REVIEW

■ To review skills and concepts taught in the unit, have students complete the Unit 5 Review on pages 188 and 189. If they need more help with a skill or concept, have them turn to the appropriate pages for a review of the lesson.

■ Have students write six sentences about an art show. Then have them revise and edit their writing to apply what they learned in the unit. For example, they might use pronouns to replace some of the nouns. They might rewrite pronouns and verbs as contractions. They might use relative pronouns or relative adverbs. Have students proofread sentences for correct capitalization and punctuation.

Unit 5 Test (pp. 190–191)

OBJECTIVE
- Assess students' understanding of the skills and concepts from Unit 5

USING THE UNIT TEST

■ Discuss the standardized-test format of the Unit Test. Review how to fill in the circle to indicate an answer choice. You may also want to review the **Test-Taking Strategies** available at **grammarworkshop.com**.

■ Have students complete the test on pages 190 and 191. Be sure they understand the directions before beginning.

An editing activity for the unit is available at grammarworkshop.com.

Capitalization, Punctuation, and Spelling

Lesson 42 (pp. 192–195)

Writing Sentences Correctly

OBJECTIVES

- Identify correctly written sentences
- Correct capitalization and punctuation in sentences
- Write the four kinds of sentences

TEACH/MODEL

■ **Learn** Read aloud the example sentences on page 192, emphasizing the tone of each. Have students say more examples of each kind of sentence. Encourage them to speak expressively, stressing the unique tone of each. Have the class identify each kind of sentence and the end punctuation each needs.

PRACTICE/APPLY

Connecting Speaking and Writing

■ Assign **Practices A–C**. Before assigning the **Write** activity in **D**, ask students to say aloud to themselves each sentence they plan to write before writing it. Review responses to **A–D** orally.

FOLLOW-UP

■ **ELL** Have students imagine that a note has been slipped under the door. Have them tell about the note, saying examples of each kind of sentence. Ask them to use their voices to show how each kind of sentence should sound.

CCSS Language 1f, 2a, 3a, 3b. (See pp. T6–7.)

Additional practice, quizzes, and activities for each lesson are available at **grammarworkshop.com**.

Lesson 43 (pp. 196–199)

Capitalizing Proper Nouns

OBJECTIVES

- Identify and write proper nouns correctly
- Correct errors in capitalization
- Write sentences using proper nouns

TEACH/MODEL

■ **Learn** After discussing the examples on page 196, have students give other examples of each kind of proper noun and tell what letters should be capitalized. Explain that short words such as *the*, *to*, *a*, and *of* that are part of the name are *not* capitalized. (*the Empire State Building*)

PRACTICE/APPLY

Connecting Speaking and Writing

■ Assign **Practices A–C**. Before assigning the **Write** activity in **D**, ask students to say aloud to themselves each sentence they plan to write before writing it. Review responses to **A–D** orally.

FOLLOW-UP

■ **ELL** Use examples (*a day, Arbor Day*) to help students distinguish between common and proper nouns. Have students say other proper nouns. Discuss how the capitalization of proper nouns can help readers better understand the meanings of sentences.

■ **Writing** Have students write five sentences, giving directions to a theater or stadium. Ask them to include one person's name, one place name, one holiday, one day of the week, and one title of respect.

CCSS Language 1f, 2a; Writing 2, 4. (See pp. T6–7.)

Additional practice, quizzes, and activities for each lesson are available at **grammarworkshop.com**.

Lesson 44 (pp. 200–203)

Abbreviations

OBJECTIVES

- Write abbreviations for days, months, names, and addresses correctly
- Correct errors in abbreviations
- Write messages using abbreviations

TEACH/MODEL

■ **Learn** Discuss the abbreviations at the top of page 200. Have students use the abbreviations to spell the following: the name of the street they live on, the month in the day's date, their state's name, the title of respect in the principal's name. Have them also state their own names using an initial.

PRACTICE/APPLY

Connecting Speaking and Writing

■ Assign **Practices A–C**. Before assigning the **Write** activity in **D**, ask students to say aloud to themselves each sentence they plan to write before writing it. Review responses to **A–D** orally.

FOLLOW-UP

■ **ELL** Explain that when people read aloud abbreviations for days or months, they usually say the whole word. Have students read aloud the abbreviations on page 200 for the months and days of the week, saying the full word that each abbreviation stands for.

■ **Writing** Ask students to write sentences for an invitation to a party, using and abbreviating a title of respect, an address, the names of a month and a day of the week, an initial, and a state name.

CCSS Language 1f, 2a. (See pp. T6–7.)

Lesson 45 (pp. 204–207)

Titles

OBJECTIVES

- Write titles of books, magazines, newspapers, songs, and poems correctly
- Correct errors in the capitalization and treatment of titles

TEACH/MODEL

■ **Learn** Invite students to read aloud the titles at the top of page 204. Discuss which words *are* and which *are not* capitalized. Then discuss how each title is set off. Ask students to look around the room to find a variety of the print materials mentioned. Discuss the title of each, pointing out any unimportant words that *are* and *are not* capitalized. Point out that verbs in titles are always capitalized.

PRACTICE/APPLY

Connecting Speaking and Writing

■ Assign **Practices A–C** and the **Write** activity in **D**. Review responses to **A–D** orally.

FOLLOW-UP

■ **Writing** Have students write five sentences about a talent show. Ask students to include titles of a magazine, a book, a newspaper, a poem, and a song. Have them use the review on page 206 as a model.

CCSS Language 2a. (See pp. T6–7.)

Lesson 46 (pp. 208–211)

Commas in a Series

OBJECTIVES

- Use commas to separate words in a series
- Correct errors in the use of commas in a series
- Combine sentences by putting words in a series

TEACH/MODEL

■ **Learn** Discuss the use of commas in the example sentences on page 208. Then say sentences with a series of three days or actions. Have students name the things in each series and tell how to punctuate each.

PRACTICE/APPLY

Connecting Speaking and Writing

■ Assign **Practices A–C**. Before assigning the **Write** activity in **D**, ask students to say aloud to themselves each sentence they plan to write before writing it.

■ Review responses orally. In **D**, students should recognize that the writing sounds better when the short, choppy sentences are combined.

FOLLOW-UP

■ **ELL** Ask students to read aloud sentences from **A**, **B**, and **C**. Instruct students to practice pausing slightly after each comma.

■ **Writing** Ask students to write five sentences about a neighborhood tag sale. Ask students to include a series of three things or actions in each sentence.

CCSS Language 1f; Writing 4, 10. (See pp. T6–7.)

Lesson 47 (pp. 212–215)

More Commas

OBJECTIVES

- Use commas in direct address and after introductory words
- Correct errors in the use of commas
- Write a script using direct address and introductory words

TEACH/MODEL

■ **Learn** Discuss commas in the example sentences on page 212. Then have pairs of students converse. One speaker should call another by name and ask a question. The second speaker should reply, starting with an introductory word such as *no, yes*, or *well*. Instruct speakers to pause briefly to indicate where each comma would go. Write and display the exchange, using the example sentences as a model.

PRACTICE/APPLY

Connecting Speaking and Writing

■ Assign **Practices A–C**. Before assigning the **Write** activity in **D**, ask students to say aloud to themselves each sentence they plan to write before writing it. Review responses to **A–D** orally.

FOLLOW-UP

■ **ELL** Have partners work together to read aloud the conversation in activity **C**. Ask them to pause briefly after each comma and to read their lines with expression.

■ **Writing** Have students write six sentences friends might say to each other over the phone. Each sentence should start with an introductory word or contain the name of someone being spoken to.

CCSS Language 1f, 3c; Writing 4, 5, 10. (See pp. T6–7.)

Additional practice, quizzes, and activities for each lesson are available at **grammarworkshop.com.**

Lesson 48 (pp. 216–219)

Parts of a Letter

OBJECTIVES

- Write the parts of friendly letters and business letters correctly
- Correct the use of capitalization and punctuation in a letter
- Write a letter

TEACH/MODEL

■ **Learn** Discuss the labeled parts of each letter on page 216 and how the parts follow the capitalization and punctuation rules given on the page. Help students to find the letter part that each rule applies to.

PRACTICE/APPLY

Connecting Speaking and Writing

■ Assign **Practices A–C**. Before assigning the **Write** activity in **D**, ask students to say aloud to themselves each sentence they plan to write before writing it.

■ Review responses orally. In **A–C**, have students tell how each letter part should be capitalized and punctuated. In **D**, have them tell whether they wrote a friendly letter or a business letter, read it, and then tell how they capitalized and punctuated the letter parts.

FOLLOW-UP

■ **Writing** Have students write short, friendly letters to friends or family members. Ask students to use proper form, with all parts that should be in a letter, and to punctuate and capitalize correctly.

CCSS Language 1f, 2a; Writing 4, 10. (See pp. T6–7.)

Lesson 49 (pp. 220–223)

Quotations

OBJECTIVES

- Use quotations marks around a speaker's words
- Correct capitalization and punctuation in quotations
- Write quotations correctly

TEACH/MODEL

■ **Learn** Discuss the rules and example sentences on page 220. Ask a student to say a short statement about the classroom. Write and display it as a quotation with no capitalization or punctuation. (*ed said the walls are blue*) Work with the class to punctuate and capitalize the quotation. Invite other students to say a question, an exclamation, and a command. Work together to punctuate each.

PRACTICE/APPLY

Connecting Speaking and Writing

■ Assign **Practices A–C**. Before assigning the **Write** activity in **D**, ask students to say aloud to themselves each sentence they plan to write before writing it. Review responses to **A–D** orally.

FOLLOW-UP

■ **ELL** Have students read aloud the conversations in **D**. Ask students to read each speaker's words with expression to show how the person might really sound.

■ **Writing** Have students write five sentences about a parent and child who disagree about something. Ask students to use a person's exact words in each sentence.

CCSS Language 2a, 2b, 3c. (See pp. T6–7.)

Additional practice, quizzes, and activities for each lesson are available at **grammarworkshop.com**.

Lesson 50 (pp. 224–227)

Words Often Misspelled

OBJECTIVES

- Distinguish between *there, they're, their; it's, its; you're, your; to, two, too; tail, tale;* and *right, write*
- Correct errors in the use and spelling of homophones
- Write a short book report that expresses an opinion and includes homophones

TEACH/MODEL

■ **Learn** With the class, read the sentences at the top of page 224. Discuss and compare the meanings and spellings of the homophones. Point out the contractions and the possessive pronouns. Elicit a new oral sentence for each homophone.

PRACTICE/APPLY

Connecting Speaking and Writing

■ Assign **Practices A–C**. Before assigning the **Write** activity in **D**, ask students to say aloud to themselves each sentence they plan to write before writing it.

■ Review responses orally. In **D**, ask students to read aloud their short book report. Have others identify and spell each homophone they hear. Then ask if they would read the book based on the opinion expressed in the report.

FOLLOW-UP

■ **ELL** Review the meanings of the homophones. Then present them in oral sentences one at a time. Have students identify the homophone in each and spell it.

CCSS Language 1g, 2d; Writing 1, 4, 10. (See pp. T6–7.)

Lesson 51 (pp. 228–231)

Words Often Confused

OBJECTIVES

- Use and spell *advice, advise; desert, dessert; proof, prove; all ready, already; further, farther*
- Correct the spelling of words that are often confused
- Write sentences using words that are often confused

TEACH/MODEL

■ **Learn** Point out that *advice* is a noun, and *advise* is a verb. Say, "I ask my friends for *advice*. They *advise* me to audition for the play." Explain that in the first sentence, the sentence structure tells the reader that the missing word is a noun. In the second sentence, the missing word is a verb.

PRACTICE/APPLY

Connecting Speaking and Writing

■ Assign **Practices A–C**. Before assigning the **Write** activity in **D**, ask students to say aloud to themselves each sentence they plan to write before writing it. Review responses to **A–D** orally.

FOLLOW-UP

■ **ELL** Have students say sentences with the ten words in **A**. Encourage them to reread the meanings if they need to.

■ **Writing** Have students write a sentence for each word in **A**. Then ask them to read each sentence to a partner, who should spell the word in **A** correctly.

CCSS Language 1g, 2d; Writing 2. (See pp. T6–7.)

Unit 6 Review (pp. 232–233)

Lessons 42–51

OBJECTIVE

- **Review skills and concepts from Unit 6, Lessons 42–51**

USING THE UNIT REVIEW

■ To review skills and concepts taught in the unit, have students complete the Unit 6 Review on pages 232 and 233. If they need more help with a skill or concept, have them turn to the appropriate pages for a review of the lesson.

FOLLOWING THE UNIT REVIEW

■ Have each student write a friendly letter inviting a relative to a school talent show. Ask students to use proper form for a friendly letter. Challenge them to try to include a title, a quotation, an abbreviation, and a series. Have them revise and edit their writing to apply what they learned in the unit. For example, they might add quotation marks around a speaker's words or fix capitalization of a title. Have them proofread their letters for correct form, capitalization, and punctuation.

Unit 6 Test (pp. 234–235)

OBJECTIVE

- **Assess students' understanding of the skills and concepts from Unit 6**

USING THE UNIT TEST

■ Discuss the standardized-test format of the Unit Test. Review how to fill in the circle to indicate an answer choice. You may also want to review the **Test-Taking Strategies** available at **grammarworkshop.com**.

■ Have students complete the test on pages 234 and 235. Be sure they understand the directions before beginning.

Proofreading Checklist ☑

Grammar and Usage

- ❑ *Did I use complete sentences?*
- ❑ *Did I correct all run-on sentences?*
- ❑ *Did the verbs I use agree with their subjects?*
- ❑ *Did I use the correct pronouns?*
- ❑ *Did I use adjectives, adverbs, and prepositions correctly?*

Punctuation and Capitalization

- ❑ *Did I begin each sentence with a capital letter?*
- ❑ *Did I end each sentence with the correct end mark?*
- ❑ *Did I use commas, quotation marks, apostrophes, and other punctuation marks correctly?*
- ❑ *Did I capitalize proper nouns and the pronoun* **I***?*

Spelling

- ❑ *Did I spell every word correctly?*
- ❑ *If a word is a homophone, did I use the correct one?*

For a printable version, see **grammarworkshop.com.**

Test-Taking Strategies ☑

- ❑ *Read each item carefully and completely before trying to answer it. Be sure you understand what you need to do. Then think about each possible answer.*
- ❑ *Ask yourself which answer seems to fit best.*
- ❑ *Always check each answer after you have marked it.*
- ❑ *Remember that some answers may seem right, but other answers might be better choices.*
- ❑ *If you are uncertain about an answer, put a check mark (✓) next to that row. Then go on to the next item.*
- ❑ *After you have answered all the items you are sure of, answer all the items you skipped.*
- ❑ *Check that you are filling in the correct circle.*
- ❑ *Before the test is over, make sure you have answered every item.*
- ❑ *Don't be concerned about the time running out. Just relax and answer the questions. Your teacher will tell you how much time you have left.*
- ❑ *Use a soft pencil to mark the answers.*
- ❑ *Fill in only one circle for each item. Make sure you fill it completely.*
- ❑ *If you change your mind about an answer, erase it completely. Then mark your new answer.*

For a printable version, see **grammarworkshop.com.**

Grammar Workshop

Common Core Enriched Edition

Level Orange

Beverly Ann Chin, Ph.D.
Senior Series Consultant
Professor of English
University of Montana
Missoula, MT

Sadlier

Reviewers

The publisher wishes to thank the following teachers for their thorough review and thoughtful comments on portions of the series prior to publication.

Timothy Beaumont
Maplewood, New Jersey

Renea Boles
Flourtown, Pennsylvania

Stacy Donaghy
Little Rock, Arkansas

Christine Ganey
New York, New York

Maria James
San José, California

Stephanie Richardson
Compton, California

Nancy Wahl
New York, New York

Roseanne Williby
Omaha, Nebraska

Photo Credits

age fotostock/Andre Seale: 80. Alamy/Ablestock: 218; Bill Brooks: 113; CuboImages srl/Pasicc: 61; D. Hurst: 17 *left*; image100: 60; Wm. Baker/GhostWorks Images: 198. The American Library Association: 34. Animals Animals/Earth Scenes/Michael Fogden: 117. AP Photo/Pablo Martinez Monsivais: 170. Corbis/Bettmann: 16, 94; Jim Erickson: 172; Ocean: 180. Dreamstime/Starper: 82. Getty Images/AFP: 62; Dorling Kindersley/Steve Lyne: 89; Iconica/Diehm: 8; Iconica/Guy Bubb: 184; Iconica/Simon Wilkinson: 112; Lifesize/Mike Powell: 140; Photodisc: 70, 130; Photographer's Choice/PattiMcConville: 40; Stockbyte: 77; Stone/photo & co: 128; Stone/S Purdy Matthews: 125; Stone+/Tim Flach: 45; Taxi/Tony Anderson: 46; The Image Bank/Gary Vestal: 24. Incorporated Research Institute for Seismology/www.iris.edu: 192. iStockphoto.com/engineer89: 90; kycstudio: 17 *center*. Levi Strauss & Co. Archives: 17 *right*. Masterfile/Jeremy Woodhouse: 20. Punchstock/Digital Vision: 76, 88, 120, 124, 126; National Geographic: 169; Photodisc: 10, 48, 64, 152, 163, 194; Photographer's Choice RF: 209; Stockbyte: 208. Used under permission from Shutterstock.com/Dario Sabljak: 217; David Dea: 22; David MacFarlane: 53; Enrique Sallent: 171; Glenda M. Powers: 144; iofoto: 118; Ivanou Allaksandr: 86; Johanna Goodyear: 155; LaurensT: 30; Lisa C. McDonald: 176; mundoview: 28; Otna Ydur: 229; Peder Digre: 160; PHB.cz (Richard Semik): 31; Poznyakov: 230; Roland Loeffler: 196; Stephen Aaron Rees: 216; Tina Rencelj: 177; William Yuey: 168. Superstock/age fotostock: 81, 114, 228; Creatas: 84; Peter Barritt: 92. Thinkstock/Fuse: 183; Jupiterimages: 182. www.goodtimestove.com: 13.

Illustrators

Ron Berg: 18, 32, 65, 66, 72, 73, 164, 165, 167, 220, 223. Ken Bowser: 11, 42, 68, 69, 95, 132, 134, 135, 143, 212, 213, 214. John Ceballos: 49, 50, 100, 101, 102, 210. Mena Dolobowsky: 78, 145, 147. CD Hullinger: 104, 106, 148, 150, 178, 200, 201, 202. Nathan Jarvis: 12. Martin Lemelman: 96, 98, 99, 185, 186, 204, 206. Zina Saunders: 26, 116, 119, 122. Sam Ward: 44. Paul Weiner: 136, 138, 139, 224, 225, 227.

For additional online resources, go to grammarworkshop.com **and enter the Student Access Code: GW13SGYK6BVN**

Address inquiries to Permissions Department, William H. Sadlier, Inc., 9 Pine Street, New York, New York 10005-4700.

S® is a registered trademark of William H. Sadlier, Inc.

Printed in the United States of America.

ISBN: 978-1-4217-1054-9
3456789 RRDH 16 15 14

CONTENTS

UNIT 3 Verbs

UNIT 4 Adjectives, Adverbs, and Prepositions

UNIT 5 PRONOUNS

UNIT 6 CAPITALIZATION, PUNCTUATION, AND SPELLING

(See page ii for the student access code.)

- Interactive Quiz for Every Lesson
- Extra Practice for Every Lesson
- Proofreading Worksheets for Every Unit

NOTE TO STUDENTS

You already know how to read, speak, and write English. So why should you learn grammar?

What Is Grammar?

Like all languages, English has rules about how words can be put together in sentences. Learning these rules will help you to speak and write so that everyone understands you. When you study grammar, you learn that words in English can be grouped into different parts. These parts include nouns, verbs, adjectives, adverbs, and pronouns. Grammar tells you how to put these parts together correctly.

How Will Grammar Help You?

Knowing grammar will help you to become a better reader, speaker, and writer. Knowing how language works will help you to read with more understanding. It will help you to express your feelings and ideas clearly. Your writing will be easier to follow. You will also make fewer mistakes when you do homework and take tests.

What Is Grammar Workshop?

Grammar Workshop is designed to teach you the rules of English and to give you lots and lots of practice. This book is called a WORKSHOP because it teaches in ways that make you work. You don't just read and memorize. You have to Learn, Practice, and Write.

Ready, Set, Go Grammar!

Now it's time to get started. Have fun, learn those rules—and go grammar!

Lesson 1: Kinds of Sentences

LEARN

A **sentence** is a group of words that expresses a complete thought.

- There are four kinds of sentences.

A **declarative sentence** makes a statement.
It ends with a period (.).

We watched a movie about volcanoes.

An **interrogative sentence** asks a question.
It ends with a question mark (?).

Have you ever seen a volcano?

An **imperative sentence** gives a command.
It ends with a period (.).

Stay away from active volcanoes.
Please be careful.

An **exclamatory sentence** shows strong feelings.
It ends with an exclamation mark (!).

How amazing that would be!
Wow, the colors are so bright!

- Every sentence begins with a capital letter and ends with a punctuation mark. The end punctuation you use depends on the kind of sentence you write.

PRACTICE

A *Read each sentence. Write* ***declarative, interrogative, imperative,*** *or* ***exclamatory*** *to tell what kind of sentence it is.*

1. What an incredible sight that is! exclamatory
2. Hot melted rock, gas, and steam burst from the volcano. declarative
3. Watch how the hot ash and lava flow down the mountain. imperative

 CCSS Language 2a, 3b. (See pp. T6–7.)

PRACTICE A *continued*

4. What is lava? ______interrogative______
5. Lava is hot liquid rock that comes out of a volcano. ______declarative______
6. Wow, a lava flow looks so dangerous! ______exclamatory______
7. Please leave the area immediately. ______imperative______
8. One famous volcano is Mount Vesuvius in Italy. ______declarative______
9. Will Mount Vesuvius erupt again? ______interrogative______
10. I hope not! ______exclamatory______

B *Add the correct end punctuation to each sentence. Then write **declarative, interrogative, imperative,** or **exclamatory** to tell what kind of sentence it is.*

1. We learned more about volcanoes __.__ ______declarative______
2. Wow, they can be so destructive __!__ ______exclamatory______
3. Fortunately, they do not erupt very often __.__ ______declarative______
4. What are the warning signs of an eruption __?__ ______interrogative______
5. One sign is a loud explosion __.__ ______declarative______
6. Hey, that was such a loud clap __!__ ______exclamatory______
7. You really scared me __!__ ______exclamatory______
8. Move out of the path of the lava __.__ ______imperative______
9. Look at the volcanic ash __.__ ______imperative______
10. Please tell me more about volcanoes __.__ ______imperative______
11. What else would you like to know __?__ ______interrogative______
12. Are there any volcanoes in our state __?__ ______interrogative______

Remember

A **declarative sentence** makes a statement.
An **interrogative sentence** asks a question.
An **imperative sentence** gives a command.
An **exclamatory sentence** shows strong feelings.

C *Here is a conversation among some friends on a hike. The dialogue has three missing capital letters and seven missing or incorrect end marks. Look for the mistakes and correct them. Use the proofreading marks in the box.*

Bianca Mount Rainier is the highest peak in the state of Washington.

Danny exactly how tall is it?

Bianca Read that sign over there

Maria Wow, it's 14,410 feet high

Bianca we'll only climb a thousand feet or so.

Maria What a relief that is

Danny Wait for me, you two.

Bianca Did you know that Mount Rainier is a volcano

Maria Are you serious.

Bianca the last major eruption was about 500 years ago.

Danny Will it erupt again soon!

Bianca The scientists say no

Maria Let's hurry up anyway.

Danny You can't be too careful!

Proofreading Marks

^	Add
⊙	Period
ℓ	Take out
≡	Capital letter
/	Small letter

Did you correct ten mistakes with capital letters and end marks?

 CCSS Language 3b. (See pp. T6–7.)

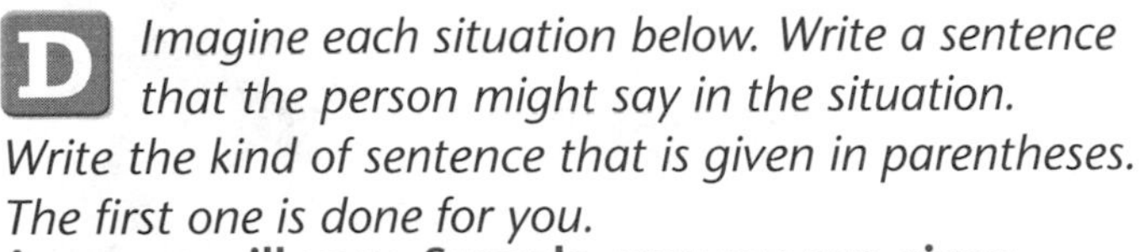

WRITE

Additional Resources at grammarworkshop.com

D *Imagine each situation below. Write a sentence that the person might say in the situation. Write the kind of sentence that is given in parentheses. The first one is done for you.*

Answers will vary. Sample answers are given.

Situation 1 Ms. Murray is teaching about volcanoes. She makes this statement about volcanoes. (declarative)

Ms. Murray *Hot ash or lava can erupt from a volcano.*

Situation 2 Your classmate Janet does not understand something about volcanoes. She raises her hand and asks a question. Write the question she asks. (interrogative)

Janet **Do all volcanoes have lava inside?**

Situation 3 Lois is another classmate. She is very surprised by a fact she learns about volcanoes. Write the statement she makes to show her surprise. (exclamatory)

Lois **What an amazing fact that is!**

Situation 4 Your friend Jerry hears that you have drawn some pictures of a volcano. He lets you know that he wants to look at them. Write the statement he makes. (imperative)

Jerry **Please show me your drawings.**

Situation 5 Luis thinks your drawings are really great. He wants to display them in some way. Write the question he asks. (interrogative)

Luis **Can we hang up your drawings on the bulletin board?**

CCSS Language 1f, 2a, 3b. (See pp. T6–7.)

Proofreading Checklist ☑

- ❑ *Did you begin each sentence with a capital letter?*
- ❑ *Did you end each sentence with the correct end mark?*

Lesson 2: Complete Subjects and Predicates

LEARN

A **simple sentence** expresses a complete thought. It has a subject and a predicate.

- The **subject** tells *whom* or *what* the sentence is about.
  Maggie asks many questions.

The **predicate** tells what the subject *does* or *is*.
  Maggie **asks many questions**.

- The **complete subject** includes all the words in the subject part of the sentence. The **complete predicate** includes all the words in the predicate part of the sentence.

The complete subject or complete predicate can be one word or more than one word.

Complete Subject	Complete Predicate
Our little sister Maggie	smiles.
She	takes things apart.
My mom and dad	call her "the inventor."
All real inventors	are explorers.
The pictures in this book	gave us ideas.

PRACTICE

A *Read each sentence. Write **complete subject** or **complete predicate** to tell which part of the sentence is in **boldface**. The first one is done for you.*

1. **Benjamin Franklin** was a great inventor. ___complete subject___
2. **His inventions** are part of our everyday lives. ___complete subject___
3. Ben **needed two pairs of eyeglasses**. ___complete predicate___
4. One pair **was for reading**. ___complete predicate___

5. **The other pair** was for seeing things at a distance. complete subject
6. **Franklin** hated carrying two pairs of glasses. complete subject
7. He **invented new glasses that solved the problem**. complete predicate
8. **Ben** put half of a lens for distance on top. complete subject
9. He **put half of a lens for reading on the bottom**. complete predicate
10. We **call these glasses "bifocals."** complete predicate

B *Read each sentence. Draw a line between the complete subject and the complete predicate. Underline the complete subject once and the complete predicate twice. The first one is done for you.*

1. Ben Franklin|invented a new kind of stove.
2. The new stove|got hot fast.
3. The new invention|warmed every part of a room.
4. The Franklin stove|was safer than a fire in a fireplace.
5. It|burned less wood than other stoves.
6. People|use Ben's stove even today.
7. Ben Franklin|experimented with unusual ideas, too.
8. This busy scientist|tested one idea in a pond.
9. Ben|tied a kite to himself.
10. He|swam in the pond.
11. The wind|blew the kite.
12. The kite|pulled Ben across the pond.

Franklin stove

C *Write a complete subject or a complete predicate to complete each sentence. Choose a subject or predicate from the box, or use a subject or predicate of your own. Write your sentence on the lines provided, adding the correct end punctuation.*

Remember

The **complete subject** tells *whom* or *what* the sentence is about.

The **complete predicate** tells what the subject *does* or *is*.

the gasoline engine	business and trade
turned nighttime into day	let people record information
early clocks	made travel much easier and safer
certain inventions	

Answers will vary. Sample answers are given.

1. have changed the world completely.

   Certain inventions have changed the world completely.

2. The invention of writing

   The invention of writing let people record information.

3. grew quickly after the invention of money.

   Business and trade grew quickly after the invention of money.

4. The first maps

   The first maps made travel much easier and safer.

5. helped people manage time better.

   Early clocks helped people manage time better.

6. made cars and trucks possible.

   The gasoline engine made cars and trucks possible.

7. The electric lightbulb

   The electric lightbulb turned nighttime into day.

CCSS Language 1f. (See pp. T6–7.)

WRITE

D *The computer is another invention that is changing our world. Use what you know about computers to complete each sentence. Add a complete subject or a complete predicate to each group of words. Write each sentence on the lines provided. Check a dictionary if you need help spelling a word.*

Answers will vary. Sample answers are given.

1. The invention of the computer ______

The invention of the computer has made a big difference in our lives.

2. use personal computers at home. ______

People of all ages use personal computers at home.

3. Our school computers ______

Our school computers are always busy.

4. play games on computers. ______

My friends and I play games on computers.

5. The computers in the library ______

The computers in the library help people find books.

6. find information for reports and homework on the Internet. ______

Students find information for reports and homework on the Internet.

7. Modern cars, televisions, and music players ______

Modern cars, televisions, and music players have computers inside.

8. solve problems with computers. ______

Scientists solve problems with computers.

CCSS Language 1f, 2a, 2d.
(See pp. T6–7.)

Proofreading Checklist ☑

- ❑ *Does each sentence begin with a capital letter?*
- ❑ *Does each sentence end with a period or other end mark?*
- ❑ *Does each sentence have a subject and a predicate?*

Lesson 3: Simple Subjects

LEARN

- The **simple subject** is the most important word in the complete subject. The simple subject tells exactly *whom* or *what* the subject is about.
- Sometimes the subject of a sentence is just one word. Sometimes it is a name. Then the simple subject and the complete subject are the same. Most of the time, however, the simple subject is part of the complete subject.

In the chart below, the simple subjects are shown in **boldface**.

Helen Keller sitting at a desk

Complete Subject	Complete Predicate
The school **librarian**	gave me a book.
The **book**	was about Helen Keller.
Helen Keller	lost her hearing and sight.
She	needed a special teacher.

PRACTICE

A *The complete subject in each sentence is in* ***boldface****. Circle the simple subject in the complete subject. Write it on the line.*

1. **This book** is about Helen Keller's remarkable life. book
2. **Helen Keller** became ill at the age of 19 months. Helen Keller
3. **The mysterious illness** left her blind and deaf. illness
4. **Anne Sullivan** was Helen's teacher. Anne Sullivan
5. **The gifted teacher** taught Helen how to read and write. teacher
6. **Helen** graduated from college in 1904 with Anne's help. Helen
7. **The two women** traveled around the world. women

PRACTICE **A** *continued*

8. **The proud student** told people her story. student

9. **Large audiences** learned an important lesson from her. audiences

10. **An independent life** is possible even with physical challenges. life

B *Underline the complete subject in each sentence. Then circle the simple subject, and write it on the line.*

1. Levi Strauss made the first blue jeans in the 1870s. Levi Strauss
2. He was born in a part of Europe called Bavaria. He
3. This area is now a part of Germany. area
4. Strauss moved to New York in 1847. Strauss
5. Levi joined the family clothing business. Levi
6. The young man brought the business to California. man
7. Many people searched for gold in California. people
8. The gold miners bought the pants Levi made. miners
9. A heavy blue fabric made the pants strong. fabric
10. The family business expanded quickly. business
11. Many Americans wanted the waist overalls. Americans
12. "Waist overalls" was the old name for jeans. overalls

Remember

The **simple subject** is the most important word in the complete subject.

C *Write a complete subject to complete each sentence. Choose a complete subject from the box, or use a complete subject of your own. Then circle the simple subject.*

Answers will vary. Suggested answers are given.

Most readers	Exciting historical events	
The person	A biography	Everyday events

A (biography) tells the story of a person's life. **The (person)** might be an artist, an athlete, or a president. **Most (readers)** enjoy biographies very much. **Exciting historical (events)** come alive in a well-written biography. **Everyday (events)** can be interesting, too.

A biographer	These written records	
The actual writing	Most authors	Research

Most (authors) work very hard on biographies. **(Research)** is the first part of their job. **A (biographer)** must read old letters, diaries, and news stories about a person. **These written (records)** reveal a great deal about the person. **The actual (writing)** can take years and years.

WRITE

Sometimes two related sentences have the same predicate.

Lena read a biography of Harriet Tubman.
Her friend read a biography of Harriet Tubman.

When this happens, you can combine the subjects and form one sentence. Use the word *and* to join the subjects. Combining the sentences in this way will make your writing smoother.

Lena **and** her friend read a biography of Harriet Tubman.

D *Each pair of sentences below has the same predicate. Combine the sentences by joining the subjects.*

1. Harriet Tubman lived in slavery. Her family lived in slavery.
   Harriet Tubman and her family lived in slavery.

2. Hardship shaped their lives. Struggles shaped their lives.
   Hardship and struggles shaped their lives.

3. Harriet Tubman escaped. Her parents escaped.
   Harriet Tubman and her parents escaped.

4. Slave owners looked for Tubman. The police looked for Tubman.
   Slave owners and the police looked for Tubman.

5. Tubman never got caught. The slaves with her never got caught.
   Tubman and the slaves with her never got caught.

6. Careful planning led to her success. Quick thinking led to her success.
   Careful planning and quick thinking led to her success.

**Go back to the sentences you wrote.
Underline the subjects you combined.
Circle the word that joins them.**

Lesson 4: Simple Predicates

LEARN

- The **simple predicate** is the most important word in the complete predicate. The simple predicate tells exactly what the subject *does* or *is*.
- Sometimes the predicate of a sentence is just one word. Then the simple predicate and the complete predicate are the same. Most of the time, however, the simple predicate is part of the complete predicate.

In the chart below, the simple predicates are shown in **boldface**.

Complete Subject	Complete Predicate
Everyone	**read**.
All of us	**searched** for information.
Our class	**planned** a trip to Ellis Island.
Ellis Island	**is** in New York City.
We	**rode** a ferryboat to the island.
Many tourists	**visit** the immigration museum.

PRACTICE

A *The complete predicate in each sentence is in* ***boldface****. Circle the simple predicate in the complete predicate. Write it on the line.*

1. This small island **is in New York Harbor.** is
2. Samuel Ellis **owned the island at one time.** owned
3. The federal government **built a fort there in 1811.** built
4. The fort **became an immigrant center in 1892.** became
5. Immigrants **went there for inspections.** went

PRACTICE A *continued*

6. The government used **the center for 62 years.** used
7. Ellis Island closed **officially in November 1954.** closed
8. A new project began **in 1984.** began
9. The Island reopened **as a museum.** reopened
10. Over a million people visit **the museum each year.** visit

B *Underline the complete predicate in each sentence. Then circle the simple predicate, and write it on the line.*

1. Huge numbers of immigrants came to New York City. came
2. About eight million entered the city from 1855 to 1890. entered
3. Many groups arrived at Ellis Island. arrived
4. Most people left poor conditions back home. left
5. The newcomers wanted better lives in America. wanted
6. Some immigrants brought family members with them. brought
7. Others traveled by themselves. traveled
8. Many immigrants crossed the ocean by steamship. crossed
9. The ships docked at the piers. docked
10. Doctors examined the immigrants for illnesses. examined
11. Inspectors requested the proper papers. requested
12. Some passengers got special treatment. got
13. Officials checked them aboard the ships. checked
14. The inspections lasted for hours. lasted
15. Most immigrants passed inspection. passed

Remember

The **simple predicate** is the most important word in the complete predicate.

C *Write a complete predicate to complete each sentence in this diary entry. Choose a complete predicate from the box, or use a complete predicate of your own. Then circle the simple predicate.*

asked us lots of questions
showed us our new home
cried with happiness
was over at last
carried us to my uncle's apartment
held her torch high above us
took us to Ellis Island

Dear Diary,

Today our ship steamed into New York Harbor. The beautiful Statue of Liberty **(held) her torch high above us**. My mother and I **(cried) with happiness**. Our long voyage **(was) over at last**!

A small ferryboat **(took) us to Ellis Island**. There the officials **(asked) us lots of questions**. Finally, we were free to go.

An underground train **(carried) us to my uncle's apartment**. He **(showed) us our new home**. Our new life in America is beginning at last!

WRITE

Sometimes two related sentences have the same subject.

Mom studied history.
Mom shared what she knew.

When this happens, you can combine the predicates and form one sentence. Use the word *and* to join the predicates. Combining the sentences in this way will make your writing smoother.

Mom studied history **and** shared what she knew.

D *Each pair of sentences below has the same subject. Combine the sentences by joining the predicates.*

1. The United States changed. The United States grew. ____
The United States changed and grew.

2. Millions of immigrants left Europe. Millions of immigrants came here. ____
Millions of immigrants left Europe and came here.

3. A father often came first. A father sent for his family later. ____
A father often came first and sent for his family later.

4. The immigrants usually lived in big cities. The immigrants worked in jobs there.
The immigrants usually lived in big cities and worked in jobs there.

5. New York City had the most immigrants. New York City became the largest city.
New York City had the most immigrants and became the largest city.

Go back to the sentences you wrote. Underline the predicates you combined. Circle the word that joins them.

Lesson 5: Compound Sentences

LEARN

- A **simple sentence** has one subject and one predicate. It expresses one idea.

  The National Zoo is in Washington, D.C.

- Sometimes two simple sentences contain related ideas. You can combine these sentences to make a **compound sentence**. Use a connecting word such as *and, but,* or *or* to join the sentences.

  RELATED SENTENCES

  The National Zoo is huge. It has animals from all over the world.

  COMPOUND SENTENCE

  The National Zoo is huge, **and** it has animals from all over the world.

  RELATED SENTENCES

  Most zoos do not have pandas. The National Zoo does.

  COMPOUND SENTENCE

  Most zoos do not have pandas, **but** the National Zoo does.

  RELATED SENTENCES

  Would you like to go to the zoo? Would you rather see a movie?

  COMPOUND SENTENCE

  Would you like to go to the zoo, **or** would you rather see a movie?

The connecting words *and, but,* and *or* are called coordinating conjunctions. A comma (,) always goes before the conjunction in a compound sentence.

PRACTICE

A *Read each sentence. Write **simple** if the sentence is made up of only one idea. Write **compound** if the sentence is made up of two related ideas.*

1. Pandas feed mostly on bamboo plants. simple
2. A panda's head is white, but its eyes and ears are black. compound
3. Are pandas in the raccoon family, or are they true bears? compound

 CCSS Language 2c. (See pp. T6–7.)

PRACTICE A *continued*

4. Pandas are endangered, but people are working to protect them. **compound**
5. Grizzly bears walk slowly, but they can run fast. **compound**
6. Grizzlies eat many kinds of plants, and they eat fish, too. **compound**
7. A polar bear's coat is waterproof. **simple**
8. Polar bears are excellent swimmers. **simple**
9. Black bears are commonly found in the eastern United States. **simple**
10. Keep away from black bears, or you might get hurt. **compound**

B *Read each incomplete compound sentence. Underline the sentence below that best relates to it. Then combine the related sentences to form a compound sentence. Write the compound sentence on the line.*

1. Adult pandas weigh several hundred pounds, but _____.
   Pandas are in the bear family. Newborns weigh just one pound.
   Adult pandas weigh several hundred pounds, but newborns weigh just one pound.
2. Brown bears eat meat, or _____.
   The tips of their hairs are white. They eat plants, insects, and fish.
   Brown bears eat meat, or they eat plants, insects, and fish.
3. Grizzly cubs can climb trees, but _____.
   Adult grizzlies cannot. They like honey.
   Grizzly cubs can climb trees, but adult grizzlies cannot.
4. Polar bears live near the water, and _____.
   They have small ears. They hunt seals there.
   Polar bears live near the water, and they hunt seals there.
5. A brown bear has a shoulder hump, and _____.
   Grizzly bears are brown bears. It has very long claws.
   A brown bear has a shoulder hump, and it has very long claws.

C *One zoo posted this list of rules for visitors. The compound sentences on the list have six mistakes. Look for the mistakes and correct them. Use the proofreading marks in the box.*

Remember

A **simple sentence** has one subject and one predicate. It expresses one idea.

A **compound sentence** is formed by joining two simple sentences with a coordinating conjunction such as *and*, *but*, or *or*.

ZOO RULES

Enjoy your visit! Our zoo is a wonderful place to explore and these rules will keep you safe and happy.

- Please don't feed the animals. Our animals have special diets and human food can make them sick.
- Pets are not allowed at the zoo but guide dogs are permitted.
- Railings and fences protect you and they also keep our animals safe. Never extend fingers and arms through fences.
- Visitors may carry personal digital devices but they must use headphones. Noise can disturb both animals and people.
- Don't litter. Place all your trash in the bins or our zoo won't be a pleasant place to visit.

Proofreading Marks

^	Add
⊙	Period
ᘓ	Take out
≡	Capital letter
/	Small letter

Did you correct six mistakes in the compound sentences?

CCSS Language 2c. (See pp. T6–7.)

Combining Sentences

WRITE

D *Each pair of sentences below contains related ideas. Combine the sentences to form a compound sentence. Use the coordinating conjunction in parentheses to join them. Remember to put a comma before the joining word. The first one is done for you.*

1. Zookeepers know more about how an animal lives. They build better zoos. (and)

Zookeepers know more about how an animal lives, and they build better zoos.

2. Animals move around freely. People can still get a good view of them. (but)

Animals move around freely, but people can still get a good view of them.

3. Conditions must be just right in a zoo. Animals get sick. (or)

Conditions must be just right in a zoo, or animals get sick.

4. Polar bears need icy cold water. Lions need warm temperatures. (but)

Polar bears need icy cold water, but lions need warm temperatures.

5. Zoo animals need to stay busy. They will become bored and unhappy. (or)

Zoo animals need to stay busy, or they will become bored and unhappy.

6. Apes search for their own food in today's zoos. Some zoo elephants even paint pictures. (and) **Apes search for their own food in today's zoos, and some zoo elephants even paint pictures.**

7. The field feels as if it is the giraffes' natural home. There is lots of room to roam. (and)

The field feels as if it is the giraffes' natural home, and there is lots of room to roam.

8. Modern zoos are difficult to build and run. They're worth it. (but)

Modern zoos are difficult to build and run, but they're worth it.

CCSS Language 2c. (See pp. T6–7.)

Lesson 6: Complex Sentences

LEARN

- You have learned about compound sentences. Compound sentences combine related ideas using a connecting word such as *and, but,* or *or.*

  A **complex sentence** also combines related ideas. The ideas are joined by a **subordinating conjunction**. Look at the sentence below.

  The canyon is wide **because** the river has eroded its walls.

  The subordinating conjunction *because* joins the two related ideas.

The following **subordinating conjunctions** are often used to connect related ideas.

Subordinating Conjunctions			
after	although	because	before
since	until	when	while

- The subordinating conjunction may come in the middle of the sentence.

  Plains are mostly flat **although** some have small hills.

- The subordinating conjunction may come at the beginning of the sentence.

  Although some have small hills, plains are mostly flat.

  Notice that when the first idea in the sentence begins with a subordinating conjunction, a comma follows that idea.

PRACTICE

A *Read each sentence. Write **complex** if the sentence is made up of two related ideas joined by a subordinating conjunction. Write **not complex** if it is not a complex sentence.*

1. After we made the last turn, we reached the mountain. complex
2. We wanted to see the mountain because it is so majestic. complex
3. A mountain is higher than the area around it. not complex

CCSS Language 1f, 2a. (See pp. T6–7.)

4. The taller mountains reach into the colder layers of the atmosphere. **not complex**

5. Since the mountain slope is gentle, it is perfect for skiing. **complex**

6. Mountains take millions of years to form. **not complex**

7. A mountain can form when Earth's crust bends. **complex**

8. Unlike mountains, the plains are low and flat. **not complex**

9. Because they are low-lying areas, plains can flood easily. **complex**

10. Plains may be surrounded by small hills or mountains. **not complex**

B *Read each complex sentence. Write the subordinating conjunction that joins the two related ideas. The first one is done for you.*

1. When an earthquake happens, you can take steps to be safe. When

2. You should take cover until the ground stops shaking. **until**

3. Since earthquakes sometimes happen under the ocean, you may see waves on the surface. **Since**

4. A tsunami can take place after an earthquake strikes. **after**

5. Some cities are prepared for an earthquake because they have had so many. **because**

6. Although some earthquakes are dangerous, most are not. **Although**

7. Scientists could study an earthquake better when they had the latest tools. **when**

8. Before an earthquake hits, some animals seem nervous. **Before**

9. We saw a wide crack in the ground while we were hiking. **while**

10. The ground cracked because parts of the earth had split apart. **because**

C *Write a subordinating conjunction to complete each sentence. Choose a subordinating conjunction from the box, or use a subordinating conjunction of your own.*

Remember

A **complex sentence** is formed by joining two related ideas with a subordinating conjunction.

after	although	because	before
since	until	when	while

Answers may vary. Suggested answers are given.

1. Thomas went to Costa Rica **because** he wanted to see a volcano.
2. **Although** I have read about volcanoes, I haven't seen one.
3. Thomas showed us his photographs **after/when** he returned from his trip.
4. **Since/Because** she is a park ranger at Denali National Park, Aunt Mary can tell us about glaciers.
5. Glaciers leave rocks behind **while/after** they move across the land.
6. **Until/Before** we traveled to Alaska last spring, I had never seen a glacier.
7. I read books about glaciers **before/when** we took our trip.
8. I saw one of these large sheets of ice **when/after** our plane landed.
9. I put on a heavy coat **because/since** it is cold on top of a glacier.
10. **Although** there once were many glaciers in America, there are few today.
11. **Since/Because** some glaciers contain a lot of air, they can look blue.
12. We heard loud noises **when** pieces of a glacier broke off.

WRITE

D *Imagine a beautiful island that you want people to visit. Use the items below to create a persuasive article about the island. Be sure to use complete sentences. Check a dictionary if you need help spelling a word.*

Answers will vary. Sample answers are given.

1. because the island is far away

   Because the island is far away, you will travel by plane.

2. after you arrive

   You will never want to leave after you arrive!

3. since so much water surrounds the island

   Since so much water surrounds the island, you will have lots of beaches to visit.

4. when you are at the beach

   Look for playful dolphins when you are at the beach.

5. although there is a volcano

   Although there is a volcano, it is not active.

6. until you see the amazing flowers here

   You haven't seen anything so pretty until you see the amazing flowers here.

7. while you are at the beach

   Make sure you go snorkeling or diving while you are at the beach.

8. before you leave

   Before you leave, take many pictures so you don't forget this beautiful island.

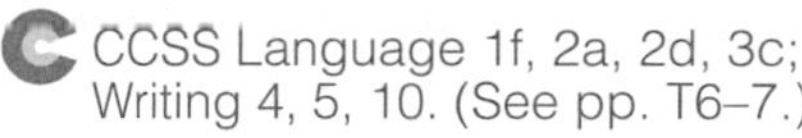

Proofreading Checklist ✓

- ☐ *Does each sentence use correct capitalization?*
- ☐ *Does each sentence that begins with a subordinating conjunction have a comma after the first idea?*

Lesson 7: Correcting Fragments and Run-ons

LEARN

- A **fragment** is an incomplete sentence. The subject or predicate might be missing. To correct this kind of fragment, add a subject or a predicate.

  FRAGMENT Bought a children's book.

  SENTENCE My sister bought a children's book.

  Add a subject.

  FRAGMENT The book.

  SENTENCE The book is for my brother.

  Add a predicate.

- A **run-on sentence** is two complete sentences that run together. One way to correct a run-on sentence is to make two separate sentences. Another way is to make a compound sentence.

  RUN-ON
  She likes to draw she wants to be an artist.

  CORRECTED SENTENCE
  She likes to draw. She wants to be an artist.

  two separate sentences

  CORRECTED SENTENCE
  She likes to draw, and she wants to be an artist.

  compound sentence

PRACTICE

A *Read each group of words. Circle **sentence, fragment,** or **run-on** to describe it.*

1. Lane Smith is an illustrator. (sentence) fragment run-on

2. The young artist. sentence (fragment) run-on

3. He loved to draw pictures he loved baseball. sentence fragment (run-on)

4. He is grateful to his teachers. (sentence) fragment run-on

5. They encouraged him they helped him. sentence fragment (run-on)

 CCSS Language 1f, 2c. (See pp. T6–7.)

PRACTICE A *continued*

6. One of his teachers. *sentence* *(fragment)* *run-on*

7. Tried out different art supplies. *sentence* *(fragment)* *run-on*

8. This artist has a great imagination. *(sentence)* *fragment* *run-on*

B *Make each fragment a complete sentence by matching it with the correct subject or predicate. Write the letter of the words you choose on the line.*

b 1. *The Tale of Peter Rabbit* — **a.** is Beatrix Potter.

a 2. The author's name — **b.** is a well-known children's book.

e 3. wrote the story in a letter. — **c.** The letter

c 4. was for a little boy who was sick. — **d.** later turned the story into a book.

d 5. Potter — **e.** Beatrix

Write each run-on sentence as a compound sentence.

6. Beatrix Potter made the story longer she redrew the pictures, too.
Beatrix Potter made the story longer, and she redrew the pictures, too.

7. She wanted to make books for children she wanted to make them easy to hold.
She wanted to make books for children, and she wanted to make them easy to hold.

8. Beatrix made the books little she used sturdy paper.
Beatrix made the books little, and she used sturdy paper.

Write each run-on sentence as two separate sentences.

9. Beatrix Potter grew up in England drawing was her favorite hobby.
Beatrix Potter grew up in England. Drawing was her favorite hobby.

10. Beatrix had a younger brother both children loved plants and animals.
Beatrix had a younger brother. Both children loved plants and animals.

CCSS Language 1f, 2c. (See pp. T6–7.)

C *Leah wrote this report. It contains three fragments and three run-on sentences. Use the proofreading marks in the box to correct the mistakes. Add a subject or predicate to correct each fragment. Write each run-on sentence as a compound sentence or as two separate sentences.*

Remember

A **fragment** is an incomplete sentence.

A **run-on sentence** is two complete sentences that run together.

Answers will vary. Suggested answers are given.

Proofreading Marks

^	Add
⊙	Period
ℓ/	Take out
≡	Capital letter
/	Small letter

Thousands of children's books are published each
year. Most of them have good illustrations. However,
The medal
only one book gets the Caldecott Medal. goes to the
best illustrator of a children's book.

The Caldecott Medal is a very special honor.
The American Library Association presents the award.
and
Librarians study the year's new children's books, they
vote on the best one.

The first Caldecott Medal was given in 1938. Since
The prize
then, many great illustrators have won it. Encourages
artists to draw fine pictures for young readers.

Sometimes, you might see a gold Caldecott Medal
tells you the book is a winner.
on a book. This medal. Take a minute to look inside it.
You're sure to find some outstanding illustrations.

Did you correct three fragments and three run-on sentences?

 CCSS Language 1f, 2c. (See pp. T6–7.)

WRITE

D *Add a subject or predicate to each fragment to make a complete sentence. Write the sentence on the line.*

Answers may vary. Suggested answers are given.

1. A book's illustrations.

   A book's illustrations are important.

2. Add interest to the story.

   These pictures add interest to the story.

3. Show the mood and feelings in a story, too.

   They show the mood and feelings in a story, too.

4. Drawings, paintings, and photographs.

   Drawings, paintings, and photographs are different kinds of illustrations.

5. Photographs.

   Photographs appear in many nonfiction books.

6. My favorite book illustrator.

   My favorite book illustrator is Lane Smith.

7. The Caldecott Medal.

   The Caldecott Medal honors great illustrators.

8. Are fun to read.

   Children's books are fun to read.

9. Books without illustrations.

   Books without illustrations are for older readers.

10. Are on display in the library.

    Many books are on display in the library.

CCSS Language 1f, 2c. (See pp. T6–7.)

Unit 1 Review
Lessons 1–7

Kinds of Sentences (pp. 8–11) *Read each sentence. Write **declarative, interrogative, imperative,** or **exclamatory** to tell what kind of sentence it is.*

1. A tornado hit the town yesterday. **declarative**
2. Did you see the tornado? **interrogative**
3. Look at these photos. **imperative**
4. How lucky we were! **exclamatory**

Complete Subjects and Predicates (pp. 12–15) *Read each sentence. Draw a line between the complete subject and the complete predicate. Underline the complete subject once and the complete predicate twice.*

5. A tornado | looks like a dark funnel-shaped cloud.
6. Winds | whirl around at high speeds.
7. These dangerous storms | move in a narrow path across the earth.
8. The twisting cloud | picks up dirt from the ground.

Simple Subjects (pp. 16–19) *Read each sentence. Underline the complete subject. Then circle the simple subject.*

9. About 700 tornadoes occur in the United States each year.
10. These powerful storms damage everything in their path.
11. The gusty winds uproot trees.
12. Some automobiles fly through the air for hundreds of feet.

Simple Predicates (pp. 20–23) *Read each sentence. Underline the complete predicate. Then circle the simple predicate.*

13. Most tornadoes hit the midwestern states.
14. Certain weather conditions produce these storms.

15. Weather scientists (track) tornadoes.

16. The scientists (announce) tornado warnings whenever possible.

Compound Sentences (pp. 24–27) *Read each sentence. Write **simple** if the sentence is made up of only one idea. Write **compound** if the sentence is made up of two related ideas.*

17. Most tornadoes occur on hot and humid days. simple

18. Warm air rises rapidly, and sometimes it begins to spin. compound

19. This spinning air sometimes forms a tornado. simple

20. The tornado can stay in the air, or it might touch down on the ground. compound

Complex Sentences (pp. 28–31) *Read each sentence. Write **complex** if it is a complex sentence. Write **not complex** if it is not a complex sentence.*

21. Although most tornadoes last only a few minutes, they can cause great damage. complex

22. The Fujita scale or F-scale measures a tornado's intensity. not complex

23. An F5 rating on the F-scale stands for the greatest wind strength any tornado can have. not complex

24. A tornado warning will be issued when radar spots powerful winds. complex

Correcting Fragments and Run-ons (pp. 32–35) *Read each group of words. Write **sentence, fragment,** or **run-on** to describe it.*

25. A storm cellar gives the best protection from a tornado a basement is the next safest place. run-on

26. The National Weather Service. fragment

27. Always keep away from windows during a tornado. sentence

28. Warns people about tornadoes. fragment

Unit 1 Test

DIRECTIONS *Fill in the circle next to the sentence that shows the correct use of capital letters and end punctuation. The first one is done for you.*

1.
- ○ Many foods come from all over the world
- ○ Did potatoes come from Peru.
- ○ chocolate was a favorite food in Mexico?
- ● How I love chocolate!

2.
- ○ Did peanuts first grow in North America!
- ● Are they members of the pea family, or do they belong to a different group?
- ○ Spanish explorers brought peanuts to Europe?
- ○ Wow, peanuts really got around

3.
- ○ Native Americans grew corn, peppers, and squash
- ○ bananas are native to South America!
- ● Are you sure about that?
- ○ I will know, after I read this encyclopedia article.

4.
- ○ Peppers are called chilies in Mexico
- ○ try a bite of this.
- ○ Wow, it's really hot?
- ● I love hot peppers on pizza.

5.
- ● Are the tomato and the potato related?
- ○ People once thought tomatoes were poisonous?
- ○ what a silly idea that is!
- ○ How did they make pizza without tomatoes.

6.
- ○ Pumpkins are American, too?
- ● Wow, those pumpkins are heavy!
- ○ did Native Americans share pumpkins with early settlers?
- ○ When did people first carve jack-o'-lanterns

7.
- ○ turkey is another American food.
- ○ Was it the main dish at the first Thanksgiving.
- ● The turkey almost became our national bird.
- ○ have you ever seen a wild turkey

8.
- ○ Explorers searched for new lands?
- ○ They often discovered new foods on their journeys
- ● Tell me which American foods you like best.
- ○ our meals would be boring without such foods!

DIRECTIONS *Read the paragraphs, and look carefully at each underlined part. Fill in the circle next to the answer choice that shows the correct use of capital letters and end punctuation. If the underlined part is already correct, fill in the circle for "Correct as is." The first one is done for you.*

The high mountains of Peru are cold. The Incas could not grow corn there but they (9) could grow potatoes. How did those potatoes get to Europe! the (10) early Spanish explorers of Peru brought them to Spain in the 1530s. What a success potatoes were at first, wealthy people (11) had parties just to try the new food

Then some questions arose. Did potatoes cause disease, or did they (12) poison the soil? For a while, many Europeans believed potatoes were dangerous. Fortunately, people got over such a silly idea. They planted potatoes widely and soon the crop (13) was plentiful. How important the new crop turned out to be many Europeans (14) had enough food for the first time.

9.
- ● there, but they
- ○ there. but they
- ○ there, But they
- ○ Correct as is

10.
- ○ Europe the
- ○ Europe. The
- ● Europe? The
- ○ Correct as is

11.
- ○ first, wealthy people
- ● first! Wealthy people
- ○ first. Wealthy people
- ○ Correct as is

12.
- ○ disease or did they
- ○ disease? or did they
- ○ disease, Or did they
- ● Correct as is

13.
- ● widely, and soon the crop
- ○ widely, And soon the crop
- ○ widely. and soon the crop
- ○ Correct as is

14.
- ○ be. Many Europeans
- ○ be, many Europeans
- ● be! Many Europeans
- ○ Correct as is

Lesson 8: Common and Proper Nouns

LEARN

- A **noun** is a word that names a person, place, or thing. A **common noun** names any person, place, or thing.
  The **girl** visited the **fountain** in the **park**.
- A **proper noun** names a specific person, place, or thing. It can be one word or more than one word.
  Julia visited **Bethesda Fountain** in **Central Park**.
- Each important word in a proper noun begins with a capital letter.

	Common	Proper
Person	teacher	Ms. Jones
Place	city	Los Angeles
Thing	statue	Statue of Liberty

Bethesda Fountain in Central Park

- Ideas such as *fear* and *greed* are called **abstract nouns**. You can't see or touch them, but they are still nouns. Abstract nouns are always common nouns.
  Greed was his undoing.

PRACTICE

Match each common noun with a proper noun. Write the letter of the proper noun on the line.

Common Nouns	Proper Nouns
b 1. month	a. Mexico
a 2. country	b. October

 CCSS Language 2a. (See pp. T6–7.)

PRACTICE A *continued*

d 3. holiday — c. Venus

c 4. planet — d. Fourth of July

e 5. building — e. White House

h 6. state — f. Asia

f 7. continent — g. Abraham Lincoln

i 8. day of the week — h. Nebraska

j 9. lake — i. Monday

g 10. president — j. Lake Charles

B *Read each sentence. Write **common** if the noun in **boldface** is a common noun. Write **proper** if it is a proper noun.*

1. Dora visited **Yellowstone National Park** last summer. proper
2. The **park** lies mainly in Wyoming. common
3. Is it the largest national park in the **United States**? proper
4. The park's geysers attract many **visitors**. common
5. Water from inside the earth shoots out of a **geyser**. common
6. **Old Faithful** is the most famous geyser. proper
7. Spectators feel great **excitement** when this geyser erupts. common
8. People visit the **Mammoth Hot Springs**, too. proper
9. **Dora** hiked up to Yellowstone Lake. proper
10. Her **love** of Yellowstone is apparent. common

CCSS Language 2a. (See pp. T6–7.)

Remember

Each important word in a proper noun begins with a capital letter.

C *Dora wrote this letter to her grandmother. She made twelve mistakes when writing common and proper nouns. Look for the mistakes and fix them. Use the proofreading marks in the box.*

Proofreading Marks	
^	Add
⊙	Period
ℓ/	Take out
≡	Capital letter
/	Small letter

Dear Grandma,

Can you imagine a Canyon 18 miles wide and a mile deep? Well, if you were here in Grand Canyon national Park in arizona, you wouldn't have to. You could be hiking in it with us!

The Trip is not all hiking, though. On tuesday, we rafted down the Colorado river for about 10 Miles! We only got wet twice, and we got to see some Sheep. We might take a mule Trip tomorrow to a place called Phantom ranch. That sounds scary, but I still want to go.

We will be home by september 1st, and I will see you at our picnic on Labor day. I can't wait to tell you more about the trip!

Love,

Dora

Did you correct twelve mistakes?

 CCSS Language 2a. (See pp. T6–7.)

Revising Sentences

WRITE

Sometimes your sentences might have nouns that are not clear or specific.

Our train travels along the **river**.
We can see **boats** on the water.

You can replace these nouns with nouns that are more descriptive. The words you choose can be either common or proper nouns.

Our train travels along the **Hudson River**.
We can see **sailboats** on the water.

D *In each sentence below, change the word or words in* ***boldface*** *to a more descriptive noun. Use either a common noun or a proper noun. Write the new sentence on the line.*

Answers may vary. Sample answers are given.

1. I would like to visit **a city** some day.

   I would like to visit San Francisco some day.

2. There is a really famous **thing** there.

   There is a really famous bridge there.

3. I will probably invite **a friend** to go with me.

   I will probably invite Paul to go with me.

4. We could pack **food** for lunch.

   We could pack sandwiches for lunch.

5. We will bring some **fruit** for snacktime, too.

   We will bring some apples for snacktime, too.

6. We would send postcards to **a teacher**.

   We would send postcards to Ms. Wilson.

7. During the trip home, we would play **a game**.

   During the trip home, we would play checkers.

Go back to the sentences you wrote. Circle the more descriptive nouns you used.

Lesson 9: Singular and Plural Nouns

LEARN

- Nouns can be singular or plural. A **singular noun** names one person, place, or thing. A **plural noun** names more than one person, place, or thing.

SINGULAR	I visited an **exhibit** at the county fair.
PLURAL	I visited three **exhibits** at the county fair.

- Follow these rules to make plural nouns.
  - Add *-s* to most singular nouns.

SINGULAR	bird	bee	flower	vegetable
PLURAL	bird**s**	bee**s**	flower**s**	vegetable**s**

  - Add *-es* when a singular noun ends in *s, ss, ch, sh,* or *x*.

SINGULAR	bus	dress	porch	dish	ax
PLURAL	bus**es**	dress**es**	porch**es**	dish**es**	ax**es**

  - When a singular noun ends in a vowel and *y*, add *-s*.

SINGULAR	boy	key	holiday
PLURAL	boy**s**	key**s**	holiday**s**

  - When a singular noun ends in a consonant and *y*, change the *y* to *i*, and add *-es*.

SINGULAR	lady	family	cherry
PLURAL	lad**ies**	famil**ies**	cherr**ies**

PRACTICE

A *Write the plural form of each noun.*

1. wish ______wishes______
2. bunny ______bunnies______
3. patch ______patches______
4. donkey ______donkeys______
5. tax ______taxes______
6. celebration ______celebrations______
7. guess ______guesses______
8. song ______songs______
9. party ______parties______
10. fox ______foxes______

CCSS Language 2d. (See pp. T6–7.)

B *Write the plural form of the noun in parentheses to complete each sentence.*

1. Many **counties** in our state hold fairs each summer. (county)
2. Different farm **groups** help pay for the events. (group)
3. Tourists arrive in cars and **buses**. (bus)
4. The **events** at the fair are always interesting. (event)
5. Some **businesses** sell products to the visitors. (business)
6. **Boxes** of prize-winning fruits and vegetables fill one building. (box)
7. The apples and **peaches** always look delicious. (peach)
8. You can sample the homemade jams and **jellies**. (jelly)
9. **Glasses** of fresh-squeezed juice are on sale, too. (glass)
10. **Sandwiches** made with local cheeses are popular. (sandwich)
11. Most children and **babies** love the animal exhibits. (baby)
12. Horses and **ponies** fill one huge barn. (pony)
13. Visitors look at the colorful chickens and **turkeys**. (turkey)
14. The best cows and sheep win blue ribbons for **prizes**. (prize)
15. We look forward to the fair for **months**. (month)

CCSS Language 2d. (See pp. T6–7.)

C *Ron wrote this report. He made nine mistakes when writing nouns. Sometimes he misspelled plural nouns. At other times, he used a plural noun for a singular noun or a singular noun for a plural noun. Use the proofreading marks to correct these mistakes.*

Remember

If a noun ends in *s, ss, ch, sh,* or *x*, add -*es* to form the plural.

If a noun ends in a consonant and *y*, change the *y* to *i*, and add -*es* to form the plural.

Proofreading Marks

^	Add
⊙	Period
ℓ	Take out
≡	Capital letter
/	Small letter

Many ~~communitys~~ communities today celebrate *Cinco de Mayo*. These words are Spanish for the "Fifth of May." On May 5, 1862, the Mexican army defeated a much larger French army. The Mexican people were proud of this important victory, and the day became a ~~holidays~~ holiday.

Cinco de Mayo celebrates Mexican history and culture. In some large ~~city,~~ cities ~~official~~ officials organize a big fiesta, or festival. In Los Angeles, almost a million residents attend. ~~Boy~~ Boys and girls in colorful ~~costumees~~ costumes perform folk dances. Bands play traditional music. Different ~~business~~ businesses prepare Mexican ~~dishs~~ dishes for the crowd. Parades are also usually part of the big day.

Cinco de Mayo is a great way for ~~familys~~ families and neighbors to remember their heritage and have fun, too!

C CCSS Language 2d. (See pp. T6–7.)

Did you correct nine mistakes with nouns?

WRITE

Singular and plural nouns can appear in the subject or the predicate of a sentence. Sometimes you can combine two related sentences by joining the nouns. Use the conjunction *and* or *or* to join the nouns.

Cowboys ride in the rodeo.
Cowgirls ride in the rodeo.
Cowboys **and** cowgirls ride in the rodeo.

The rodeo will take place in the United States.
The rodeo will take place in Canada.
The rodeo will take place in the United States **or** Canada.

D *Combine each pair of sentences by joining nouns in the subject or predicate. Use the conjunction in parentheses to join the nouns.*

1. Rodeo is based on traditions from the United States. Rodeo is based on traditions from Mexico. (and) ______
   Rodeo is based on traditions from the United States and Mexico.

2. The events developed from chores on ranches. The events developed from activities on ranches. (and) ______
   The events developed from chores and activities on ranches.

3. Rodeo riders enter contests. Rodeo riders enter races. (or) ______
   Rodeo riders enter contests or races.

4. The cowboys might perform first. The cowgirls might perform first. (or) ______
   The cowboys or cowgirls might perform first.

5. Audiences enjoy the action. Audiences enjoy the excitement. (and) ______
   Audiences enjoy the action and excitement.

Look back at the sentences you wrote. Underline the nouns you joined in the subject or predicate.

Lesson 10: Irregular Plural Nouns

LEARN

- Some nouns have **irregular plurals**. In most cases, the spelling of the singular noun changes to form the plural.

SINGULAR	man	woman	child	tooth
PLURAL	men	women	children	teeth
SINGULAR	foot	goose	mouse	ox
PLURAL	feet	geese	mice	oxen

- In a few cases, the plural noun and the singular noun are the same.

SINGULAR One **deer** nibbles the grass.
PLURAL Three **deer** stand and watch.

SINGULAR This **sheep** is white.
PLURAL The other two **sheep** are brown.

SINGULAR A **moose** swam across the lake.
PLURAL Several **moose** live on the island.

PRACTICE

A *Read each sentence. Write **singular** if the noun in **boldface** is a singular noun. Write **plural** if it is a plural noun.*

1. The **children** in our class went to the wildlife refuge. plural
2. A friendly **man** met us at the entrance. singular
3. Several Canada **geese** were swimming in the pond. plural
4. A single **moose** stood at the water's edge. singular
5. We were as quiet as **mice**, but it still ran away. plural
6. Two **women** showed us a tree cut down by a beaver. plural
7. What sharp **teeth** that beaver must have! plural
8. At sunset, a **deer** came down to the water to drink. singular

CCSS Language 2d. (See pp. T6–7.)

PRACTICE A *continued*

9. Three other **deer** soon followed. plural

10. An **ox** stood alone in the field. singular

B *Write the plural form of the noun in parentheses to complete each sentence.*

1. Twelve geese are honking in the sky above. (goose)

2. Three women look up at the big birds. (woman)

3. A group of deer is eating from a bush. (deer)

4. The animals use their teeth to tear the leaves. (tooth)

5. Several mice chewed the bark from this young tree. (mouse)

6. Many tiny feet left prints in the mud. (foot)

7. The four children point with excitement across the lake. (child)

8. Two huge moose are standing on the other side. (moose)

9. At a farm museum, two men tell us about the past. (man)

10. Two oxen pull a plow in a field. (ox)

11. A flock of sheep grazes in a meadow nearby. (sheep)

12. A family of mice races across the field. (mouse)

CCSS Language 2d. (See pp. T6–7.)

Remember

For most **irregular plurals**, the spelling of the singular noun changes to form the plural.

C *Connie wrote this poem about the first day of spring. She made six mistakes when forming irregular plural nouns. Look for the mistakes, and fix them. Use the proofreading marks in the box.*

The First Day of Spring

The first day of spring can't be beat!
I smile at all the people I meet.
The other children *~~childs~~ are smiling, too.*
We all go together to the zoo.
The reindeer *~~reindeers~~ and lions are having fun.*
They all seem glad that winter is done.
The bighorn sheep *~~sheeps~~ don't say, "Baa," today.*
Instead, they're yelling, "Hip, Hip, Hooray!"
Up in the sky, six geese *~~gooses~~ are squawking.*
It almost sounds as if they're talking
About spring to the men *~~mans~~ and* women *~~womens~~ below,*
But what they're saying, we'll never know.

Proofreading Marks

^	Add
⊙	Period
ℓ	Take out
≡	Capital letter
/	Small letter

Did you correct six irregular plural nouns?

CCSS Language 2d. (See pp. T6–7.)

WRITE

Read these rhymes about irregular plural nouns. Then write three rhymes of your own. Use the words in parentheses in your rhymes.

Answers may vary. Sample answers are given.

One bird is a goose,
And two are called geese.
But the plural of moose
Can never be meese!

The singular is man,
The plural is men.
But the plural of pan
Just cannot be pen!

1. **I have one left and one right foot.** (foot)
That makes two feet. (feet)
If I have one left and one right boot, (boot)
Does that make two beet? (beet)

2. **We call one an ox.** (ox)
We call more than one oxen. (oxen)
We call one a fox, (fox)
But don't call two of them foxen! (foxen)

3. **One of these is called a mouse.** (mouse)
Two of them are known as mice. (mice)
One of these is called a blouse, (blouse)
But more than one is never blice! (blice)

CCSS Language 2d; Writing 4, 10.
(See pp. T6–7.)

Proofreading Checklist ☑

- ❑ *Did you use the words in parentheses in your rhymes?*
- ❑ *Did you spell the real singular and plural nouns correctly?*

Lesson 11: Possessive Nouns

LEARN

A **possessive noun** is a noun that shows who or what has something.

Janet's mother teaches quilting.
She displayed the **students'** quilts.

Both singular and plural nouns can be made possessive.

- To make a singular noun possessive, add an apostrophe and *-s.*

SINGULAR	Janet	family	class
SINGULAR POSSESSIVE	Janet**'s**	family**'s**	class**'s**

- To make a plural noun that ends in *-s* possessive, add only an apostrophe.

PLURAL	students	families	classes
PLURAL POSSESSIVE	students'	families'	classes'

- To make a plural noun that does not end in *-s* possessive, add an apostrophe and *-s.*

PLURAL	women	children	sheep
PLURAL POSSESSIVE	women**'s**	children**'s**	sheep**'s**

PRACTICE

A *Write the possessive form of the noun in* ***boldface.***

1. the tools owned by the **workers** — the workers' tools
2. the hats belonging to the **men** — the men's hats
3. the rugs belonging to the **museum** — the museum's rugs
4. the sizes of the **frames** — the frames' sizes
5. the clay belonging to the **potter** — the potter's clay
6. the quilt owned by **Mia** — Mia's quilt

CCSS Language 2d. (See pp. T6–7.)

7. the smocks used by the **painters** — the painters' smocks
8. the purchases of the **tourists** — the tourists' purchases
9. the design of the **building** — the building's design
10. the collection owned by **Gus** — Gus's collection

B *Write the possessive form of the noun in parentheses that correctly completes each sentence.*

1. Our town's first craft fair was a great success. (town)
2. Our neighbors' projects were on display. (neighbors)
3. Some women's embroidered pillows were in the show. (women)
4. Mr. Moss's hand-carved chairs attracted a crowd. (Mr. Moss)
5. His birdhouses attracted the children's attention. (children)
6. Sharon's aunt is a weaver. (Sharon)
7. She uses wool from a local farmer's sheep. (farmer)
8. The sheep's wool is soft. (sheep)
9. A potter's wheel turned slowly in one area. (potter)
10. A man's hands slowly shaped clay into a vase. (man)
11. The vase's shape was almost perfect! (vase)
12. All the artists answered visitors' questions. (visitors)

C *David wrote about a class trip to a glassblower's workshop. He made seven mistakes when writing possessive nouns. Look for the mistakes, and fix them. Use the proofreading marks in the box.*

Remember

A **possessive noun** shows who or what owns or has something.

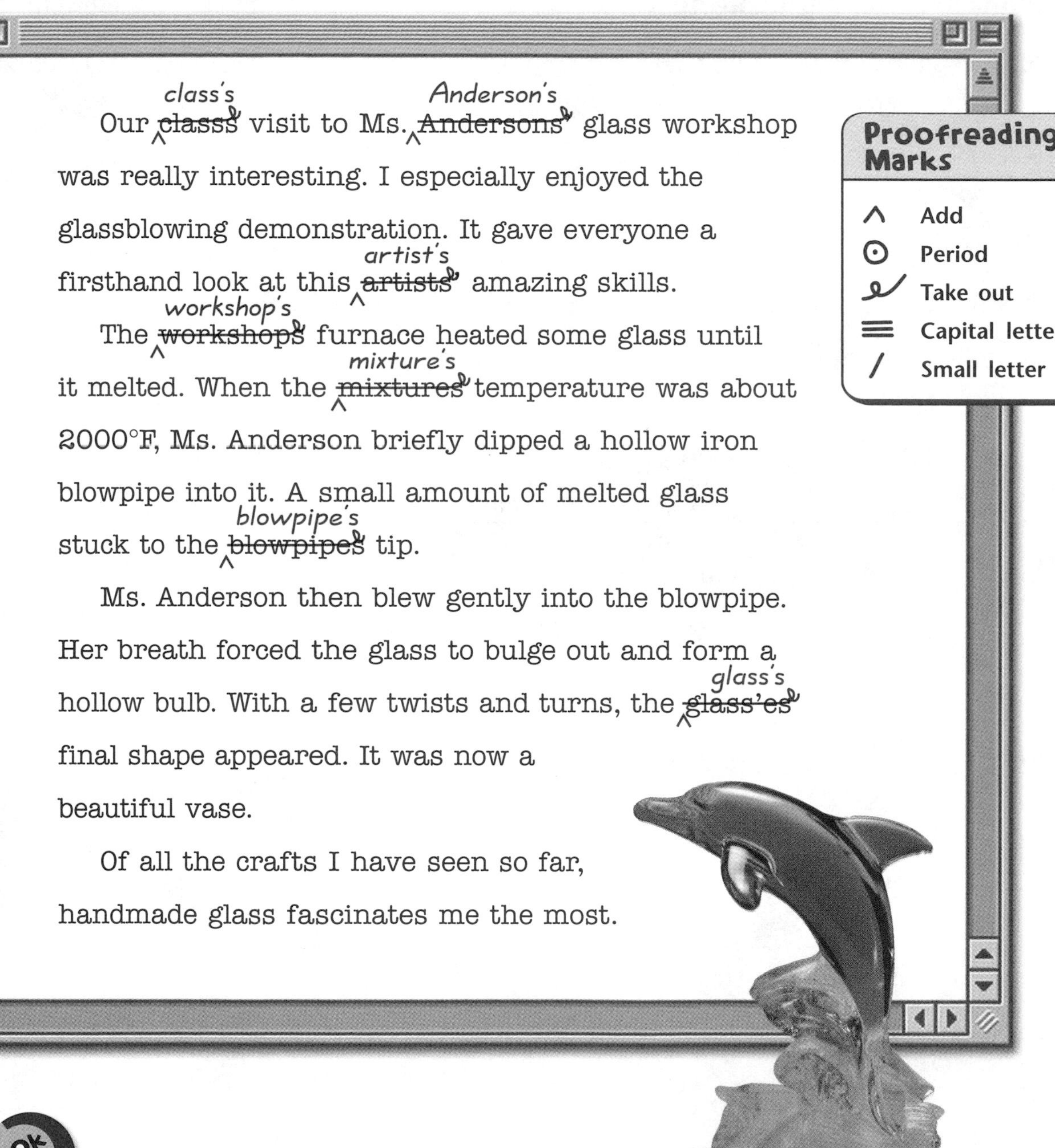

Our ~~classs~~ class's visit to Ms. ~~Andersons~~ Anderson's glass workshop was really interesting. I especially enjoyed the glassblowing demonstration. It gave everyone a firsthand look at this ~~artists~~ artist's amazing skills.

The ~~workshops~~ workshop's furnace heated some glass until it melted. When the ~~mixtures~~ mixture's temperature was about 2000°F, Ms. Anderson briefly dipped a hollow iron blowpipe into it. A small amount of melted glass stuck to the ~~blowpipes~~ blowpipe's tip.

Ms. Anderson then blew gently into the blowpipe. Her breath forced the glass to bulge out and form a hollow bulb. With a few twists and turns, the ~~glass'es~~ glass's final shape appeared. It was now a beautiful vase.

Of all the crafts I have seen so far, handmade glass fascinates me the most.

Proofreading Marks

^	Add
⊙	Period
ℓ	Take out
≡	Capital letter
/	Small letter

Look Back Did you correct seven possessive nouns?

CCSS Language 2d. (See pp. T6–7.)

WRITE

D *Rewrite each phrase using a possessive noun. Then write a sentence using the new phrase. The first one is done for you.*

Answers may vary. Sample answers are given.

1. the bright colors of the quilt *the quilt's bright colors*

The quilt's bright colors will make the room look cheerful.

2. the unusual shape of the basket **the basket's unusual shape**

The basket's unusual shape reminded us of a snake.

3. the bird feeder belonging to our class **our class's bird feeder**

Our class's bird feeder attracts many birds.

4. the clubhouse of the members **the members' clubhouse**

The members' clubhouse needed a new door.

5. the sweater belonging to the baby **the baby's sweater**

My grandmother knitted the baby's sweater.

6. the workshop of a blacksmith **the blacksmith's workshop**

Where is the blacksmith's workshop?

7. the rocking horse of the toy makers **the toy makers' rocking horse**

We saw the toy makers' rocking horse in the store window.

8. the needle of the sewing machine **the sewing machine's needle**

The sewing machine's needle was broken.

CCSS Language 1f, 2d. (See pp. T6–7.)

Proofreading Checklist ☑

- ❑ ***Did you make singular nouns possessive by adding an apostrophe and -s?***
- ❑ ***Did you make plural nouns ending in -s possessive by adding just an apostrophe?***

Unit 2 Review
Lessons 8–11

Common and Proper Nouns (pp. 40–43) *Read each sentence. Write **common** if the noun in **boldface** is a common noun. Write **proper** if it is a proper noun.*

1. The town of **Plymouth** is in Massachusetts. proper

2. Settlers called **Pilgrims** built the town. proper

3. **Native Americans** lived nearby. proper

4. Together, they celebrated a harvest **festival**. common

5. The Pilgrims set up long **tables** outdoors. common

6. Today, **actors** dress up as the Pilgrims in Plymouth. common

7. They act out the first **Thanksgiving**. proper

8. At the first Thanksgiving, the Pilgrim's showed their **appreciation** for the plentiful harvest. common

Singular and Plural Nouns (pp. 44–47) *Read each sentence. Write the plural form of the noun in parentheses.*

9. Most American (family) celebrate Thanksgiving. families

10. Traditional (dish) are important in this feast. dishes

11. Stores sell many (turkey) for the main meal. turkeys

12. (Box) of pies are piled up on shelves. Boxes

13. (Cranberry) are another specialty of the day. Cranberries

14. Cooks use them to make (sauce) and relishes. sauces

15. Guests arrive from faraway towns and (city). cities

16. Some (community) have Thanksgiving Day parades. communities

Irregular Plural Nouns (pp. 48–51) *Read each sentence. Write the plural of the noun in parentheses.*

17. There were ten (child) at our Thanksgiving dinner. **children**

18. The dining room table was over 16 (foot) long. **feet**

19. All the men and (woman) helped cook the meal. **women**

20. I couldn't wait to sink my (tooth) into the turkey! **teeth**

21. Later, we went outside and saw a flock of (goose). **geese**

22. I asked if a group of (sheep) is also called a flock. **sheep**

23. I think a group of (deer) would be a herd. **deer**

24. Ben wanted to know what to call a group of (moose). **moose**

Possessive Nouns (pp. 52–55) *Read each sentence. Write the possessive form of the noun in parentheses.*

25. Have you ever heard (Sarah Hale) name before? **Sarah Hale's**

26. She called attention to (Thanksgiving) importance. **Thanksgiving's**

27. Each (state) date for Thanksgiving was different at one time. **state's**

28. This magazine (editor) idea was to make Thanksgiving a national holiday. **editor's**

29. She told some of our (country) leaders of her plan. **country's**

30. Her idea had many (governors) support. **governors'**

31. In 1863, Hale even got the (president) attention. **president's**

32. (Abraham Lincoln) proclamation made Thanksgiving a national holiday. **Abraham Lincoln's**

Unit 2 Test

DIRECTIONS *Fill in the circle next to the sentence that shows correct spelling and the correct use of capital letters and apostrophes.*

1. ○ California is the third largest states.
○ Only Texas and alaska are larger in area.
● California has the most people.
○ What is this states capital?

2. ○ The Pacific Ocean is just west of california.
○ How beautiful the beachs must be!
● San Francisco and San Diego are on the coast.
○ These citys have natural harbors.

3. ○ Have you visited the states northern counties?
○ Ranchs, farms, and orchards dot this region.
● The Napa Valley is known for growing grapes.
○ The redwood trees' grow there.

4. ○ Amazement is your reaction when viewing these many giant tree.
● Have you heard of Inyo National Forest?
○ The worlds oldest living trees grow there.
○ Tall palm trees line Los Angeles' many boulevards.

5. ○ San Jose is one of Californias' major cities.
○ About 912,000 People live there.
○ Oakland is another Major city.
● What is Oakland's population?

6. ○ Where is Yosemite national park?
● The park is 200 miles east of San Francisco.
○ It covers over 1200 square mile's.
○ Some of our Continents highest waterfalls are there.

7. ○ Only small trees and bushs grow in desert areas.
○ Ms. jones's class is learning about desert plants.
● The class read about Joshua Tree National Park.
○ The childrens want to see this national park.

8. ● What animals roam California's forests?
○ Deers and foxs all live there.
○ The forests are also the California condors home.
○ Isn't that our countrys' largest land bird?

DIRECTIONS *Read the paragraph, and look carefully at each underlined part. Fill in the circle next to the answer choice that shows correct spelling and the correct use of capital letters and apostrophes. If the underlined part is already correct, fill in the circle for "Correct as is."*

Gold was discovered in California in 1848. News of James Marshall's discovery on the american river (9) spread like wildfire. Thousands of would-be miners from the eastern part of the United states (10) rushed to California. People with "gold fever" also sailed from countrys in europe and asia (11). In all, over 80,000 newcomers arrived in California in 1849. Some found richs, but many miners' lives (12) were filled with hardship. Still, the "forty-niners" liked California and stayed there. Success came to many of those who built businesss, ranchs, and farms (13), turning Sacramento and San Francisco into well-to-do cities (14).

9.
- ○ James Marshall's discovery on the american River
- ● James Marshall's discovery on the American River
- ○ James Marshall's discovery on the American river
- ○ Correct as is

10.
- ○ eastern part of the united states
- ○ eastern part of the united States
- ● eastern part of the United States
- ○ Correct as is

11.
- ● countries in Europe and Asia
- ○ countrys in Europe and asia
- ○ countrys in Europe and Asia
- ○ Correct as is

12.
- ○ found richs, but many miners lives
- ○ found richs, but many miners's lives
- ● found riches, but many miners' lives
- ○ Correct as is

13.
- ○ businesses, ranchs, and farms
- ● businesses, ranches, and farms
- ○ businesss, ranches, and farms
- ○ Correct as is

14.
- ○ Sacramento and San Francisco into well-to-do citys
- ○ sacramento and San Francisco into well-to-do cities
- ○ Sacramento and san francisco into well-to-do cities
- ● Correct as is

Lesson 12: Action Verbs

LEARN

- Every sentence has a subject and a predicate. The **verb** is the main word in the predicate.
- Often, the verb is a word that shows an action. An **action verb** tells what the subject does or did.

Subject	Predicate
The skier	**zooms** down the slope.
Her bright, blue skis	**flashed** in the sunlight.

PRACTICE

A *Read each sentence, and look at the predicate in **boldface**. Write the action verb in the predicate.*

1. The Olympic skiers **gather at the ski slope**. gather
2. They **wear bright, colorful outfits**. wear
3. A fan **cheers for his favorite athlete**. cheers
4. Many flags **wave in the breeze**. wave
5. Alpine skiers **race down steep mountain slopes**. race
6. One skier **moves at a speed of 70 miles per hour**. moves
7. The cross country skier **travels many kilometers**. travels
8. He **glides across the hilly landscape**. glides
9. Ski jumpers **leap long distances through the air**. leap
10. Somehow, they **land on their skis**. land

B *Draw a line between the subject and the predicate of each sentence. Then write the action verb. The first one is done for you.*

1. Many fans|watch the figure skaters. ____watch____
2. The skaters|perform their routines well. ____perform____
3. One athlete|traces a figure 8 on the ice. ____traces____
4. She|spins in the air. ____spins____
5. The three judges|score the events. ____score____
6. Couples|skate as pairs. ____skate____
7. They|choose the music for these events. ____choose____
8. Some pairs|design their own costumes. ____design____
9. The male skater|lifts his partner high in the air. ____lifts____
10. The audience|claps loudly. ____claps____
11. Ice dancers|move quickly and gracefully. ____move____
12. The skaters|competed in a separate set of events. ____competed____
13. They|danced to different kinds of music. ____danced____
14. Judges|graded their artistic skills. ____graded____
15. The excited ice dancers|waited for their scores. ____waited____

Remember
The **verb** is the main word in the predicate. The verb often shows an action.

C *Write an action verb to complete each sentence. Choose an action verb from the box, or use an action verb of your own.*

change	cheer	covers	enter	lean
look	produces	protect	push	reach
sharpen	signals	sit	swing	wear

Answers may vary. Suggested answers are given.

1. Speed skaters ___**wear**___ tight, lightweight uniforms.

2. They ___**sharpen**___ their skates before each race.

3. Some of these skaters ___**reach**___ speeds of 48 kilometers per hour.

4. Helmets ___**protect**___ their heads in case of falls.

5. Skating fans ___**enter**___ the stadium for the big race.

6. Skaters ___**lean**___ forward during the wait for the start.

7. Their eyes ___**look**___ straight ahead.

8. The official ___**signals**___ the start of the race.

9. Speed skaters ___**push**___ hard on their skates with each stroke.

10. They ___**swing**___ one arm back and forth.

11. A smooth flowing motion ___**produces**___ the best skating rhythm.

12. The racers ___**change**___ lanes during a race.

13. Each athlete ___**covers**___ the same distance that way.

14. The fans ___**sit**___ on the edge of their seats.

15. They ___**cheer**___ the exhausted winner.

WRITE

D *Read each subject for a sentence. Write a predicate to complete the sentence. Begin each predicate with an action verb. The first one is done for you.*

Answers will vary. Sample answers are given.

1. Our town's winter sports festival *begins today.*
2. Deep snow **covers the ground.**
3. The snow sculptures **sparkle in the sun.**
4. Some children **ride sleds down the hill.**
5. A few cross country skiers **pass the skaters.**
6. A horse-drawn sleigh **brings our friends to the park.**
7. Three speed skaters **race on the pond.**
8. More snow **falls during the day.**
9. Some workers **clear the paths in the park.**
10. Two ice dancers **perform for a crowd.**
11. A brave ski jumper **flies through the air.**
12. A skater **gives us a lesson.**
13. A fluffy white dog **plays in the snow.**
14. All the children **throw snowballs.**
15. Two hockey teams **play a short game.**

CCSS Language 1f. (See pp. T6–7.)

Proofreading Checklist ✓

- ❑ *Did you add a predicate to complete each sentence?*
- ❑ *Did you begin each predicate with an action verb?*

Lesson 13: Present-Tense Verbs

LEARN

- **The tense of a verb tells when an action happens. The action can happen in the present, past, or future.**

A verb in the present tense tells about an action that happens now or happens often.

Our uncle **drives** a fire truck.
Fire trucks **rush** to a fire.

- **A present-tense verb must *agree* with the subject of the sentence. The subject and the verb must both be singular or plural.**
  - **When the subject is a singular noun or *he, she,* or *it,* add *-s* to the verb.**
    A fire **spreads** quickly in a house.
    It **leaps** from room to room.
  - **When the subject is a plural noun or *I, we, you,* or *they,* do not add *-s* to the verb.**
    Firefighters **save** lives.
    They **protect** property, too.

PRACTICE

A *Choose the verb in parentheses that agrees with the subject. Then write the verb on the line.*

1. A loud siren ____wails____ in the night. (wail, wails)

2. Two fire trucks ____roar____ down our block. (roar, roars)

3. I ____spot____ the flames in a building down the street. (spot, spots)

4. The fire captain ____gives____ orders to the firefighters. (give, gives)

5. Two women ____connect____ a hose to the hydrant. (connect, connects)

6. They ____aim____ the water-filled hose at the fire. (aim, aims)

PRACTICE A *continued*

7. Other firefighters ___**break**___ the front door. (break, breaks)

8. They ___**enter**___ the burning building. (enter, enters)

9. The people inside ___**shout**___ to the firefighters. (shout, shouts)

10. We ___**hope**___ for the best. (hope, hopes)

B *Write the present-tense form of the verb in parentheses to correctly complete each sentence.*

1. A ladder company ___**arrives**___ next. (arrive)

2. The firefighters ___**raise**___ ladders up to the fifth floor. (raise)

3. One firefighter ___**sprays**___ water into the apartment. (spray)

4. She ___**sees**___ yellow flames and dark smoke. (see)

5. A police officer ___**closes**___ the street to traffic. (close)

6. She ___**calls**___ for backup on her walkie-talkie. (call)

7. I ___**hear**___ an ambulance, too. (hear)

8. The ambulance workers ___**give**___ first aid to two people. (give)

9. People ___**leave**___ the building with the help of the firefighters. (leave)

10. Families ___**stand**___ on the sidewalk. (stand)

11. Fire officials ___**check**___ every part of the building. (check)

12. They ___**find**___ the cause of the fire. (find)

13. The ladder company ___**returns**___ all the equipment to the truck. (return)

14. All the emergency workers ___**leave**___ the site at last. (leave)

15. We ___**appreciate**___ their brave work! (appreciate)

C

Ms. Wright's class wrote this list of fire-safety tips. The students made nine mistakes in subject-verb agreement. Use the proofreading marks in the box to correct the errors.

Remember

A present-tense verb must *agree* with the subject of the sentence. The subject and the verb must both be singular or plural.

Proofreading Marks

- ^ Add
- ⊙ Period
- Take out
- ≡ Capital letter
- / Small letter

Smoke detectors save lives!

In your house, each floor ~~need~~ needs a smoke detector. Test your smoke detectors once a month. The batteries usually ~~lasts~~ last about one year.

Fire extinguishers ~~puts~~ put out fires!

Small fires grow into big ones. Fire extinguishers ~~stops~~ stop small fires fast. Keep one in the kitchen and another in the basement.

Fire drills keep families safe!

Many families ~~holds~~ hold fire drills at their homes. Then each person ~~know~~ knows the safest way out during a fire. These drills ~~saves~~ save lives!

Careful adults ~~hides~~ hide matches!

Matches are useful, but young children ~~plays~~ play with them sometimes. Make sure the matches in your house are in a safe place.

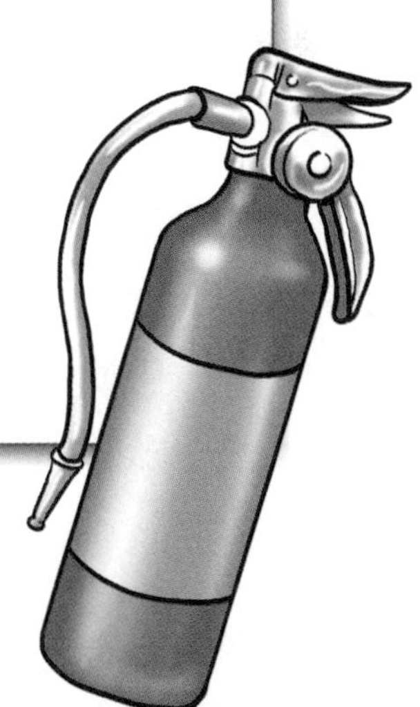

Did you correct nine verbs that did not agree with their subjects?

WRITE

D *Verbs show action. If you use descriptive verbs, your readers can see the action more clearly. In each sentence below, change the word in* ***boldface*** *to a more descriptive verb. Write the new sentence on the line. The first one is done for you.*

Answers will vary. Sample answers are given.

1. I **like** my uncle's work at the firehouse.

   I admire my uncle's work at the firehouse.

2. Some days, he **cleans** the fire truck.

   Some days, he shines the fire truck.

3. He **wipes** the equipment, too.

   He scrubs the equipment, too.

4. A loud alarm **sounds** sometimes.

   A loud alarms rings sometimes.

5. "Fire!" someone **says**.

   "Fire!" someone shouts.

6. The firefighters **move** toward their trucks.

   The firefighters run toward their trucks.

7. To get downstairs, some **go** down a pole.

   To get downstairs, some slide down a pole.

8. Seconds later, the trucks **travel** out the door.

   Seconds later, the trucks race out the door.

9. The fire trucks **head** to the fire.

   The fire trucks speed to the fire.

Go back to the sentences you wrote. Circle the descriptive verbs you used.

CCSS Language 3a. (See pp. T6–7.)

Lesson 14: More Present-Tense Verbs

LEARN

- A verb in the present tense must *agree* with the subject of the sentence. Both the subject and the verb must be either singular or plural.
- Follow these rules to make a present-tense verb agree with the subject.

For verbs that end in *ss, ch, sh, zz,* or *x*:

- **Add *-es* when the subject is a singular noun or *he, she,* or *it*.**

  press + es = press**es** — watch + es = watch**es**

  Jackie **presses** a seed into the soil. — She **watches** the seed grow.

- **Do not add *-es* when the subject is a plural noun or *I, we, you,* or *they*.**

  The students **press** seeds into the soil.

  They **watch** the seeds grow.

For verbs that end in a consonant and *y*:

- **Change *y* to *i*, and add *-es* when the subject is a singular noun or *he, she,* or *it*.**

  fly + es = fl**ies** — hurry + es = hurr**ies**

  A robin **flies** to the oak tree. — It **hurries** to its nest.

- **Do not change *y* to *i* or add *-es* when the subject is a plural noun or *I, we, you,* or *they*.**

  Robins **fly** to the oak tree.

  They **hurry** to their nests.

PRACTICE

A *Choose the verb in parentheses that agrees with the subject. Then write the verb on the line.*

1. The students ____discuss____ the signs of spring. (discuss, discusses)

2. My nose ____itches____ from pollen in the air. (itch, itches)

3. Baby birds ____hatch____ in their nests. (hatch, hatches)

4. Geese ____fly____ to their spring and summer homes. (fly, flies)

PRACTICE **A** *continued*

5. We ___watch___ the birds in the sky. (watch, watches)

6. The air conditioner ___buzzes___ on and off. (buzz, buzzes)

7. Pet owners ___brush___ shedding hair from dogs and cats. (brush, brushes)

8. Mom ___searches___ the closet for lighter clothes. (search, searches)

9. Fans ___hurry___ to baseball games. (hurry, hurries)

10. The worker ___patches___ the potholes in the road. (patch, patches)

B *Write the present-tense form of the verb in parentheses to correctly complete each sentence.*

1. Many families ___try___ to do spring cleaning in April. (try)

2. Six family members ___dress___ in old clothes. (dress)

3. Grandma ___fixes___ a broken curtain rod. (fix)

4. George ___washes___ the windows. (wash)

5. He ___reaches___ them on a stepladder. (reach)

6. The twins ___rush___ upstairs. (rush)

7. They ___wax___ the wooden floors. (wax)

8. Ms. Jones ___wishes___ the garage was neater. (wish)

9. She ___tosses___ things in boxes for a garage sale. (toss)

10. Mr. Jones ___dries___ the curtains in the sun. (dry)

11. Spring cleaning day ___passes___ quickly. (pass)

12. The adults ___relax___ at the end of the day. (relax)

Remember

A verb in the present tense must *agree* with the subject of the sentence. Both the subject and the verb must be either singular or plural.

C *Jason wrote about baseball tryouts in an e-mail to his aunt. He made seven errors in subject-verb agreement. Use the proofreading marks in the box to correct the errors.*

Proofreading Marks

^	Add
⊙	Period
ℓ	Take out
≡	Capital letter
/	Small letter

I show up for the baseball tryouts every spring, and I ^try ~~tries~~ my best. Baseball is my favorite sport, even though I am not the best player.

When I play left field, I miss a lot of balls. The high ones fly right over me. Fast grounders ^pass ~~passed~~ between my legs.

To be honest, I'm not much better at the plate. The ball ^flies ~~fly~~ right past me, and I usually strike out. Coach Jim always ^stresses ~~stress~~ one thing. "Don't tense up at the plate," he says. This time, I ^relax ~~relaxes~~. The pitcher ^pitches ~~pitch~~ a fastball right toward me. I smack the ball hard, and it sails over the fence.

The other players ^rush ~~rushes~~ toward me. I get "high fives" from everyone. Coach Jim tells me the good news. "Congratulations! You made the team," he says. It looks like I am finally on the path to being a great athlete!

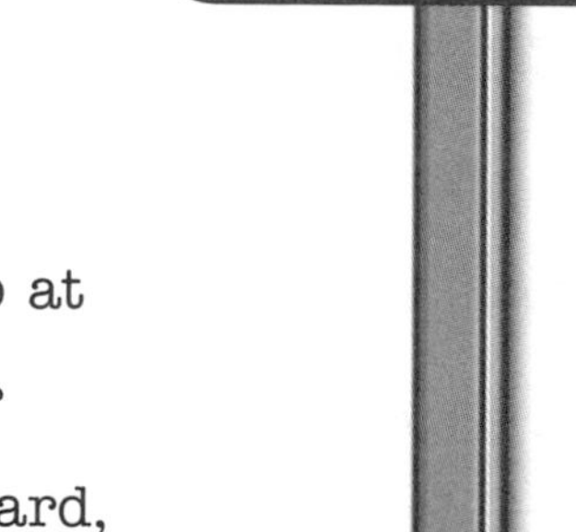

Did you correct the seven errors in subject-verb agreement?

WRITE

The verb is the main word in the predicate of a sentence. Sometimes you can combine two related sentences by joining the verbs. Use the word *and* to join the verbs.

Charlie washes quickly. Charlie dresses quickly.
Charlie washes **and** dresses quickly.

Combining sentences in this way will make your writing smoother and clearer.

D *Combine each pair of sentences by joining the verbs.*

1. People play in the park. People relax in the park.

People play and relax in the park.

2. Sue smells the cherry blossoms. Sue touches the cherry blossoms.

Sue smells and touches the cherry blossoms.

3. Children make kites. Children fly kites.

Children make and fly kites.

4. Karen grabs a football. Karen tosses a football.

Karen grabs and tosses a football.

5. Mia sees the ball. Mia catches the ball.

Mia sees and catches the ball.

6. Their friends watch them. Their friends encourage them.

Their friends watch and encourage them.

7. Mr. Ruiz observes the players. Mr. Ruiz coaches the players.

Mr. Ruiz observes and coaches the players.

Go back to the sentences you wrote. Circle the verbs that you joined.

Lesson 15: Past-Tense Verbs

LEARN

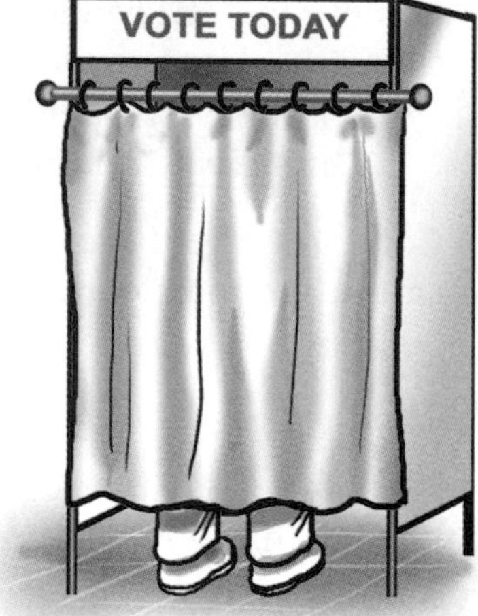

- A verb in the **past tense** tells about an action that already happened.
  The students **elected** a class president.
  I **supported** one of the candidates.
- Follow these rules to form the past tense.
  - Add *-ed* to most verbs.
    help + ed = help**ed**
    All my friends **helped** Will.
  - If a verb ends in *e*, drop the *e* and add *-ed*.
    vote + ed = vot**ed**
    The students **voted** on Tuesday.
  - If a verb ends in a consonant and *y*, change the *y* to *i*, and add *-ed*.
    hurry + ed = hurr**ied**
    They **hurried** to the voting booth.
  - For most verbs that end in one vowel followed by one consonant, double the consonant, and add *-ed*.
    stop + ed = **stopped**
    Our regular schoolwork **stopped** for the election.

PRACTICE

A *Write the past-tense form of each verb.*

1. study studied
2. grin grinned
3. push pushed
4. debate debated
5. reply replied
6. answer answered
7. decide decided
8. play played
9. clap clapped
10. carry carried

B *Write the past-tense form of the verb in parentheses to correctly complete each sentence.*

1. All the students **gathered** in the gym. (gather)
2. Our principal **explained** the election rules. (explain)
3. I **nominated** Will for class president. (nominate)
4. Will **expressed** his ideas in class meetings. (express)
5. He also **debated** the other candidate. (debate)
6. Both candidates **stepped** to the front of the room. (step)
7. Will **wanted** TVs in the cafeteria. (want)
8. Chris **described** possible school improvement projects. (describe)
9. Most students **liked** her ideas. (like)
10. The class **asked** both candidates questions. (ask)
11. I **worried** a little bit about Will's chances. (worry)
12. Chris's speech **stirred** strong feelings. (stir)
13. We **planned** a big "get out the vote" drive for Will. (plan)
14. Our teacher **tallied** the votes late Tuesday. (tally)
15. Everyone **congratulated** Chris on her victory. (congratulate)

C *Chris wrote this election speech. She spelled eight past-tense verbs incorrectly. Use the proofreading marks in the box to correct the errors.*

Remember

The spelling of some verbs changes when *-ed* is added to form the past tense. Follow the spelling rules when writing the past tense of verbs.

My fellow students,

I recently finished a term as your class president, and I ~~tryed~~ **tried** to serve you well. I ~~studyed~~ **studied** the problems we faced and worked hard to make our school better. I now need another term to finish that work.

Let me briefly describe our class's successes. The first book sale we ever organized ~~raisedd~~ **raised** over $200. We used that money for new musical instruments.

The Everyone Can Help program ~~grabed~~ **grabbed** people's attention. More than half of our classmates ~~applyed~~ **applied** for volunteer jobs in the school and community.

Our talks with the cafeteria staff ~~helpd~~ **helped**, too. Students now have healthier meal choices, and we ~~stoped~~ **stopped** wasting food.

A few of my campaign ideas ~~appearedd~~ **appeared** in the newspaper. I hope you read them and will vote for me next week.

Proofreading Marks

^	Add
⊙	Period
ℓ	Take out
≡	Capital letter
/	Small letter

Did you correct eight spelling mistakes with past-tense verbs?

WRITE

D *Read each pair of sentences below. In one sentence, the verb is in the past tense. In the other sentence, the verb is in the present tense. This switch in verb tense can cause confusion for the reader. Write each pair of sentences so that both verbs are in the same tense. The first one is done for you.*

1. The class president **represents** us. She **discussed** important issues with teachers.

The class president represents us. She discusses important issues with teachers.

Or: The class president represented us. She discussed important issues with teachers.

2. The vice president **helped** the president. He **attends** all the class meetings.

The vice president helps the president. He attends all the class meetings.

Or: The vice president helped the president. He attended all the class meetings.

3. The class secretary **recorded** notes during meetings. He **reports** news about upcoming events, too.

The class secretary records notes during meetings. He reports news about upcoming events, too. *Or:* The class secretary recorded notes during meetings. He reported news about upcoming events, too.

4. The treasurer **plans** fund-raisers. She **controlled** the class funds.

The treasurer plans fund-raisers. She controls the class funds.

Or: The treasurer planned fund-raisers. She controlled the class funds.

5. The student government **planned** activities for the class. It **provides** leadership.

The student government plans activities for the class. It provides leadership.

Or: The student government planned activities for the class. It provided leadership.

Go back to each pair of sentences you wrote.
Are the verbs in the same tense?

Lesson 16: Future-Tense Verbs

LEARN

- A verb in the **future tense** tells about an action that *will* happen. The action has not yet occurred. Use the special verb *will* to form the future tense.

  The Garcia family **will build** a new house.
  The builder and the Garcias **will discuss** the plans.

- The present, past, and future tenses are called **simple tenses**. They tell about action that happens now, in the past, and in the future.

  PRESENT Ms. Garcia **studies** the plans.
  PAST Ms. Garcia **studied** the plans.
  FUTURE Ms. Garcia **will study** the plans.

PRACTICE

A *Read each sentence. Underline the verb. Circle* **yes** *if the verb is in the future tense. Circle* **no** *if it is not.*

1. The Garcias like the builder's plans. yes no
2. They will call the builder tomorrow. yes no
3. He will supervise the workers at the site. yes no
4. The builder made a schedule already. yes no
5. The schedule shows each part of the project. yes no
6. The whole project will take about three months. yes no
7. Many different workers will order supplies. yes no
8. They haul supplies in their trucks. yes no
9. The family will move in June. yes no
10. They will rent a moving truck. yes no

B *Complete each sentence. Write the future tense of the verb in parentheses*

1. Carpenters **will build** the frame of the house. (build)
2. They **will measure** each piece of lumber. (measure)
3. Then they **will construct** each wall separately. (construct)
4. These workers **will shape** the windows and doorways, too. (shape)
5. The plumbers **will arrive** next. (arrive)
6. They **will bring** the kitchen and bathroom fixtures. (bring)
7. They **will install** the heating system, too. (install)
8. Roofers **will work** on the roof. (work)
9. They **will nail** shingles into place. (nail)
10. An electrician **will spend** a few weeks at the house. (spend)
11. She **will run** wires through the house. (run)
12. She **will test** the electrical system later. (test)
13. The painters **will start** in early June. (start)
14. They **will paint** the inside and the outside of the house. (paint)
15. The Garcias **will choose** the colors. (choose)

C *Daniel wrote this entry in his diary. He forgot to put seven verbs in the future tense. Use the proofreading marks in the box to correct the errors.*

Remember

Use the future tense to tell about an action that will happen. Use the special verb *will* to form the future tense.

Proofreading Marks

∧	Add
⊙	Period
~~e~~	Take out
≡	Capital letter
/	Small letter

Dear Diary,

I can't wait until our move next Thursday! We have already packed 30 boxes with dishes, books, clothes, and toys. We probably will pack 30 more before we're done. Mom ∧will buy some new furniture for the house after we move in.

Mom and Dad ∧will rent a truck next Wednesday. It's a 24-foot truck, so everything will fit. Uncle Jack and Aunt Rita ∧will help us load it. They ∧will drive the truck over to the new house on Thursday morning. We ∧will follow them in our family car.

Once I leave here, I know I will miss my old neighborhood. I ∧will miss my friends even more, but I know I ∧will come back for a visit. I also know I will make new friends at my new school.

Did you put seven verbs in the future tense?

WRITE

D *This builder's schedule shows the jobs that must be completed by the dates shown. On the lines below, complete the sentences about the jobs on the list. Use* ***will*** *with the verb in parentheses to form the future tense. The first one is done for you.*

May 25	Build cabinets
May 26	Paint rooms
May 27	Install light fixtures
May 28	Pave driveway
May 29	Order kitchen appliances
June 1	Test plumbing system
June 2	Check roof and gutters
June 2–3	Plant bushes
June 3–4	Inspect building
June 3–4	Clean up job site

1. (build) The carpenter *will build the cabinets.*
2. (paint) The painters **will paint the rooms.**
3. (install) The electrician **will install the light fixtures.**
4. (pave) A paving company **will pave the driveway.**
5. (order) The builder **will order the kitchen appliances.**
6. (test) The plumber **will test the plumbing system.**
7. (check) The roofer **will check the roof and gutters.**
8. (plant) Landscapers **will plant the bushes.**
9. (inspect) A building inspector **will inspect the building.**
10. (clean) The work crew **will clean up the job site.**

CCSS Language 1f. (See pp. T6–7.)

Proofreading Checklist ☑

- ❏ *Did you write a future-tense verb in each sentence?*
- ❏ *Did you use* ***will*** *to form each future-tense verb?*

Lesson 17: Linking Verbs

LEARN

- A **linking verb** links the subject of a sentence with other words that tell about the subject. A linking verb does not show action.

  A shark **is** a meat-eating fish.
  Whale sharks **are** the largest of all sharks.

- Different forms of the verb *be* are often used as linking verbs. Use the form of *be* that agrees with the subject of the sentence.

	Forms of *be*	
Subject	**Present**	**Past**
singular noun *he, she, it*	is	was
plural noun *you, we, they*	are	were
I	am	was

The tank in this room **is** huge.
Those sharks **are** hammerheads.
I **am** curious about sharks.

It **was** open all day.
They **were** popular with visitors.
I **was** busy yesterday.

PRACTICE

A *Read each sentence. Choose the linking verb in parentheses that agrees with the subject. Then write the linking verb on the line.*

1. We ____were____ at the aquarium yesterday. (was, were)

2. I ____was____ excited about the new shark exhibit. (was, were)

3. The tiger sharks ____were____ the biggest. (was, were)

4. One shark ____was____ 20 feet long. (was, were)

5. Shark teeth ____are____ razor sharp. (is, are)

6. That movie about the great white shark ____was____ terrifying! (was, were)

7. Some viewers ____were____ afraid of sharks for years. (was, were)

8. Shark attacks on humans ____are____ rare. (is, are)

9. The total number ____is____ about 100 attacks each year. (is, are)

10. About 20 attacks ____were____ deadly last year. (was, were)

B *Write the present-tense or past-tense form of* ***be*** *that correctly completes each sentence.*

1. The giant squid ____is____ one of today's rarest sea creatures.

2. Some of its tentacles ____are____ 90 feet long!

3. Long ago, sailors ____were____ afraid of the giant squid.

4. To them, it ____was____ a sea monster.

5. These days, I ____am____ very interested in giant squids.

6. Their homes ____are____ far below the ocean's surface.

7. Until recently, no photos of these creatures ____were____ available.

8. Scientists ____were____ unsure of the squid's size for a long time.

9. Some whales ____are____ enemies of the giant squid.

10. A deep, round scar on a whale ____is____ the mark of a squid attack.

11. The octopus ____is____ an ocean dweller, too.

12. It ____is____ a shy animal.

C *Jasmine wrote this report about piranhas. She made eight mistakes using linking verbs. Use the proofreading marks in the box to correct the errors.*

Remember

Different forms of the verb *be* are used as linking verbs. Use the form of *be* that agrees with the subject of the sentence.

Many people ~~is~~ are afraid of piranhas. The fear of this fish probably got started because of old movies. In old jungle movies, people ~~was~~ were often attacked by hungry piranhas.

In real life, most piranhas ~~is~~ are harmless to people. Twenty different types of piranhas live in South America. Many of them eat the fruit and nuts that fall into the water.

Red-bellied piranhas ~~is~~ are meat eaters, though. Black piranhas are meat eaters, too. Both of these fish have sharp, pointed teeth, and their jaws ~~is~~ are powerful. When the water level is high, these piranhas find plenty of food. They don't bother people.

During dry spells, the water level falls. Then the piranhas ~~is~~ are hungrier, and they ~~is~~ are more dangerous. Even so, attacks on humans are rare. Of course, we don't have to worry about piranhas in North America. Our climate ~~are~~ is too cold for these fish.

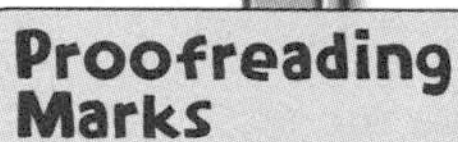

Proofreading Marks

^	Add
⊙	Period
✓	Take out
≡	Capital letter
/	Small letter

Did you correct eight linking verbs?

Red-bellied piranha

WRITE

D *Use a linking verb to join a subject from Box A to a word from Box B, and write a sentence. You can add other words to your sentence, and you can use a choice from a box more than once. An example is done for you.*
Answers will vary. Sample answers are given.

A	
the ocean	whales
dolphins	a child

B	
giants	huge
curious	mammals

1. *Whales are giants of the sea.*
2. **The ocean is a huge body of water.**
3. **Dolphins are mammals.**
4. **A child is curious about whales and dolphins.**

A	
alligators	the animal
jaws	many people

B	
similar	powerful
reptile	afraid

5. **Alligators are similar to crocodiles.**
6. **The jaws of an alligator are very powerful.**
7. **The animal is a reptile.**
8. **Many people are afraid of alligators.**

Proofreading Checklist ☑

- ☐ *Did you use a linking verb in each sentence?*
- ☐ *Did you use the correct form of the linking verb **be**?*

Lesson 18: Main Verbs and Helping Verbs

LEARN

- A verb can be more than one word. In this kind of verb, the most important word is the **main verb**. The **helping verb** usually works with the main verb to tell *when* the action happened. The helping verb always comes before the main verb.

  The moviemakers **are arriving** today.
  They **have unpacked** their equipment.
  They **will shoot** scenes for a movie in our town.

The main verb and the helping verb form a **verb phrase**. In the verb phrases above, the main verbs are *arriving, unpacked,* and *shoot*. The helping verbs are *are, have,* and *will*.

- Here are some common helping verbs.

am	was	has
is	were	have
are	will	had

- The verbs *can, may, must,* and *should* are called **modals**. These verbs are also helping verbs.

  can dance   may sing   must act   should direct

PRACTICE

A *Read each sentence, and look at the verb in* **boldface**. *Write the helping verb and the main verb on the lines.*

	Helping Verb	*Main Verb*
1. The movie company **has hired** a famous director.	has	hired
2. The director **is making** an adventure film.	is	making
3. A chase **will occur** in the movie.	will	occur
4. Several stunt performers **are preparing** for the scene.	are	preparing

CCSS Language 1c. (See pp. T6–7.)

	Helping Verb	*Main Verb*
5. The director **may film** the scene today.	may	film
6. The movie stars **should greet** their fans.	should	greet
7. People in the crowd **were cheering** for them.	were	cheering
8. I **am standing** near the cameras.	am	standing
9. The director **has planned** every detail.	has	planned
10. He **had started** work on the movie months ago.	had	started

B *Underline the verb in each sentence. If the verb is more than one word, be sure to underline both the main verb and helping verb. Then write the verb on the line.*

1. The writers can make some last-minute changes. can make

2. The director had asked for the changes. had asked

3. The crew tests the equipment. tests

4. A makeup artist is applying makeup to the stars. is applying

5. Electricians must check the cables before the scene is filmed. must check

6. Some stunt performers have signaled to the director. have signaled

7. An assistant director has requested quiet on the set. has requested

8. The director shouts, "Action!" shouts

9. The cameras are filming the scene. are filming

10. The star jumps into a speedboat. jumps

11. She has practiced this move many times. has practiced

12. An exciting chase scene begins. begins

Remember

A **helping verb** works with the main verb to tell *when* an action happened.

C *Write a helping verb and main verb to complete each sentence in this e-mail. Choose verbs from the box, or use verbs of your own.* **Answers will vary. Sample answers are given.**

must walk	was explaining	has promised	are filming
have watched	will appear	has scheduled	will begin

Casey,

Something amazing has just happened! As a result, I **will appear** (1) in a movie.

As I **was explaining** (2) to you yesterday, some moviemakers **are filming** (3) some scenes here in Fairport. The project is an action-adventure movie. Mom and I **have watched** (4) the filmmakers three times this week.

Earlier today, we went down to the marina to watch again. The director saw us and asked if we wanted to be extras in a scene. In the scene, we **must walk** (5) down a long dock. When we reach the middle of the dock, a big speedboat chase **will begin** (6).

The director **has scheduled** (7) us for 8 o'clock tomorrow morning. Mom **has promised** (8) her that we will be there early. Look for me in the near future at your favorite movie theater!

CCSS Language 1c. (See pp. T6–7.)

WRITE

D *Write a sentence to answer each question. Include both a helping verb and a main verb in each of your sentences. The first one is done for you.*

Answers will vary. Sample answers are given.

1. How many movies have you watched this month?

I have watched three movies this month.

2. What movie have you enjoyed recently?

I have enjoyed [title of movie] recently.

3. What movie was playing last week in your community?

[Title of movie] was playing last week.

4. What actors were starring in the movie?

[Actors' names] were starring in the movie.

5. What movie is showing this week?

[Title of movie] is showing this week.

6. Where is the movie playing?

The movie is playing at the [name of theater].

7. At about what time will this movie start?

The movie will start at [time of day].

8. Who may join you?

My [friend(s), relative(s), or individual name(s)] may join me.

9. Which actor has created the funniest characters?

[Name of actor] has created the funniest characters.

Proofreading Checklist ☑

CCSS Language 1c. (See pp. T6–7.)

- ❑ *Did you answer each question with a complete sentence?*
- ❑ *Did you use a helping verb and a main verb in each sentence?*

Lesson 19: Using Helping Verbs

LEARN

- **The past tense is often formed by adding *-ed* to a verb. Another way to show a past action is to use the helping verbs *has, have,* or *had* with the past-tense form of the main verb.**

  Our grade **has published** a school newspaper.
  The students **have worked** hard on it.
  We **had studied** newspapers in social studies for weeks.

- **Be sure to use the helping verb that agrees with the subject of the sentence.**

Subject	Present	Past
singular noun *he, she, it*	has	had
plural noun *I, you, we, they*	have	had

PRACTICE

A *Write **yes** or **no** to tell if the helping verb agrees with the subject of the sentence.*

1. Our class has decided to publish a newspaper. yes
2. A few years ago, another class had published a school newspaper. yes
3. We has learned a lot from looking at those earlier news articles and editorials. no
4. Our staff members have selected Mike and Teresa as the head editors. yes
5. They has asked our teacher for help. no
6. Each student have volunteered for a job. no

7. Jon have prepared an article about our new principal, Ms. Gray. ___no___
8. He had interviewed her last week. ___yes___
9. Laura had photographed the new playground. ___yes___
10. She had borrowed her dad's digital camera for the assignment. ___yes___

B *Draw a line under the helping verb in parentheses that correctly completes each sentence.*

1. We (has, had) named our paper *The Student News* earlier in the week.
2. Now we (has, have) renamed it *The Dover School Newsflash*.
3. Ginny (has, have) used her layout skills to design the paper.
4. She (have, had) sharpened her skills in a class last year.
5. Finally, I (has, have) finished my article about the cafeteria food.
6. Yesterday, Miki (have, had) asked me to rewrite it.
7. My first draft (have, had) lacked facts and details.
8. Our teacher (has, have) suggested many story ideas to Miki.
9. She (has, have) assigned stories to writers, too.
10. Tim (has, have) roamed around the school looking for news.
11. By last week's deadline, he (have, had) talked to almost everyone.
12. This week, Ramon (has, have) decided to write an advice column.
13. Many classmates (has, have) handed him funny letters to answer.
14. The twins (has, have) edited most of the stories.
15. They (has, have) learned so much about grammar and punctuation.

C *Sasha wrote this news story. In five of the sentences, the helping verbs **has** and **have** do not agree with the subject. Find the mistakes, and use the proofreading marks to correct them.*

Remember
Use *has* with a singular noun and with *he, she,* and *it*. Use *have* with a plural noun and with *I, you, we,* and *they*.

Proofreading Marks

^	Add
⊙	Period
↩	Take out
≡	Capital letter
/	Small letter

First-Time Racer Wins Pinewood Derby

The Pinewood Derby was held tonight in the school gym. Over two dozen participants entered the race.

Mr. Edward Ryan has held these derby races for 25 years. He ~~have~~ ^has never seen a race with such fast times before.

The big winner is first-time racer Brian Little! He ~~have~~ ^has finished with a best time of 3.15 seconds.

What helped Brian win? Brian says, "I ~~has~~ ^have talked with some winning pinewood racers. They ~~has~~ ^have given me some tips, and tips from good racers help a lot."

By coming in first, Brian ~~have~~ ^has earned the right to go to the regional race in Springfield next month. "I can't wait," he said. In the meantime, he has started to make his car faster!

Did you make five helping verbs agree with the subjects?

WRITE

D *Think about something exciting that happened to someone you know. Write seven sentences to tell what happened. Use past-tense verbs with the helping verbs* ***has, have,*** *or* ***had*** *in your sentences. Check a dictionary if you need help spelling a word.*
Answers will vary. Sample answers are given.

1. Coach Sue Townes had traveled to New York City.
2. She had participated in the New York City Marathon.
3. The event had occurred in November.
4. She has returned with many interesting facts and stories to share.
5. People had lined the streets to watch.
6. Spectators had cheered the runners.
7. We have listened to the exciting details of her trip.

CCSS Language 2d; Writing 3. (See pp. T6–7.)

Proofreading Checklist ☑

- ❑ *Did you use **has, have,** or **had** with the past tense of verbs?*
- ❑ *Did you use **has** when the subject of the sentence was a singular noun or **he, she,** or **it**?*
- ❑ *Did you use **have** when the subject of the sentence was a plural noun or **I, you, we,** or **they**?*

Lesson 20: **Progressive Forms of Verbs**

LEARN

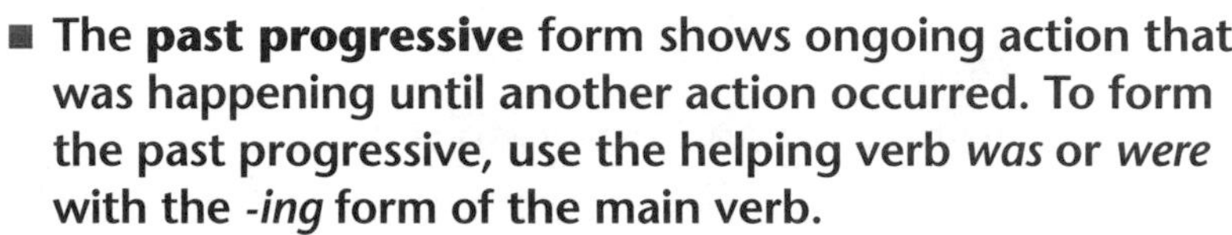

- **You have learned about the present, past, and future verb tenses. Each of these tenses has a progressive form. The progressive form shows that an action is ongoing.**

- **The present progressive form shows ongoing action that is still happening when the words are written. To form the present progressive, use the helping verb *am, is,* or *are* with the *-ing* form of the main verb.**

  I **am studying** about different periods in art.
  Our teacher **is explaining** how an art movement begins.
  Beth and Tom **are looking** at a painting from the Impressionist art period.

- **The past progressive form shows ongoing action that was happening until another action occurred. To form the past progressive, use the helping verb *was* or *were* with the *-ing* form of the main verb.**

  The librarian **was arranging** the books as we entered.
  We **were reading** when the books started to fall.

- **The future progressive form shows ongoing action that will happen in the future. To form the future progressive, use the helping verb *will be* with the *-ing* form of the main verb.**

  Our class **will be discussing** Impressionism this week.

- **Notice the subject-verb agreement in the sentences above.**

PRACTICE

A *Underline the progressive form of the verb in each sentence.*

1. We are learning about different forms of art.

2. Our art teacher was showing us different ways to hold a paintbrush when the bell rang.

3. We will be painting our own landscapes this week.

4. I am going to the pond near my house to draw.

CCSS Language 1b. (See pp. T6–7.)

PRACTICE A *continued*

5. Nick and Luna will be joining me at the pond tomorrow.

6. I was outlining a tree when a duck knocked over my easel.

7. My friends were laughing so hard that no one helped me pick up my painting.

8. Now Luna is sketching a picture of the duck.

9. I am thinking about painting the flowers instead of the trees.

10. Nick will be using the Impressionist style for his landscape.

B *Read each sentence. Choose the helping verb in parentheses that correctly completes the sentence. Then write the helping verb on the line.*

1. Jacob and I **are** working on a presentation on Claude Monet. (is, are)

2. Our librarian **is** gathering art books for us to examine. (is, are)

3. I **am** researching Monet's life and works of art. (am, is)

4. Jacob **is** reading about the start of the Impressionist movement. (is, were)

5. Later, we **will be** creating an Impressionist painting of a garden. (was, will be)

6. We **will be** preparing a slideshow of Monet's paintings, too. (was, will be)

7. Jacob and I **were** giving our presentation when the fire alarm sounded. (was, were)

8. I **was** walking home when I saw brochure for a Monet exhibit in Paris. (was, were)

9. We **were** talking about Monet's beautiful paintings when Dad came home. (is, were)

10. Now I **will be** dreaming about a trip to Paris, the birthplace of Impressionism. (are, will be)

C *Here is a report on the Impressionist painter, Claude Monet. Write the correct present, past, or future progressive form of a verb to complete each sentence. Choose a verb from the box, or use a verb of your own.* **Answers will vary. Sample answers are given.**

Remember

The **progressive forms** of verbs show ongoing action. To decide which helping verb to add, think about when the action began or will begin.

hope   inspire   learn   live   teach   visit

Proofreading Marks

^	Add
⊙	Period
ℓ	Take out
≡	Capital letter
/	Small letter

This month in art class, we **are learning** about the Impressionist painter Claude Monet. He is a French painter who lived from 1840 to 1926. While Monet **was visiting** the Louvre, a museum in Paris, he saw painters copying famous masterworks, like the Mona Lisa. Unlike them, Monet drew what he saw in his own way.

Monet was not the only one in France to paint like this. Others painted this way, too. All these artists **were living** in Paris at that time, and they became friends. Instead of sharp clean lines, the Impressionist painters used rapid, blurred brushstrokes. These artists developed a whole new style of art.

Monet is known for his use of color and the way he painted light. Still today, his artwork **is inspiring** artists to think in new ways. I **am hoping** to become an artist like Monet. My dream is that one day, I **will be teaching** young artists about his work.

CCSS Language 1b. (See pp. T6–7.)

WRITE

Look at the picture below. Using the progressive forms of verbs, write a story based on the picture. Include at least four different progressive forms. Use a dictionary to help with spelling.

Answers will vary. A sample answer is given.

Today Antonia **is going** to the pier with her mom. They watch as the smaller boats float calmly on the water. They **are waiting** for the larger sailboats. They **will be drawing** these boats as they pass by.

Then, while Antonia and her mom **were sketching** the waves, a large boat with huge sails came gliding by. It was the largest sailboat Antonia had ever seen. While her mother **was viewing** the craft, Antonia started to sketch it. She told her mom that she **was trying** to capture the magnificence of the boat. Her mom said, "**I am loving** what I see. Your boat is as grand and splendid as the real one."

By the pier, Antonia finished her drawing while her mother stood nearby and watched.

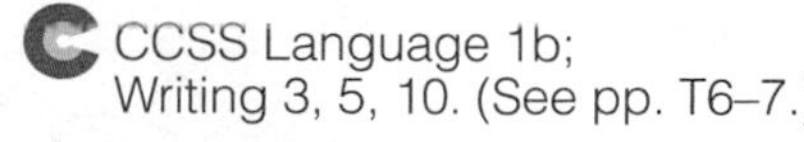

Proofreading Checklist ☑

- ❑ *Did you use* ***am, is,*** *and* ***are*** *for present progressive forms?*
- ❑ *Did you use* ***was*** *or* ***were*** *for past progressive forms?*
- ❑ *Did you use* ***will be*** *for future progressive forms?*

Lesson 21: Irregular Verbs

LEARN

- **Irregular verbs** do not add *-ed* to show the past tense. Instead, the spelling of an irregular verb changes to form the past tense. The spelling of many irregular verbs changes again when they are used with the helping verbs *has, have,* or *had*.

- There are many irregular verbs. Here are ten of them.

  PRESENT — I **begin** to read Aesop's fables.
  PAST — I **began** to read Aesop's fables.
  PAST WITH *HAVE* — I **have begun** to read Aesop's fables.

Present	Past	Past with *has, have, or had*
begin	began	has, have, or had begun
bring	brought	has, have, or had brought
come	came	has, have, or had come
do	did	has, have, or had done
eat	ate	has, have, or had eaten
give	gave	has, have, or had given
grow	grew	has, have, or had grown
make	made	has, have, or had made
say	said	has, have, or had said
swim	swam	has, have, or had swum

PRACTICE

A *Write the verb in parentheses that correctly completes each sentence.*

1. A kind butcher had ___given___ a hungry dog some meat. (gave, given)
2. The dog ___brought___ the meat to a bridge over a river. (bring, brought)
3. Before he ___began___ to eat, the dog looked down. (began, begun)

CCSS Language 2d. (See pp. T6–7.)

PRACTICE A *continued*

4. In the water below the bridge, another dog **swam** into view. (swam, swum)

5. This dog had **come** to the river with meat, too. (came, come)

6. He stopped and slowly **ate** his meat. (ate, eaten)

7. The dog on the bridge **grew** greedy. (grew, grown)

8. He **made** a sudden move toward the meat reflected in the water. (make, made)

9. As soon as he had **done** that, the real meat dropped into the river. (did, done)

10. The hungry dog **ate** nothing that night. (ate, eaten)

B *Write the past form of the verb in parentheses to correctly complete each sentence.*

1. A tired, hungry wolf had just **swum** across a river. (swim)

2. A farmer's dog **began** barking at the wolf. (begin)

3. "I have **come** a long way," growled the wolf. (come)

4. "I have **eaten** nothing for days," he said. (eat)

5. The kind dog **brought** the wolf some food. (bring)

6. "You must like it here," the wolf **said**. (say)

7. "The farmer has **done** a lot for me," replied the dog. (do)

8. "What has **made** that mark on your neck?" the wolf asked next. (make)

9. "I have **grown** so fat that my chain is too tight," explained the dog. (grow)

10. "I would never have **given** up my freedom for a chain," the wolf said. (give)

C *Evan wrote this version of an old fable called "The Fox and the Goat." He made seven mistakes with the past forms of irregular verbs. Use the proofreading marks in the box to correct the errors.*

Remember The spelling of an irregular verb changes in the past tense or when used with *has, have,* or *had.*

Fox had fallen into a well. He ~~swum~~ swam around for a while, but he couldn't get out.

After a while, Goat came along. He had ~~brung~~ brought a bucket to get some water. "What are you doing down there, Fox?" Goat asked.

Fox looked serious. "Haven't you heard about the drought?" he asked.

Goat ~~gived~~ gave a shrug. "What drought?" he asked.

"The water shortage has ~~growed~~ grown really bad all over the country," Fox said. "In fact, this may be the last water left anywhere. If I were you, Goat, I'd jump in!"

Well, the foolish goat ~~done~~ did just that. As soon as Goat was in the well, Fox jumped on his back. Then he climbed up onto Goat's horns and out of the well.

"I'm so glad you ~~come~~ came along," Fox called down to Goat. "You have ~~maked~~ made my day! But next time, look before you leap!"

Proofreading Marks

^	Add
⊙	Period
℘	Take out
≡	Capital letter
/	Small letter

Did you correct seven mistakes with irregular verbs?

 CCSS Language 2d. (See pp. T6–7.)

WRITE

D *Complete the sentences in the fable below with past forms of irregular verbs. Use forms of the verbs in the chart on page 96. Then write a few sentences of your own to finish the fable. Use past forms of irregular verbs in some of your sentences.*

The ants were hard workers. All summer long, they had **grown** grain and vegetables in their large garden. Once fall came, they **brought** the food inside and stored it. They had **done** everything possible to prepare for the cold months of winter.

Grasshopper, on the other hand, **did** very little all summer and fall. When the weather was hot, he **swam** in the pond. When he was hungry, he **ate** fresh berries off the bushes.

Winter **came** early that year, and Grasshopper **began** to worry. No berries **grew** on the bushes now, and he had no food in his house. With his stomach growling, Grasshopper paid a visit to the ants.

"What has **brought** you here today, Grasshopper?" asked one of the ants.

Story endings will vary. A sample is given.

Grasshopper said that he had come to ask for help. He was sorry that he had done so little to get ready for winter. The ants gave Grasshopper food to eat, and they invited him to stay with them.

CCSS Language 2d; Writing 3, 4, 10. (See pp. T6–7.)

Proofreading Checklist ☑

❑ *Did you use the correct past forms of the irregular verbs?*

Lesson 22: More Irregular Verbs

LEARN

- **Irregular verbs** do not form the past tense by adding *-ed*. Instead, the spelling of an irregular verb changes when the past tense is formed. The spelling may change again when the irregular verb is used with the helping verbs *has, have,* or *had*.

PRESENT People **write** tall tales today.

PAST People **wrote** tall tales in the past.

PAST WITH *HAVE* People **have written** tall tales for a long time.

Present	Past	Past with *has, have, or had*
break	broke	has, have, or had broken
draw	drew	has, have, or had drawn
drive	drove	has, have, or had driven
fly	flew	has, have, or had flown
ride	rode	has, have, or had ridden
sing	sang	has, have, or had sung
take	took	has, have, or had taken
tell	told	has, have, or had told
throw	threw	has, have, or had thrown
write	wrote	has, have, or had written

PRACTICE

A *Write the verb in parentheses that correctly completes each sentence.*

1. Cowboys have ___told___ tall tales about Pecos Bill. (tell, told)
2. They have ___sung___ about how he was raised. (sang, sung)
3. The coyotes ___took___ Bill to the Texas plains. (took, taken)

CCSS Language 2d. (See pp. T6–7.)

PRACTICE A *continued*

4. Bill ____rode____ faster than any other cowboy. (rode, ridden)

5. He ____drove____ the biggest cattle to market. (drove, driven)

6. No cowboy had ever ____thrown____ a lasso so well! (threw, thrown)

7. One tale has ____told____ of a terrible drought. (tell, told)

8. Pecos Bill had ____ridden____ up into the sky on his horse. (rode, ridden)

9. He had ____driven____ some storm clouds over to Texas. (drove, driven)

10. He ____broke____ them open so the rain would fall. (broke, broken)

B *Write the past form of the verb in parentheses to correctly complete each sentence.*

1. Almost everyone ____rode____ railroads in the early 1900s. (ride)

2. People ____wrote____ songs and tall tales about John Henry. (write)

3. Many tales have ____told____ about his incredible strength. (tell)

4. Henry ____drove____ spikes into the wooden boards that hold down railroad tracks. (drive)

5. His huge sledgehammer ____flew____ through the air. (fly)

6. Some people have ____written____ that Henry could swing two hammers at once! (write)

7. A folksinger ____sang____ about Henry's contest with a new power drill. (sing)

8. Henry's boss had ____taken____ the drill to the work site. (take)

9. The amazing contest ____drew____ a large crowd. (draw)

10. Even after the power drill had ____broken____, John Henry was still working. (break)

CCSS Language 2d. (See pp. T6–7.)

Remember

The spelling of an irregular verb changes in the past tense or when used with *has, have,* or *had*.

C *Sam wrote this story about Paul Bunyan, another hero of many tall tales. Sam made eight mistakes with the past forms of irregular verbs. Use the proofreading marks in the box to correct the errors.*

Proofreading Marks

^	Add
⊙	Period
ℓ/	Take out
≡	Capital letter
/	Small letter

Paul Bunyan ~~throwed~~ threw down his ax. Then he ~~taked~~ took a deep breath. "What a job!" he said. It had ~~took~~ taken a week, but the giant logger and his big blue ox Babe were finally done. They had cleared the trees out of the Great Forests. People would now call this area the Great Plains.

"To float these logs down to my sawmill in Louisiana," Paul said, "we need a river." Paul hitched a plow to Babe and ~~drived~~ drove her and the plow down to New Orleans. Believe it or not, that's how the Mississippi River got started!

"Step more lightly," Paul ~~telled~~ told Babe. Every so often, her heavy hoofs ~~breaked~~ broke through the rocky ground, and streams of oil ~~flyed~~ flew up. Those were the first oil wells.

How do I know these things? Babe told me about them herself, and I have ~~wrote~~ written down everything she said.

Did you correct eight mistakes with irregular verbs?

 CCSS Language 2d. (See pp. T6–7.)

WRITE

D *The tall tale below tells what Paul Bunyan might do in today's world. Complete the sentences in the story with past forms of irregular verbs. Use forms of the verbs in the chart on page 100. Then write a few sentences of your own to complete the story. Use past forms of irregular verbs in your sentences.*

Paul Bunyan and the Trees

Last year, Paul Bunyan **drove** across the country in a supersized truck. He **flew** over other areas of the world in a jumbo jet. Along the way, Paul **took** a long, hard look at the places he passed. What he saw almost **broke** his heart!

Actually, it was the lack of trees that almost **drove** Paul crazy. "People have always **told** tall tales about my logging," he moaned. "They have even **sung** songs about me and Babe working together. Maybe we have **taken** this logging business too seriously. Now it's time to plant some trees!" **Story endings will vary. A sample is given.**

Paul Bunyan threw his axes and chain saws into a big trash can. Then he told Babe to start planting trees. Paul and Babe drove across the country planting trees. Everyone they met told them to keep up the good work.

CCSS Language 2d; Writing 3, 4, 10. (See pp. T6–7.)

Proofreading Checklist ☑

- ❑ *Did you use the correct past forms of irregular verbs?*
- ❑ *Did you use the correct form of the verb with **has, have,** and **had**?*

Lesson 23: Contractions with *Not*

LEARN

A **contraction** is made by joining two words together. An apostrophe (') takes the place of any letters that are left out. Some contractions are formed by joining a verb with the word *not*.

are + not = **aren't**
Some common beliefs about health **aren't** true.

will + not = **won't**
Carrots **won't** improve your eyesight.

Notice that the spelling of the verb *will* changes when it is combined with *not* to form the contraction *won't*

Contractions with *not*			
is not	**isn't**	do not	**don't**
are not	**aren't**	does not	**doesn't**
was not	**wasn't**	did not	**didn't**
were not	**weren't**	cannot	**can't**
has not	**hasn't**	could not	**couldn't**
have not	**haven't**	should not	**shouldn't**
had not	**hadn't**	would not	**wouldn't**
will not	**won't**		

PRACTICE

A *Write the contraction for each pair of words.*

1. was not wasn't

2. cannot can't

3. does not doesn't

4. is not isn't

5. are not aren't

6. were not weren't

PRACTICE A *continued*

7. did not **didn't**
8. had not **hadn't**
9. could not **couldn't**
10. will not **won't**

B *Write a contraction for the word or words in parentheses to complete each sentence.*

1. Eating lots of carrots **won't** turn your skin orange. (will not)
2. Worrying **doesn't** turn a person's hair gray. (does not)
3. Too much chocolate **isn't** the cause of pimples. (is not)
4. Foods **don't** cause all skin problems. (do not)
5. Colds **aren't** caused by bad weather. (are not)
6. You **can't** get the flu unless you are exposed to a virus. (cannot)
7. Staying in bed **won't** help you get over a cold faster. (will not)
8. Standing on your head **hasn't** ever cured the hiccups. (has not)
9. Touching a frog **doesn't** cause warts. (does not)
10. Scientists **haven't** found any evidence for this idea. (have not)
11. Everyone wishes you **wouldn't** crack your knuckles. (would not)
12. We **shouldn't** believe every health and diet tip we hear! (should not)

C *Dana and Ian wrote this fact sheet listing other untrue ideas about diet and health. In it, they made eight mistakes with contractions. Use the proofreading marks in the box to correct the errors.*

Remember
When you join two words in a contraction, an apostrophe takes the place of any letters that are left out.

The Truth About Diet and Health

- Drinking coffee won't stunt your growth. Even so, caffeine ~~shouldnt~~ shouldn't be part of a young person's diet.
- Eating carrots ~~doesnt~~ doesn't improve your eyesight. However, the vitamin A in carrots does help eyes stay healthy.
- Going outside with wet hair ~~wont~~ won't make you catch a cold. Colds ~~are'nt~~ aren't caused by wet hair or windy weather. They are caused by viruses.
- Watching TV ~~doesnt~~ doesn't damage your eyes. However, people who spend too much time watching TV probably ~~dont~~ don't get enough exercise.
- Reading in dim light ~~isnt~~ isn't a cause of bad eyesight. Good lighting, however, makes reading much easier!
- Crossing your eyes ~~cant~~ can't make you permanently cross-eyed. But why do it? It's hard to see that way!

Proofreading Marks

^	Add
⊙	Period
℘	Take out
≡	Capital letter
/	Small letter

Did you correct eight mistakes with contractions?

WRITE

D *Read each sentence. Then rewrite it, using one or more contractions formed with* ***not****. Make any other changes that are necessary for the new sentence to make sense. The first two are done for you.*

Answers will vary. Sample answers are given.

1. If you do exercise regularly, you will get in shape.

If you don't exercise regularly, you won't get in shape.

2. Your scrape has healed because you have taken care of it.

Your scrape hasn't healed because you haven't taken care of it.

3. My muscles have gotten stronger because I have exercised.

My muscles haven't gotten stronger because I haven't exercised.

4. If you do get eight hours of sleep, you will feel rested tomorrow.

If you don't get eight hours of sleep, you won't feel rested tomorrow.

5. If you have eaten breakfast, you will have the energy you need.

If you haven't eaten breakfast, you won't have the energy you need.

6. Sue did get enough vitamins because she did eat fresh fruit and vegetables.

Sue didn't get enough vitamins because she didn't eat fresh fruit and vegetables.

7. If you had acted recklessly, you would have gotten hurt.

If you hadn't acted recklessly, you wouldn't have gotten hurt.

8. If you get caught in the rain, you will need an umbrella.

If you don't get caught in the rain, you won't need an umbrella.

Proofreading Checklist ☑

- ❑ *Did you use one or more contractions with* ***not*** *in each sentence you wrote?*
- ❑ *Did you use an apostrophe in place of letters that are left out?*

Unit 3 Review
Lessons 12–23

Action Verbs (pp. 60–63) *Underline the action verb in each sentence.*

1. Musicians play many different instruments in orchestras.
2. A conductor leads the orchestra.
3. Orchestras entertain people.

Present-Tense Verbs (pp. 64–71) *Write the present tense of the verb in parentheses to correctly complete each sentence.*

4. Ellen (tighten) the strings of her violin. **tightens**
5. The clarinet player (remove) his instrument from its case. **removes**
6. The conductor (discuss) the music with the orchestra. **discusses**
7. Each musician (study) the music carefully. **studies**
8. The ushers (guide) people to their seats. **guide**
9. My sister (reach) her seat just in time. **reaches**

Past-Tense Verbs (pp. 72–75) *Write the past tense of the verb in parentheses to correctly complete each sentence.*

10. Early orchestras (accompany) singers. **accompanied**
11. Composers (plan) music for more and more instruments. **planned**
12. Some early orchestras (include) more than 100 musicians. **included**

Future-Tense Verbs (pp. 76–79) *Write the future tense of the verb in parentheses to correctly complete each sentence.*

13. We (go) to a concert next Friday night. **will go**
14. The musicians (play) works by Mozart. **will play**
15. A large crowd (attend) this performance. **will attend**

Linking Verbs (pp. 80–83) *Underline the linking verb that agrees with the subject of the sentence.*

16. Drums (is, are) percussion instruments.

17. Another percussion instrument (is, are) the xylophone.

18. I (am, is) a trombone player.

Main Verbs and Helping Verbs (pp. 84–91) *Underline the helping verb in each sentence.*

19. Jamie should distribute the sheet music.

20. The musicians are turning the pages.

21. The conductor will answer our questions.

Progressive Forms of Verbs (pp. 92–95) *Underline the progressive form of the verb in each sentence. Then write it on the line.*

22. Members of the orchestra are playing their scales. are playing

23. Reilly and Marvin were talking about classical music. were talking

24. The store will be delivering new music stands. will be delivering

Irregular Verbs (pp. 96–103) *Underline the correct verb in parentheses to complete each sentence.*

25. Our orchestra (began, begun) today's practice at two o'clock.

26. All the members have (took, taken) their seats.

27. Jesse had (wrote, written) one of the songs we will perform.

Contractions with *Not* (pp. 104–107) *Read each sentence. Write the words in **boldface** as a contraction.*

28. Some of the instruments **are not** in tune. aren't

29. We **do not** get discouraged. don't

30. Our performance **will not** be perfect until we practice more. won't

Unit 3 Test

DIRECTIONS *Fill in the circle next to the sentence that spells and uses verbs or contractions correctly.*

1.
- ○ Rain clouds has formed in the sky.
- ● The wind began to blow harder.
- ○ Suddenly, the rain splashs down on the sidewalk.
- ○ A boy hurrys home.

2.
- ● The storm has driven everyone indoors.
- ○ Heavy rain drumed down on our roof.
- ○ Mom and I didnt close our windows in time.
- ○ The raindrops varyed in size.

3.
- ○ The rain has stoped now.
- ○ The sky have cleared suddenly.
- ○ A rainbow appear in the sky.
- ● Our neighbors may come outside to see it.

4.
- ○ The rain has provideed the trees and plants with water.
- ● It washes the sidewalks, too.
- ○ Some rain rushs off into streams and rivers.
- ○ The sun's heat evaporate the rest of it.

5.
- ○ The clouds have growed dark again.
- ○ The heavy rain poures down once more.
- ○ The neighbors has scurried indoors again.
- ● We don't like these heavy rainstorms.

6.
- ○ Snow were falling all night.
- ○ Snowflakes begun to fall.
- ○ The snowstorm isnt over yet.
- ● The children are throwing snowballs in the air.

7.
- ○ The roads was icy yesterday.
- ○ People was driving carefully.
- ○ My grandmother watch the weather report.
- ● We must play indoors today.

8.
- ○ Our class will made a rain gauge.
- ● A rain gauge is a weather tool.
- ○ It measure the amount of rainfall.
- ○ Kit has bring a coffee can for the project.

DIRECTIONS *Read the paragraph, and look carefully at each underlined part. Fill in the circle next to the answer choice that shows the correct spelling and use of verbs or contractions. If the underlined part is already correct, fill in the circle for "Correct as is."*

The water cycle supplies (9) Earth with its water. In the cycle, moist air rises from the ground. The moisture takes the form of water vapor, and the vapor is carried high into the sky. Here the air was cooler (10). The cool air cann't hold (11) as much water as the warmer air below. The water vapor changes (12) from vapor into droplets. These tiny droplets forms (13) clouds. Eventually, this moisture will falls (14) to Earth as rain. Snow will fall instead if the temperature has dropped low enough.

9. ○ The water cycle supply
○ The water cycle supplys
○ The water cycle have supplied
● Correct as is

10. ● the air is cooler
○ the air are cooler
○ the air were cooler
○ Correct as is

11. ○ cool air cant hold
● cool air can't hold
○ cool air can'nt hold
○ Correct as is

12. ○ The water vapor change
○ The water vapor changees
○ The water vapor changies
● Correct as is

13. ● These tiny droplets form
○ These tiny droplets has formed
○ These tiny droplets formes
○ Correct as is

14. ○ this moisture fall
○ this moisture had fall
● this moisture will fall
○ Correct as is

Lesson 24: Adjectives

LEARN

- An **adjective** is a word that describes a noun. It can tell *what kind*, and it can also tell *how many*. An adjective usually comes before the noun it describes.

  WHAT KIND We visited a **large** refuge.

  HOW MANY **Several** birds live in the refuge.

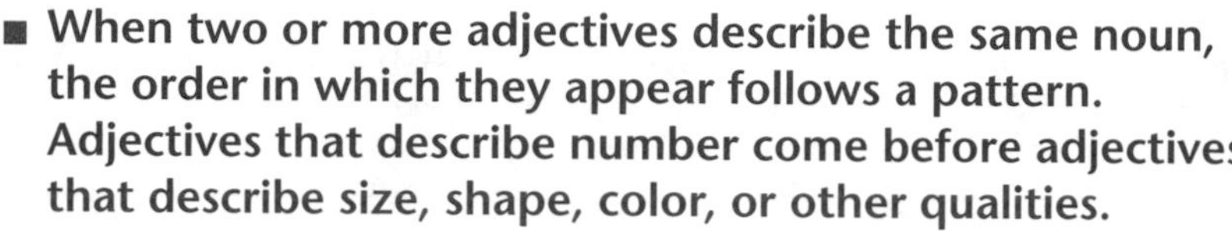

- When two or more adjectives describe the same noun, the order in which they appear follows a pattern. Adjectives that describe number come before adjectives that describe size, shape, color, or other qualities.

  Two white swans have built a nest there.
  They used **many dry** twigs to make the nest.

- An adjective can also come after the noun it describes. This usually happens when the adjective follows a form of the verb *be*.

  The swan's nest is **round**.
  The eggs are **white**.

PRACTICE

A *Circle the adjective(s) that describe the noun in **boldface**. Then write the adjective(s) on the line.*

1. A patient **swan** sits on the nest. patient
2. She protects three small **eggs**. three small
3. The nest is near a beautiful **lake**. beautiful
4. The swan chose a safe **location** for the nest. safe
5. Tall **grass** surrounds the nest. Tall
6. Few **enemies** bother the birds here. Few

  CCSS Language 1d. (See pp. T6–7.)

PRACTICE A *continued*

7. The **eggs** are large. large

8. The babies have sharp **beaks**. sharp

9. Their beaks break the hard **eggshells**. hard

10. Soon the **babies** are free. free

B *Circle the adjective(s) in each sentence, and underline the noun that they describe. Then write the adjective(s) on the line.*

1. Several ducks live near the lake. Several

2. Their feathers are waterproof. waterproof

3. Their feet are webbed. webbed

4. Many hungry ducks dive for food. Many hungry

5. They eat insects and small plants. small

6. Their grassy nests are on the shore. grassy

7. The geese near the lake are noisy. noisy

8. Their honking is loud! loud

9. Five babies may follow an adult. Five

10. Their feathers are fluffy. fluffy

11. Nine geese are flying in a pattern. Nine

12. The pattern is v-shaped. v-shaped

13. The geese are watchful. watchful

14. A goose is fierce at times. fierce

15. Even the babies are bold! bold

C *Write an adjective to complete each sentence. Choose an adjective from the box, or use an adjective of your own.*

Remember
An **adjective** describes a noun. It can tell *what kind* or *how many.*

beautiful	brown	clear	cute	flat
gentle	green	happy	long	peaceful
sandy	short	soft	sunny	tall

Answers may vary. Suggested answers are given.

1. We went to the bird refuge on a **sunny** day.
2. The sky above was **clear**.
3. A **gentle** breeze rippled the water.
4. A **tall** heron waded along the shore.
5. Its legs were **long**.
6. **Beautiful** water lilies were blooming on the lake.
7. A **green** frog sat on a lily pad.
8. Its **short** croak faded into silence.
9. Seven **cute** ducklings were swimming with their mother.
10. We walked down a **sandy** path along the pond.
11. A snake slept on a **flat** rock.
12. Three **brown** hawks circled overhead.
13. The **soft** buzzing of insects filled the air.
14. The bird refuge is so **peaceful**.
15. I was **happy** to be there.

CCSS Language 1d. (See pp. T6–7.)

WRITE

Sometimes you can combine two related sentences into one sentence by moving an adjective.

In the example below, only the second sentence has an adjective. To make one smooth sentence, you can place the adjective *noisy* before the noun *blue jay* in the first sentence.

A blue jay squawked at a squirrel. The blue jay was noisy.
A noisy blue jay squawked at a squirrel.

In this example, both sentences have adjectives. You can combine the sentences by placing the adjective *big* in the second sentence after the adjective *seven* in the first sentence.

Seven turkeys hurried by. The turkeys were big.
Seven big turkeys hurried by.

D *The sentences in each pair below are related. Move the adjective from one sentence to the other to combine the sentences. Write the new sentence on the line.*

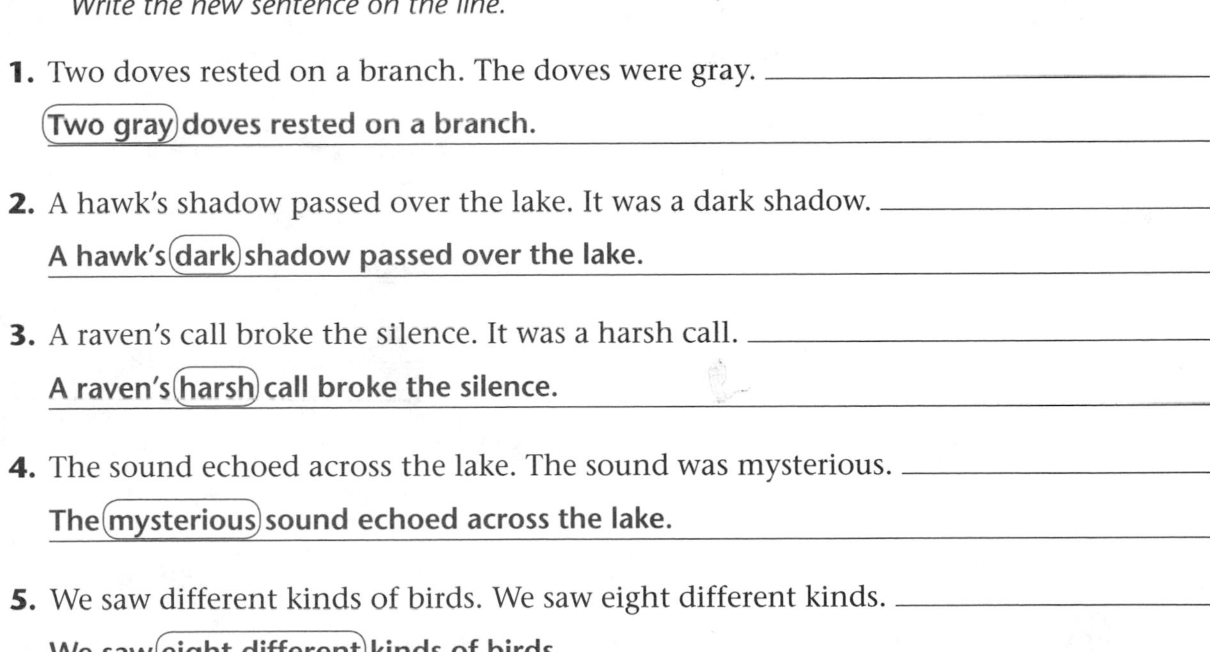

1. Two doves rested on a branch. The doves were gray.
   Two gray doves rested on a branch.

2. A hawk's shadow passed over the lake. It was a dark shadow.
   A hawk's dark shadow passed over the lake.

3. A raven's call broke the silence. It was a harsh call.
   A raven's harsh call broke the silence.

4. The sound echoed across the lake. The sound was mysterious.
   The mysterious sound echoed across the lake.

5. We saw different kinds of birds. We saw eight different kinds.
   We saw eight different kinds of birds.

Go back to the sentences you wrote. Circle the adjective or adjectives.

Lesson 25: *A, An, The*

LEARN

- The special adjectives *a, an,* and *the* are called **articles.** These small words come before nouns.

  a raccoon **an** otter **the** animals

- The articles *a* and *an* refer to any person, place, or thing. The article *the* refers to a specific person, place, or thing.

  An elephant can run faster than **a** person.
  The runner crossed **the** finish line at noon.

  - Use *a* before a singular noun that begins with a consonant sound.

    I found **a** book of interesting facts.

  - Use *an* before a singular noun that begins with a vowel sound.

    Each fact described **an** animal.

  - Use *the* before both singular and plural nouns.

    The facts about **the** insect surprised me.

PRACTICE

A *Some sentences have more than one article. Circle each article, and write it on the line. The first one is done for you.*

1. It is impossible for (a) pig to look up into (the) sky. a, the
2. (A) sleeping bear in winter can go 100 days without water. A
3. (An) ostrich never buries its head in (the) sand. An, the
4. There are more than 20 muscles in (the) ear of (a) cat. the, a
5. (An) insect buzzes because of (the) movement of its wings. An, the
6. (A) cockroach can run one meter per second. A
7. (The) pattern of (a) zebra's black-and-white stripes is formed by its hair. The, a

PRACTICE **A** *continued*

8. (A) snail can sleep for three years. ___A___
9. Wolves don't howl more often when (the) moon is full. ___the___
10. (A) shark's mouth has six to twenty rows of teeth. ___A___

B *Write the article in parentheses that correctly completes each sentence.*

1. ___An___ elephant flaps its ears to stay cool. (A, An)
2. The Chow-Chow is ___a___ dog with blue lips. (a, the)
3. Some spiders can spin ___a___ web in 30 minutes. (a, an)
4. A koala is not ___a___ bear. (a, the)
5. It is ___a___ relative of the kangaroo. (a, an)
6. Females carry their young in ___a___ pouch. (a, an)
7. A zorilla is ___an___ animal that looks like a skunk. (a, an)

Zorilla

8. Zorillas, like skunks, use odor as ___a___ defense. (a, an)
9. The American buffalo is not ___a___ buffalo at all. (a, the)
10. It is ___a___ bison. (a, an)
11. An Andean condor can have ___a___ wingspan of 10 feet. (a, an)
12. It is one of the largest flying birds in ___the___ world. (a, the)
13. The world's smallest mammal is ___a___ bat. (a, an)
14. This tiny bat is the size of ___a___ bumblebee. (a, an)
15. ___An___ ostrich is a bird that does not fly. (A, An)

C *Sean wrote a report about how certain animals communicate their emotions. In this part of the report, he used five articles incorrectly. Use the proofreading marks in the box to correct the errors.*

Remember

Use *a* before a singular noun that begins with a consonant sound. Use *an* before a singular noun that begins with a vowel sound.

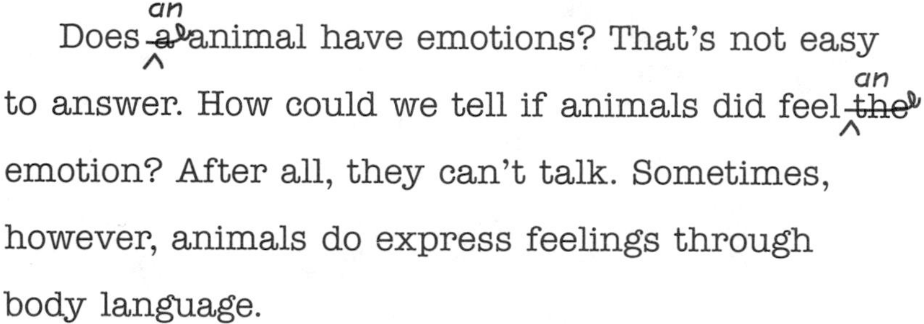

Does ~~a~~ an animal have emotions? That's not easy to answer. How could we tell if animals did feel ~~the~~ an emotion? After all, they can't talk. Sometimes, however, animals do express feelings through body language.

For example, if ~~the~~ a dog has misbehaved, it might turn its head sideways and show its neck. It might also crouch down and lift its front paw to show you it is sorry. Wolves, which are wild relatives of dogs, might also show these two types of body language.

Wolves live in ~~the~~ a pack with one strong leader. Pack members use body language to show that they recognize their leader. To your dog, you are ~~a~~ the leader of the pack, so it uses the same kind of body language with you.

Proofreading Marks

^	Add
⊙	Period
ℓ/	Take out
≡	Capital letter
/	Small letter

Did you correct five mistakes with articles?

WRITE

D *Write a sentence about each animal below. In each sentence, use an article before the animal's name, and use the information given in parentheses. After writing your sentence, go back and add an adjective to each sentence. The first one is done for you.*

Answers will vary. Sample answers are given.

1. blue whale (weighs up to 200 tons)

A blue whale weighs up to 200 tons.

(A) big blue whale weighs up to 200 tons.

2. butterfly (flaps its wings five times per second)

A butterfly flaps its wings five times per second.

(A) fluttering butterfly flaps its wings five times per second.

3. humpback whale (can eat one ton of food per day)

The humpback whale can eat one ton of food per day.

(The) hungry humpback whale can eat one ton of food per day.

4. opossum (sleeps 19 hours per day)

An opossum sleeps 19 hours per day.

(An) old opossum sleeps 19 hours per day.

5. hummingbird (can fly backwards)

The hummingbird can fly backwards.

(The) colorful hummingbird can fly backwards.

Go back to the sentences you wrote.
Circle each article you used.
Underline each adjective you added.

CCSS Language 1d, 1f. (See pp. T6–7.)

Lesson 26: Demonstrative Adjectives

LEARN

- Adjectives can tell *what kind* or *how many*. Adjectives can also tell *which one*. Adjectives that tell *which one* are called **demonstrative adjectives**.

This, that, these, and *those* are demonstrative adjectives. Use *this* and *that* before singular nouns. Use *these* and *those* before plural nouns.

This film is very popular.
That book is a favorite of young children.
These children are here for Story Time.
Those adults are waiting for them.

- *This* and *these* refer to people, places, or things that are nearby. Do not use *here* after *this* or *these.*

CORRECT The children's librarian has chosen **this book**.
INCORRECT The children's librarian has chosen **this here book**.

CORRECT **These children** want to hold the book.
INCORRECT **These here children** want to hold the book.

- *That* and *those* refer to people, places, or things that are farther away. Do not use *there* after *that* or *those.*

CORRECT Everyone will sit in **that room**.
INCORRECT Everyone will sit in **that there room**.

CORRECT **Those children** want to hear the story again.
INCORRECT **Those there children** want to hear the story again.

PRACTICE

A *Underline the demonstrative adjective in each sentence. Then write it on the line.*

1. The new library is on this block. this

2. It used to be in that old building. that

3. Let's use those computers to search the online catalog. those

PRACTICE **A** *continued*

4. <u>These</u> books are novels by Laura Ingalls Wilder. **These**

5. Ask <u>that</u> librarian if you need help to find a book. **that**

6. <u>These</u> picture books belong in the children's section. **These**

7. <u>Those</u> volunteers will sort the books by author. **Those**

8. <u>This</u> room is the Listening Room. **This**

9. Use <u>these</u> earphones to listen to music. **these**

10. Let's make a reservation to use <u>this</u> equipment again. **this**

B *Write the demonstrative adjective in parentheses that correctly completes each sentence.*

1. Look at the picture in **this** book about New York City. (this, these)

2. It shows **that** building across the street. (this, that)

3. **That** famous structure is the 42nd Street Library. (That, Those)

4. The library was built on **those** two blocks over there. (this, those)

5. Look at **those** marble lions at the library entrance. (that, those)

6. **This** big cat next to me is nicknamed Patience. (This, That)

7. **That** big cat on the other side is nicknamed Fortitude. (This, That)

8. Let's go up **these** stone steps and into the main entrance. (this, these)

9. **This** magnificent library has eleven reading rooms. (This, Those)

10. Readers can find some useful books in **these** reading areas. (this, these)

11. There are 42 oak tables in **that** huge room. (that, these)

12. Up to 16 people can sit at each of **those** oak tables. (this, those)

C *Angie wrote this script for a tour of the new town library. She made six mistakes when using demonstrative adjectives. Use the proofreading marks in the box to correct the errors.*

Remember
This and *these* refer to people, places, or things that are nearby. *That* and *those* refer to people, places, or things that are farther away.

Proofreading Marks

^	Add
⊙	Period
ℓ	Take out
≡	Capital letter
/	Small letter

Welcome to our new library! We'll begin our tour in the reference section. These ~~here~~ books all around us are reference books. You'll find dictionaries, encyclopedias, and atlases on the shelves. ^That ~~This~~ woman standing over there is Ms. Charles. She is our reference librarian.

In that corner over there, we see the periodical room. Newspapers and magazines are called periodicals. Everyone can go there to read those ~~there~~ magazines and papers.

The library is a great place to do research. ^Those ~~These~~ computers against the far wall are for everyone to use. ^This ~~That~~ sheet of paper in my hand lists the rules for computer use.

Finally, here we are in the media section. For many people, ^this ~~that~~ is their favorite part of the library. Audiobooks, videos, eReaders, and eBooks are available. You can borrow them just like books!

Did you correct six mistakes with demonstrative adjectives?

WRITE

D *Imagine you are giving a tour of your classroom from where you sit. Start by listing two things or areas of the classroom that are near you. Then list two things or areas of the classroom that are farther away. A sample is done for you.*
Answers will vary. Sample answers are given.

Near	***Farther Away***
the library corner	our new computer
the art center	the interactive whiteboard

Now write a sentence with a demonstrative adjective that tells something about the things or areas of the classroom you have listed. You can use the sample below as a model.

1. This area on the left is the library corner. We have books on many subjects on these shelves.

2. The art center is right next to me. This is my favorite place in the classroom.

3. Over in the far corner is our new computer. The school bought that computer for us last year.

4. Next to our new computer are the interactive whiteboard and projector. Those pieces of equipment are new, too.

CCSS Language 1f, 3a.
(See pp. T6–7.)

Proofreading Checklist ☑

- ☐ *Did you use **this** and **these** to refer to things that are nearby?*
- ☐ *Did you use **that** and **those** to refer to things that are farther away?*

Lesson 27: Comparing with Adjectives

LEARN

- **Adjectives can compare people, places, and things. Adjectives that compare tell how things are different from each other.**
  Lions are **stronger** than leopards.
  Lions are the **strongest** big cat.

  - **Add *-er* to most adjectives to compare two people, places, or things.**
    strong + er = strong**er**
  - **Add *-est* to most adjectives to compare more than two people, places, or things.**
    strong + est = strong**est**

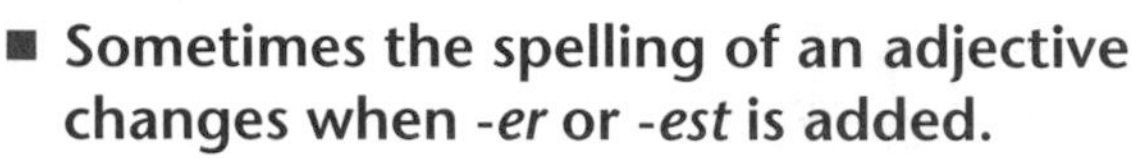

- **Sometimes the spelling of an adjective changes when *-er* or *-est* is added.**

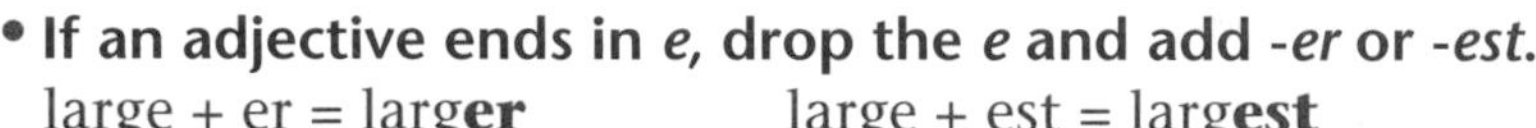

  - **If an adjective ends in *e*, drop the *e* and add *-er* or *-est*.**
    large + er = larg**er** large + est = larg**est**
  - **If an adjective ends in a consonant and *y*, change the *y* to *i* and add *-er* or *-est*.**
    hungry + er = hungr**ier** hungry + est = hungr**iest**
  - **If an adjective ends in one vowel followed by a consonant, double the consonant and add *-er* or *-est*.**
    big + er = big**ger** big + est = big**gest**

PRACTICE

A *In Column A, add* ***-er*** *to each adjective. In Column B, add* ***-est*** *to each adjective. Remember to make the necessary spelling changes before adding* ***-er*** *and* ***-est***.

	A		*B*
1. cold	colder	**6.** warm	warmest
2. wild	wilder	**7.** simple	simplest
3. scarce	scarcer	**8.** late	latest
4. tiny	tinier	**9.** shady	shadiest
5. hot	hotter	**10.** thin	thinnest

B *Write the form of the adjective in parentheses that correctly completes each sentence.*

1. Lions are the **largest** members of the cat family. (large)
2. Lions are **stronger** than humans. (strong)
3. They can drag **heavier** weights than people can. (heavy)
4. They are **mightier** than any other cat. (mighty)
5. Lions are not the **fastest** of the big cats. (fast)
6. They are usually **slower** than their prey. (slow)
7. A zebra, for example, is **swifter** than a lion. (swift)
8. Vision is the **sharpest** of a lion's five senses. (sharp)
9. A lion can see in **dimmer** light than you can. (dim)
10. A lion's night vision is **keener** than its prey's night vision. (keen)
11. Hunting at night is **easier** than hunting during the day. (easy)
12. A female lion is **smaller** than a male lion. (small)
13. Females are **fiercer** hunters than males. (fierce)
14. Of all the cats, lions have the **loudest** roar. (loud)
15. Many people think that lions are the **grandest** animals of all. (grand)

C *Lena wrote this report about tigers. She made seven mistakes when using and spelling adjectives that compare. Use the proofreading marks in the box to correct the errors.*

Remember

Add *-er* to an adjective to compare two people, places, or things. Add *-est* to compare more than two.

Proofreading Marks	
∧	Add
⊙	Period
ℓ/	Take out
≡	Capital letter
/	Small letter

Tigers are an endangered animal. Three kinds of tigers have become extinct. Six other kinds survive. Of these six groups, the ~~larger~~ largest are the Siberian tigers.

About 400 Siberian tigers are found in Asia. A ~~biger~~ bigger population lives in eastern Russia. These big cats survive in some of the ~~icyest~~ iciest forests on Earth.

Most Bengal tigers live in India, but a ~~smallest~~ smaller population is found in Nepal. Bengal tigers tend to live in the ~~hotest~~ hottest and wettest regions of India.

Indochinese tigers live mainly in the jungles of Thailand. There may be ~~fewwer~~ fewer than 1500 left.

Sumatran tigers are a fourth type of tiger. About 400 of them live on the island of Sumatra. Of all the types, these have the ~~darker~~ darkest coats.

Finally, there are the Malaysian tiger and the South China tiger, the rarest kind. None may be left in China.

Did you correct seven adjectives that compare?

WRITE

D *Follow the directions below to write groups of three sentences. In your first sentence, use the adjective in parentheses. In your second sentence, use the adjective with* ***-er****. In your third sentence, use the adjective with* ***-est****. The first one is done for you.*

Answers will vary. Sample answers are given.

1. Use the following information about weight to compare these three big cats. (heavy)

Cheetah 160 pounds **Lion** 400 pounds **Siberian tiger** 700 pounds

A cheetah is heavy.

A lion is heavier than a cheetah.

The Siberian tiger is the heaviest of the three cats.

2. Use the following information about top speeds to compare these three cats. (fast)

Leopard 36 mph **Lion** 50 mph **Cheetah** 70 mph

A leopard is fast.

A lion is faster than a leopard.

The cheetah is the fastest of the three cats.

3. Use the following information about body length (including the tail) to compare these three big cats. (long)

Leopard 6 feet **Cheetah** 7 feet **Lion** 9 feet

A leopard is long.

A cheetah is longer than a leopard.

The lion is the longest of the three cats.

Proofreading Checklist ☑

- ❑ *Did you use an adjective with* ***-er*** *to compare two of the big cats?*
- ❑ *Did you use an adjective with* ***-est*** *to compare the three big cats?*

Lesson 28: Comparing with *More* and *Most*

LEARN

The words *more* and *most* are often needed when comparing adjectives of two or more syllables.

- **Use *more* with adjectives when comparing two people, places, or things.**
  Football is **more popular** than soccer in the United States.
- **Use *most* with adjectives when comparing more than two people, places, or things.**
  Soccer is the **most popular** sport in the world.
- **Do not add *-er* or *-est* to an adjective when you use *more* or *most* to compare.**

CORRECT	Jean is **more patient** than Debbie.
INCORRECT	Jean is **more patienter** than Debbie.
CORRECT	Carlos has the **most awesome** kick.
INCORRECT	Carlos has the **most awesomest** kick.

PRACTICE

A *Change each adjective in Column A to compare two. Change each adjective in Column B to compare more than two. Write the new adjectives on the lines.*

A		B	
1. honest	more honest	**6.** generous	most generous
2. active	more active	**7.** loyal	most loyal
3. complex	more complex	**8.** difficult	most difficult
4. responsible	more responsible	**9.** basic	most basic
5. famous	more famous	**10.** independent	most independent

B *Complete each sentence. Add* ***more*** *or* ***most*** *to the adjective in parentheses. Write the words on the line.*

1. Why is soccer the **most popular** game in the world? (popular)
2. Many fans claim soccer is **more exciting** than baseball. (exciting)
3. According to them, it is also **more enjoyable** than football. (enjoyable)
4. Soccer is the **most active** game I have ever played. (active)
5. In football, breaks in the action are **more frequent** than in soccer. (frequent)
6. Nonstop action is soccer's **most appealing** feature. (appealing)
7. Other sports have **more complicated** rules than soccer. (complicated)
8. The rules for football are probably the **most complex** of all. (complex)
9. As a result, football is **more challenging** to learn than soccer. (challenging)
10. Soccer also has the **most basic** equipment of any team sport. (basic)
11. That helps make it the **most affordable** sport of all. (affordable)
12. Baseball equipment is **more expensive** than soccer equipment. (expensive)
13. Setting up a football field is **more demanding** than setting up a soccer field. (demanding)
14. Soccer fans may be the **most spirited** sports fans in the world. (spirited)
15. They may also be the **most loyal** fans in the world. (loyal)

C *Eric wrote this journal entry about playing soccer. He made six mistakes when he used adjectives to compare. Use the proofreading marks in the box to correct the errors.*

Remember

Do not add *-er* or *-est* to an adjective when you use *more* or *most* to compare.

Proofreading Marks

^	Add
⊙	Period
℘	Take out
≡	Capital letter
/	Small letter

Everyone wants to win at soccer. Winning, however, is not my most ^important ~~importantest~~ goal. Learning teamwork, playing fairly, and having fun are my main reasons for playing. To me, being in top shape is a more ^important ~~importanter~~ goal than being on the top team.

Of the dozens of soccer leagues in the state, ours has the best teams. We play against the most ^skillful ~~skillfullest~~ athletes in our age group. Win or lose, I enjoy the competition. And when the season is over, I know I've improved. My passes are ^more ~~most~~ accurate than before, and I understand the game a little better.

Now that the season is about to start, I am looking forward to the ^most ~~more~~ exciting year the team has ever had. Even though I play mainly for the love of the game, I also hope it is the ^most ~~more~~ successful season ever!

Did you correct six mistakes in adjectives that compare?

WRITE

D *Write three sentences to compare the three sports in each group. In your first sentence, use the adjective in parentheses. In your second sentence, use* ***more*** *with the adjective. In your third sentence, use* ***most*** *with the adjective. The first one is done for you.*
Answers will vary. Sample answers are given.

1. tennis baseball golf (exciting)

Golf is exciting to watch.

Tennis is more exciting than golf.

Baseball is the most exciting of the three sports.

2. kickball dodgeball softball (enjoyable)

Kickball is an enjoyable game.

Softball is a more enjoyable game than kickball.

Dodgeball is the most enjoyable game of all.

3. basketball hockey football (challenging)

Basketball is a challenging game.

Football is more challenging than baseball.

Hockey is the most challenging game of all.

4. diving figure skating swimming (graceful)

Swimming is a graceful sport.

Diving is a more graceful sport than swimming.

Figure skating is the most graceful of the three sports.

CCSS Language 1f.
(See pp. T6–7.)

Proofreading Checklist ☑

❑ *Did you use* ***more*** *with an adjective to compare two sports?*
❑ *Did you use* ***most*** *with an adjective to compare three sports?*

Lesson 29: Comparing with *Good* and *Bad*

LEARN

■ **The adjectives *good* and *bad* have special forms for comparing.**

Adjective	Compare Two	Compare More Than Two
good	better	best
bad	worse	worst

- **Use *better* when comparing two people, places, or things. Use *best* when comparing more than two.**

  A dog makes a **good** pet.
  A cat makes a **better** pet than a dog.
  A parrot makes the **best** pet of all.

- **Use *worse* when comparing two people, places, or things. Use *worst* when comparing more than two.**

  The rain brought **bad** weather.
  The sleet brought **worse** weather.
  The ice storm brought the **worst** weather of all.

PRACTICE

A *Underline the form of **good** or **bad** in each sentence. Then write the word on the line.*

1. Walking my dog Lucky is the best way for me to exercise. best
2. Walking Lucky is better than playing softball. better
3. Lucky and I took the worst shortcut to the park. worst
4. The path was worse than the road we always take. worse
5. It was the worst idea I ever had. worst

PRACTICE A *continued*

*Write the form of **good** or **bad** in parentheses that correctly completes each sentence.*

6. Our pet rabbit did the ___worst___ thing yesterday. (worse, worst)

7. Was it ___worse___ than what he did last week? (worse, worst)

8. Eating flowers in the garden was the ___worst___ thing he ever did. (worse, worst)

9. We must put a ___better___ fence around the flower bed. (better, best)

10. The ___best___ kind of fence is one with no openings. (good, best)

B *Write the form of the adjective in parentheses that correctly completes each sentence.*

1. The forest is the ___best___ place to see woodland animals. (good)

2. Morning is a ___good___ time of day to see a deer. (good)

3. A hot afternoon is the ___worst___ time. (bad)

4. Did you know that some flowers have a ___bad___ smell? (bad)

5. The ___worst___ ones of all smell like rotting meat. (bad)

6. This ___bad___ odor attracts flies. (bad)

7. Is the odor ___worse___ than the odor of a skunk? (bad)

8. Look up to get an even ___better___ view of the birds. (good)

9. This trail leads to the ___best___ spot for bird-watching. (good)

10. It is a ___better___ trail than the rocky one. (good)

11. This picture of the rabbit is ___worse___ than the first one. (bad)

12. Still, it is ___better___ than the picture of the woodpecker. (good)

C *Martin wrote this report about a class trip. He made six mistakes using the different forms of **good** and **bad**. Use the proofreading marks in the box to correct the errors.*

Remember

Use *better* and *worse* to compare two people, places, or things. Use *best* and *worst* to compare more than two people, places, or things.

Proofreading Marks

^	Add
⊙	Period
ℓ/	Take out
≡	Capital letter
/	Small letter

Last week, our class visited the new aquarium. It has the ~~better~~ best exhibit of ocean life I've ever seen.

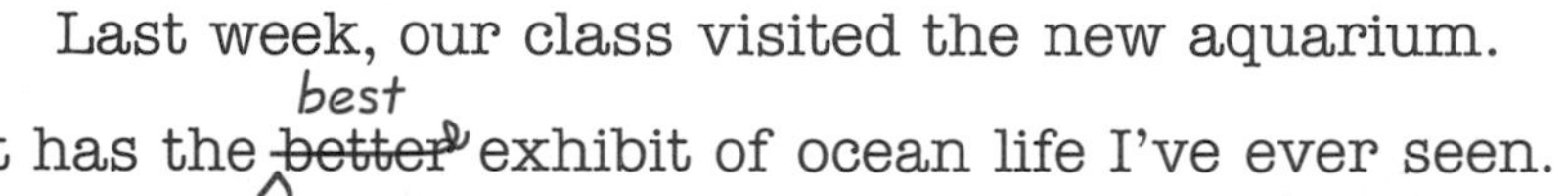

During our visit, we had the best tour ever. First, our tour guide took us to see a film about rare and dangerous animals. Then she took us to see something even ~~best~~ better than the tour. She led us to a circular fish tank that had a spiral ramp wrapped around it. The tank was four floors high and filled with a variety of fish, sharks, and sea turtles. It was awesome! Unfortunately, I was standing next to a baby carriage. The baby inside was crying really loudly. It was the ~~worse~~ worst spot of all to be standing. Then I saw that Paula's spot was ~~worst~~ worse than mine. She was standing behind a man who was 6 feet tall!

I really enjoyed this class trip. The ~~better~~ best part was watching a diver feed the animals in the tank. The ~~worse~~ worst part was having to leave the aquarium.

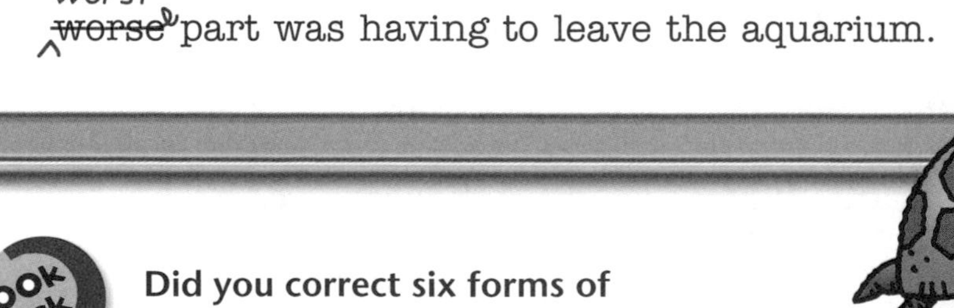

Did you correct six forms of *good* and *bad*?

WRITE

D *Write about a trip you took with your class. Tell where you went and what you saw. Describe the best part and worst part of the trip. Include the words* ***better****,* ***best****,* ***worse****, and* ***worst*** *in your descriptions. Check a dictionary if you need help spelling a word.*

Answers will vary.

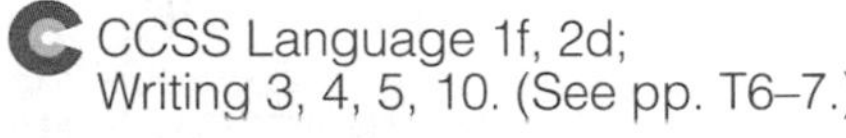
CCSS Language 1f, 2d;
Writing 3, 4, 5, 10. (See pp. T6–7.)

Proofreading Checklist ☑

- ❑ *Did you use* ***better*** *and* ***worse*** *to compare two people, places, or things?*
- ❑ *Did you use* ***best*** *and* ***worst*** *to compare more than two?*

Lesson 30: Adverbs

LEARN

- An **adverb** is a word that generally describes a verb. Adverbs describe verbs by telling *how, when,* or *where* an action happens. Many adverbs end in *-ly*.

HOW	The news reporters work **hard**. They check the facts **carefully**.
WHEN	The evening news will begin **soon**. The team **always** prepares in advance.
WHERE	The news van rushes **ahead**.

Notice that adverbs can come before or after the verbs they describe.

- Here are some adverbs that tell *how.*

slowly	suddenly	quietly	well	badly
fast	together	hard	easily	quickly

- Here are some adverbs that tell *when.*

yesterday	often	always	then	usually
next	tomorrow	later	soon	recently

- Here are some adverbs that tell *where.*

here	there	outside	below	near
upstairs	locally	everywhere	ahead	far

PRACTICE

A *Circle the adverb that describes the verb in* **boldface**. *Write whether the adverb tells* ***how, when,*** *or* ***where.***

1. Aunt Sonia (always) **wanted** to be a reporter. ___when___
2. She (recently) **got** her wish. ___when___
3. (Today), she **is** a reporter at a TV news studio. ___when___
4. Many other reporters **work** (there) with her. ___where___
5. The news director **plans** the assignments (carefully). ___how___

PRACTICE A *continued*

6. Aunt Sonia (often) **interviews** people. when
7. She **tries** (hard) to ask good questions. how
8. She **travels** (everywhere) for stories. where
9. A camera crew (usually) **follows** her. when
10. (Later), she **writes** the news story. when

B *Circle the adverb in each sentence, and underline the verb that it describes. Then write the adverb on the line.*

1. Aunt Sonia visited city hall (recently). recently
2. Her news crew went (there) to cover the city spelling bee. there
3. Over 100 students (usually) enter the event. usually
4. I (gladly) participated in the spelling bee. gladly
5. I was (always) a good speller. always
6. I (bravely) attempted each spelling. bravely
7. I spelled many words (correctly). correctly
8. My aunt smiled (happily). happily
9. One student (finally) won the bee. finally
10. Everyone clapped (wildly) for the winner. wildly
11. Aunt Sonia interviewed the winner (afterwards). afterwards
12. (Then) she interviewed some other students. Then
13. The camera crew filmed (steadily). steadily
14. I looked (directly) into the camera. directly
15. Watch for me (tonight) on the news. tonight

Remember

An **adverb** describes a verb by telling *how, when,* or *where* an action happens.

C *Write an adverb to complete each sentence. Choose an adverb from the box, or use an adverb of your own. The clue in parentheses will help you. The first one is done for you.*

Answers may vary. Suggested answers are given.

clearly	fairly	far	locally	next	usually

1. News reporters must describe events ___clearly___. (how)
2. They must also present stories ___fairly___. (how)
3. Facts are ___usually___ double-checked at the studio. (when)
4. News editors decide which stories to cover ___next___. (when)
5. Reporters might investigate stories ___locally___ or nationally. (where)
6. They might travel near or ___far___ for a story. (where)

always	anywhere	correctly	quickly	sometimes	well

7. News video can take viewers ___anywhere___. (where)
8. The video should work ___well___ with the story. (how)
9. A news anchorperson ___always___ reads the news. (when)
10. A good anchor reads each story ___correctly___. (how)
11. The anchor ___sometimes___ interviews people on air. (when)
12. Thanks to the news broadcast, we ___quickly___ learn what is happening. (how)

WRITE

D *Adverbs make sentences clearer and more interesting. Read these sentences from a news report about a snowstorm. Then rewrite each one, adding an adverb. Your adverb should tell how, when, or where an action happens. The first one is done for you.*

Answers will vary. Sample answers are given.

1. The worst snowstorm in 40 years hit Riverview.

   The worst snowstorm in 40 years hit Riverview yesterday.

2. The snow fell for over 24 hours.

   The snow fell heavily for over 24 hours.

3. Snowplows are working to clear the streets.

   Snowplows are working hard to clear the streets.

4. All city schools will close.

   All city schools will close today.

5. City officials are checking weather reports.

   City officials are checking weather reports frequently.

6. More snow and strong winds will arrive.

   More snow and strong winds will arrive tonight.

7. Also, temperatures are falling.

   Also, temperatures are falling rapidly.

8. We can't expect any relief!

   We can't expect any relief soon!

Go back to the sentences you wrote. Circle the adverbs that you added.

CCSS Language 3a. (See pp. T6–7.)

Lesson 31: Comparing with Adverbs

LEARN

- An **adverb** can compare two or more actions.
  - Add *-er* to most one-syllable adverbs to compare two actions.
    Jason runs **faster** than I do.
  - Add *-est* to most one-syllable adverbs to compare more than two actions.
    Tran runs **fastest** of all the students in our class.
- The words *more* and *most* can also be used with adverbs to compare. Use *more* and *most* with most adverbs that have two or more syllables, including adverbs that end in *-ly*.
  - Use *more* with adverbs to compare two actions.
    Ian leaps **more gracefully** than Tai.
  - Use *most* with adverbs to compare more than two actions.
    Of all the athletes in our school, Megan leaps **most gracefully**.
  - Do not add *-er* or *-est* to an adverb when you use *more* or *most*.

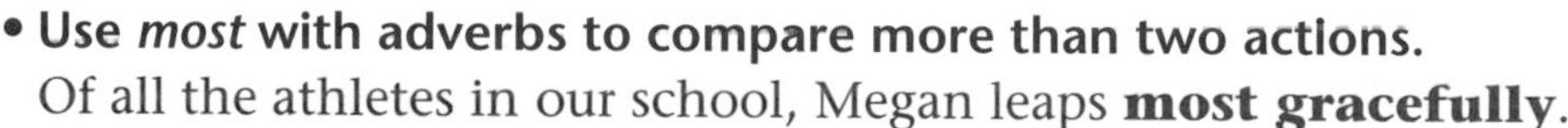

PRACTICE

A *Write the adverb in parentheses that correctly completes each sentence.*

1. Our track club practices harder in spring than in winter. (harder, hardest)
2. Saturday is the day we begin earliest. (earlier, earliest)
3. Today, I jogged longer than I did yesterday. (longer, longest)
4. Beginners should run more slowly than experienced runners. (more slowly, most slowly)
5. Of all the members in our club, Sonia can jump highest. (higher, highest)

PRACTICE **A** *continued*

6. Runners must breathe **more deeply** than walkers. (more deeply, most deeply)

7. I run **more comfortably** on grass than on the sidewalk. (more comfortably, most comfortably)

8. Of all the club runners, Alex practices **most frequently**. (more frequently, most frequently)

9. Of the three clubs, ours trains **most seriously** for the 5-kilometer race. (more seriously, most seriously)

10. We have competed **more successfully** than we did last year. (more successfully, most successfully)

B *Write the form of the adverb in parentheses that correctly completes each sentence.*

1. Of the eight runners in the 100-meter race, Alberto ran **fastest**. (fast)

2. I sprinted **more quickly** than Neil did. (quickly)

3. The high jump took **longer** to organize than the 5-kilometer race. (long)

4. I've practiced **harder** this year than last year. (hard)

5. Fans cheered **louder** for the long jump than for the 5-kilometer race. (loud)

6. Of all the races, I cheered **most wildly** for the relay. (wildly)

7. In the long jump, Nilda jumped **more confidently** than Rachel. (confidently)

8. Of the many sprinters, Lin ran **most rapidly**. (rapidly)

9. She certainly ran **more smoothly** than I did. (smoothly)

10. I hope our team performs **more impressively** than any other team. (impressively)

C *Jenna wrote this story for the sports section of her school newspaper. She made six mistakes when using adverbs that compare. Use the proofreading marks in the box to correct the errors.*

Remember

Add *-er* or *-est* to most one-syllable adverbs to compare. Use *more* or *most* with most adverbs that have two or more syllables.

The Track and Field Festival at Town Park on April 1 was a big success. Of the three track clubs, the Lions performed ~~more~~ most successfully. "All the athletes performed more skillfully than last year," Coach Chen said.

Over twelve runners took part in the 5-kilometer race. Jan Ruiz ran ~~most~~ fastest. As usual, she also ran the most gracefully of all the athletes.

Tom Powers took first prize in the high jump, jumping ~~more~~ higher than he did in his record jump. Of the many athletes in the long jump, Carla Allen jumped ~~farther~~ farthest.

All three clubs had teams in the relay race. The Aces ran fastest. They also handed off the baton more ~~smoothlier~~ smoothly than the Trackers.

A large crowd gathered, and people cheered more ~~loudlier~~ loudly as the day went on. All in all, the future of track in this town looks bright!

Proofreading Marks

^	Add
⊙	Period
ℓ	Take out
≡	Capital letter
/	Small letter

Did you correct six mistakes in adverbs that compare?

WRITE

Write two sentences to describe what is happening in each picture. Use the adverbs in parentheses to compare the actions of the athletes.

Answers will vary. Sample answers are given.

1. (fast) **Tim was running and jumping faster than Tom.**

2. (gracefully) **Jim jumps the most gracefully of the three athletes.**

3. (high) **Joan jumped higher than Sue.**

4. (impressively) **Of the three athletes, Lisa jumped the most impressively.**

CCSS Language 1f.
(See pp. T6–7.)

Proofreading Checklist ☑

- ❑ *Did you add -**er** or –**est** to the one-syllable adverbs?*
- ❑ *Did you use **more** or **most** with the adverbs that have two or more syllables?*

Lesson 32: Using *Good* and *Well*

LEARN

The words *good* and *well* can sometimes be confusing.

Good is an adjective that describes a noun.

Kim is a **good** cook.

Well is usually an adverb that describes a verb.

She bakes **well**, too.

Well is an adjective only when it refers to someone's health. When *well* refers to health, it describes a noun.

Kim was sick. She is **well** now.

Think about what you are describing when using *good* and *well*.

PRACTICE

A *Underline the word in parentheses that correctly completes each sentence.*

1. I'm afraid I don't cook very (good, well).

2. I thought I could make a (good, well) dinner from frozen leftovers.

3. I had promised my family a (good, well) meal.

4. Unfortunately, I didn't plan (good, well).

5. I should have taken a (good, well) look at the frozen foods.

6. I needed more time to cook them (good, well).

7. My cooking did not make a (good, well) impression on the family.

8. Fortunately, Dad had a (good, well) idea.

PRACTICE A *continued*

9. He knew that the microwave oven in the apartment next door worked (good, well).

10. We managed to cook the food quickly, thanks to our (good, well) neighbors.

B *Write* ***good*** *or* ***well*** *to complete each sentence.*

1. All young people should learn how to eat **well**.
2. Cooking is a **good** skill to have.
3. Home-cooked, healthful meals help you stay **well**.
4. Fast food from a restaurant isn't generally a **good** choice.
5. Cooking at home is a **good** way to save money.
6. Nutritious meals help a sick person get **well**.
7. Making a **good** meal is relaxing.
8. There are many **good** ways to learn to cook.
9. Everyone knows at least one **good** cook.
10. Spend time with someone who cooks **well**.
11. TV chefs prepare food very **well**, too.
12. Reading cookbooks is another **good** idea.
13. In time, you will have many **good** recipes.
14. You will learn to serve meals **well**.
15. There are plenty of **good** reasons to learn how to cook.

Cooking

C *Christopher wrote this restaurant recommendation for his aunt. He made six mistakes when using the words* ***good*** *and* ***well****. Use the proofreading marks in the box to correct the errors.*

Remember
Good **is an adjective that describes a noun.** ***Well*** **is usually an adverb that describes a verb.**

If you're looking for a ~~well~~ good restaurant, try the Lakeview House.

First of all, the owners did a good job with decorating. Old signs and photographs cover the walls. Most nights, a jazz band plays. The bands play ~~good~~ well, and the music goes ~~good~~ well with the lakefront location. My mother wasn't feeling that well when we arrived, but the music soon cheered her up.

There's always a good atmosphere at the Lakeview House. The waiters always treat the customers well. Most tables have a ~~well~~ good view of the lake, too.

Now for the most important thing–the food. My fish was delicious. It was cooked really ~~good~~ well. Even the salad was good. Mom said her grilled chicken was good, too.

The next time you want to eat out, try the Lakeview House. I think you'll have a ~~well~~ good opinion of it, too.

Proofreading Marks	
^	Add
⊙	Period
ℓ/	Take out
≡	Capital letter
/	Small letter

Did you correct six mistakes with ***good*** **and** ***well*****?**

WRITE

D *Imagine you are talking to a friend about food. Write two sentences you would say about each topic below. Use the word in parentheses in each sentence.*
Answers will vary. Sample answers are given.

1. your favorite fruit or vegetable

(good) **Bananas are a good fruit to eat.**

(well) **Eating fruits and vegetables will help you feel well.**

2. your favorite sandwich

(good) **You can make a good sandwich with bread, peanut butter, and jelly.**

(well) **I can make this sandwich well.**

3. your favorite home-cooked meal

(good) **You need chicken, rice, and vegetables for a good home-cooked meal.**

(well) **I would like to cook these foods well some day.**

4. your favorite dessert

(good) **A frozen vanilla yogurt cup is a good dessert.**

(well) **Almost anyone can make a frozen vanilla yogurt cup well.**

Now imagine you are a nutritionist writing an article about healthy eating. How might the sentences you write for the article be different from the sentences above? Discuss this question with your classmates.
Possible answers: The language in the article would be more formal. The tone of the article would not sound like a conversation.

CCSS Language 1f, 3c.
(See pp. T6–7.)

Proofreading Checklist ☑

- ❑ *Did you use the word **good** to describe nouns?*
- ❑ *Did you use the word **well** to describe verbs or to refer to someone's health?*

Lesson 33: Negatives

LEARN

- A word that means "no" is called a **negative**. The words *no, not, nothing, none, never, nowhere, nobody,* and *no one* are negatives.
  Good manners **never** go out of style.
  There is **no** reason to behave rudely.

- Contractions with *not*, such as *don't, wasn't,* and *aren't,* are also negatives.
  Many people **aren't** polite enough.
  They **don't** think about other people's feelings.

- Do not use two negatives together in a sentence. This kind of mistake is called a **double negative**. To correct a sentence with a double negative, take out one negative or replace it with a word such as *any, every, ever, anything, anywhere, anyone,* or *anybody*.

INCORRECT	**Don't never** talk during a movie.
CORRECT	**Don't** talk during a movie. **Never** talk during a movie. **Don't ever** talk during a movie.

PRACTICE

A *Write the negative word in each sentence.*

1. Don't interrupt a speaker. Don't
2. Try not to call out answers in class. not
3. Booing another team doesn't show good sportsmanship. doesn't
4. Nobody likes to lose a game. Nobody
5. Still, there's nothing worse than a sore loser! nothing
6. There is no excuse for bad behavior. no
7. Never forget to say, "Please" and "Thank you." Never

CCSS Language 3a. (See pp. T6–7.)

PRACTICE A *continued*

8. You shouldn't expect others to clean up after you. shouldn't

9. None of us should forget to write thank-you notes. None

10. There isn't any substitute for good manners. isn't

B *Write the word in parentheses that correctly completes each sentence.*

1. When it comes to manners, there isn't anywhere as important as the dinner table. (anywhere, nowhere)

2. Don't go anywhere too far when dinnertime is near. (anywhere, nowhere)

3. There isn't anyone in the kitchen. (no one, anyone)

4. No one should start eating before everyone is served. (should, shouldn't)

5. You should not ever eat too fast. (ever, never)

6. There's never any excuse for gulping down food. (no, any)

7. Don't reach for anything over someone else's plate. (nothing, anything)

8. Sometimes you don't like anything on your plate. (nothing, anything)

9. Still, nobody wants to hear any rude comments about the food. (no, any)

10. You shouldn't ever chew with your mouth open. (ever, never)

11. There shouldn't be any elbows on the table. (any, no)

12. There isn't anybody who can cook this well. (nobody, anybody)

C

Mariah wrote this essay about why manners are important. She used seven double negatives in her writing. Use the proofreading marks in the box to correct the errors.

Answers may vary. Suggested answers are given.

Remember

Do not use two negative words together in a sentence. This kind of mistake is called a **double negative**.

Mark	Meaning
^	Add
⊙	Period
(take-out mark)	Take out
≡	Capital letter
/	Small letter

A lot of people today don't have ~~no~~ any manners. They think that manners don't matter. That's where they're wrong.

Manners aren't just saying, "Please," or waiting your turn in line. Manners are about being kind and thoughtful. You don't want ~~no one~~ anyone to interrupt you, so you shouldn't interrupt ~~nobody~~ anybody else. It isn't ~~no~~ any fun having someone cut in line in front of you, so you should never cut in front of ~~nobody~~ anybody else.

People will judge you by your manners. If you don't have ~~none~~, any, people will not think well of you. Even simple actions like saying, "Thank you," will make a good impression on others.

Good manners alone have never made ~~no one~~ anyone a success. On the other hand, they haven't ever hurt anyone.

Did you correct seven double negatives?

CCSS Language 3a. (See pp. T6–7.)

Revising Sentences

WRITE

D *Rewrite each sentence by adding a negative. Your sentences should give rules for good manners online. There may be more than one way to change each sentence. The first one is done for you.*

Answers will vary. Sample answers are given.

1. It's a good idea to type e-mails in all capital letters. *It's not a good idea to type e-mails in all capital letters. Or: Don't type e-mails in all capital letters.*

2. People who type in all capital letters are being thoughtful.
People who type in all capital letters are not being thoughtful.

3. Use busy-looking, colorful type and backgrounds in your e-mails.
Don't use busy-looking, colorful type and backgrounds in your e-mails.

4. Busy-looking e-mails are easy to read.
Busy-looking e-mails are not easy to read.

5. Leave the "Subject" line in an e-mail blank.
Don't leave the "Subject" line in an e-mail blank.

6. Some people want to receive e-mail jokes and chain letters.
Some people don't want to receive e-mail jokes and chain letters.

7. Most of us want our mailboxes filled with junk mail.
Most of us don't want our mailboxes filled with junk mail.

8. Open e-mails from people you don't know.
Never open e-mails from people you don't know.

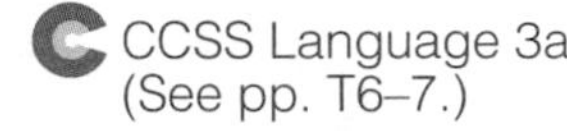

Proofreading Checklist ☑

- ❑ *Did you add a negative to each sentence you wrote?*
- ❑ *Did you avoid double negatives in your sentences?*

Lesson 34: Prepositions and Prepositional Phrases

Snowshoe hare

LEARN

- A **preposition** is a word that shows how a noun or pronoun is connected to some other word in the sentence.

  The snowshoe hare lives **in** Alaska.
  During the summer, the hare's coat is brown.
  The hare's brown coat blends **with** the ground.

Here are some common prepositions.

about	among	below	for	near	through
above	around	beside	from	of	to
across	at	by	in	off	under
after	before	down	inside	on	until
against	behind	during	into	over	with

- A **prepositional phrase** is a group of words that begins with a preposition and ends with a noun or pronoun. When a prepositional phrase comes at the beginning of a sentence, it is followed by a comma.

  After the first snowfall, the hare's coat turns white.
  The hare **with the white coat** eats its meal.
  Another snowshoe hare sits **beside it**.

Prepositional phrases add important and interesting information to sentences.

PRACTICE

A *Read each sentence. Look at each prepositional phrase in* ***boldface****. Write the preposition on the line.*

1. I read a book **about camouflage**. about
2. Camouflage lets an animal hide **from its predators**. from
3. The chameleon lives **in Asia and Africa**. in

CCSS Language 1e. (See pp. T6–7.)

4. **Among green leaves**, this lizard turns green. Among
5. **Above a brown branch**, it turns brown. Above
6. A giraffe has dark blotches **on its coat**. on
7. These blotches look like patches **of shade**. of
8. The giraffe is hard to see **under trees**. under
9. A fawn **with spots** is also hard to see. with
10. Light and shadows hide it **from view**. from

B *Underline the prepositional phrase in each sentence. Then write the preposition on the line.*

1. Some predators catch prey by surprise. by
2. Camouflage helps many of them. of
3. Frogs are hard to see on a green riverbank. on
4. They wait there for insects. for
5. The leaf-tailed gecko moves across the forest floor. across
6. To an insect, it could be a leaf. To
7. The arctic fox is white during the winter months. during
8. Quietly, it creeps over the snow. over
9. Fish below the water's surface can see the white feathers that cover a penguin's belly. below
10. These feathers look like the top of the water. of
11. This area gets bright light from the sun. from
12. Under the water, fish don't notice the penguin. Under

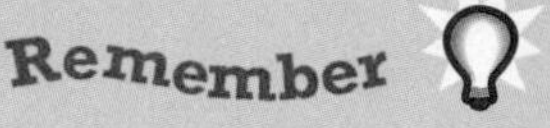

A **prepositional phrase** is a group of words that begins with a preposition and ends with a noun or pronoun.

C *Write a prepositional phrase to complete each sentence. Choose a prepositional phrase from the box, or use a prepositional phrase of your own. The first one is done for you.*

in the dry grass	on the African plains	in snowy places
down a river	against the snow	for a drink

Answers may vary. Suggested answers are given.

1. Lion cubs live *on the African plains.*
2. Their sandy-colored coats help them hide **in the dry grass.**
3. Harp seal cubs live **in snowy places.**
4. Their snow-white coats can't be seen **against the snow.**
5. A crocodile looks like a log floating **down a river.**
6. The crocodile doesn't move until some prey stops **for a drink.**

against the sand	in a swamp	with long necks
in muddy water	of the desert	on its back

7. The turtle carries its home **on its back.**
8. **In muddy water**, this shell looks like a rock.
9. Many desert birds are the color **of the desert.**
10. Their enemies can't see them **against the sand.**
11. Many swamp birds have thin bodies **with long necks.**
12. These birds look like reeds **in a swamp.**

CCSS Language 1e. (See pp. T6–7.)

WRITE

D *One way to make a sentence more interesting and helpful to a reader is to add a prepositional phrase. Add a prepositional phrase to each sentence below.*
Answers will vary. Sample answers are given.

1. My friend loves desert animals.
   My friend from Nevada loves desert animals.

2. We visit the Natural History Museum.
   We visit the Natural History Museum in the city.

3. The museum has wonderful exhibits.
   The museum has wonderful exhibits of all kinds.

4. We get a map when we arrive.
   We get a map of the museum when we arrive.

5. Finally, we find the lizard exhibit.
   Finally, we find the lizard exhibit on the fourth floor.

6. A plaque describes the snake fossils.
   A plaque on the wall describes the snake fossils.

7. A diagram gives more information.
   A diagram gives more information about the snakes.

8. We spend more than an hour here.
   We spend more than an hour with the lizards and snakes.

Go back to the prepositional phrases you added.
Circle the preposition in each one.

CCSS Language 1e, 3a. (See pp. T6–7.)

Unit 4 Review
Lessons 24–34

Adjectives (pp. 112–115) *Underline the adjective(s) in each sentence.*

1. Texas is a large state.

2. It has many famous landmarks.

3. The farmland is rich.

***A, An, The*; Demonstrative Adjectives** (pp. 116–123) *Underline the word in parentheses that correctly completes each sentence.*

4. Dallas is (a, an) city in Texas.

5. We saw (a, an) astronaut in Houston.

6. (This, These) state produces many farm products.

7. (This, These) products include corn, wheat, and other grains.

8. The cotton is harvested by (that, those) workers.

Comparing with Adjectives (pp. 124–127) *Write the form of the adjective in parentheses that correctly completes each sentence.*

9. Only California has a (big) population than Texas. bigger

10. Gaudalupe Peak is the (high) mountain in Texas. highest

11. Dallas is (large) than Austin. larger

Comparing with *More* and *Most* (pp. 128–131) *Write **more** or **most** to complete each sentence.*

12. Of the many early Native Americans in Texas, the Caddos were the most successful farmers.

13. The Jumano people are more famous for trading than for farming.

14. The Comanche were the most skillful hunters of all the groups.

Comparing with *Good* and *Bad* (pp. 132–135) *Write the form of the adjective in parentheses that correctly completes each sentence.*

15. The library has many (good) books about Texas. good

16. This encyclopedia has (good) maps than that one. better

17. This book is in the (bad) shape of all the books. worst

Adverbs (pp. 136–139) *Underline the adverb in each sentence.*

18. Spanish settlers reached Texas early.

19. They quickly built missions.

20. Texas was part of Mexico then.

Comparing with Adverbs (pp. 140–143) *Write the form of the adverb in parentheses that correctly completes each sentence.*

21. American settlers arrived in Texas (late) than Spanish settlers. later

22. By 1830, Americans were settling Texas (quickly) than Mexicans were. more quickly

23. The American settlers could buy land (cheaply) in Texas than in the United States. more cheaply

Using *Good* and *Well*; Negatives (pp. 144–151) *Underline the word in parentheses that correctly completes each sentence.*

24. Settlers came to Texas in search of a (good, well) life.

25. Farmers prepared their new fields (good, well).

26. Many Texans didn't want to be part of Mexico (no more, anymore).

27. No one could (ever, never) find a peaceful solution.

Prepositions and Prepositional Phrases (pp. 152–155) *Underline the prepositional phrase in each sentence. Then circle the preposition.*

28. For years, Texans opposed the Mexican government.

29. Later, Texas became part of the United States.

30. The history of Texas is long and interesting.

Unit 4 Test

DIRECTIONS *Fill in the circle next to the sentence that spells and uses adjectives, adverbs, and negatives correctly.*

1. ○ Sunday was hoter than Saturday.
○ It was the busyest day this year at Greenfield Park.
○ I haven't never seen so many people there.
● Everyone was having a good time.

2. ● Those two teams played on a softball field.
○ They played really good.
○ The best of the two teams scored 20 runs.
○ The worst of the two teams scored ten times.

3. ○ There wasn't no more than a light breeze.
○ People could still fly a kites.
● The box kite flew more gracefully than the hawk kite.
○ A star-shaped kite was the most prettiest.

4. ○ The park has an playground.
○ The merry-go-round was the popularest ride.
● This line was longer than usual.
○ I didn't bring no money.

5. ○ At the dog run, a beagle was the most calmest dog.
○ An sheepdog did tricks for the crowd.
○ Some dogs behaved good.
● Some behaved badly.

6. ○ Dad didn't want to get into no rowboat.
● He never feels well out on the water.
○ I handled the oars gooder this time.
○ I rowed around the lake really good.

7. ● The swimming pool was the most crowded spot.
○ Mom couldn't find a empty lane.
○ There wasn't no way to swim laps.
○ Going for a swim was the worse decision we made.

8. ● The park doesn't close until nine o'clock.
○ Usually, we leave much earlyer than that.
○ On Sunday, we weren't in no hurry to leave.
○ We were having a exciting time.

DIRECTIONS *Read the paragraphs, and look carefully at each underlined part. Fill in the circle next to the answer choice that shows the correct use and spelling of adjectives and negatives. If the underlined part is already correct, fill in the circle for "Correct as is."*

Parks are a important part (9) of a community. City parks provide open, green spaces. This spaces provide (10) good places for children and adults to enjoy the outdoors. Without such parks, many people couldn't never play sports (11), exercise outdoors, or have picnics.

State parks are usually far away. Small local parks are easier to reach (12). You can enjoy them anytime with your family and friends. I think our local park is the most friendliest place (13) in the whole neighborhood! It is the best place of all (14) for friends and neighbors to gather.

9.
- ○ a importanter part
- ○ the important part
- ● an important part
- ○ Correct as is

10.
- ● These spaces provide
- ○ That spaces provide
- ○ Those space provide
- ○ Correct as is

11.
- ○ could'nt never play sports
- ○ couldn't not play sports
- ● couldn't ever play sports
- ○ Correct as is

12.
- ○ easyer to reach
- ○ most easy to reach
- ○ more easier to reach
- ● Correct as is

13.
- ○ a more friendly place
- ● the friendliest place
- ○ the more friendlier place
- ○ Correct as is

14.
- ○ the good place of all
- ○ the better place of all
- ○ the well place of all
- ● Correct as is

Lesson 35: Subject Pronouns

LEARN

Mount Rushmore

- A **pronoun** is a word that takes the place of one or more nouns. A **subject pronoun** is used as the subject of a sentence. It tells *whom* or *what* the sentence is about.

  Jason visited Mount Rushmore.
  He photographed the giant sculpture.

  Mr. and Mrs. Gomez went with Jason.
  They enjoyed the trip.

Like nouns, subject pronouns can be singular or plural.

Singular	I	you	he	she	it
Plural	we	you	they		

- A pronoun's **antecedent** is the noun the pronoun refers to. A pronoun and its antecedent must agree in number. If the antecedent is singular, the pronoun must be singular. If the antecendent is plural, the pronoun must be plural. In the first sentence below, the singular pronoun *she* refers to the singular noun *Elena*. In the second sentence, the plural pronoun *they* refers to *Mom and Dad*.

  Elena saw my photographs. **She** saw them yesterday.
  Mom and Dad enjoy traveling. **They** always travel by train.

PRACTICE

A *Write the subject pronoun in each sentence.*

1. I visited Mount Rushmore with my grandmother. I
2. She lives in South Dakota. She
3. Have you ever been to Mount Rushmore? you

4. It shows the giant carved faces of four presidents. It
5. They are Washington, Jefferson, Lincoln, and Roosevelt. They
6. I also read about Gutzon Borglum. I
7. He designed the memorial. He
8. Did you know that workers carved with dynamite? you
9. They worked for fourteen years. They
10. We would like to go back someday. We

B *Write the subject pronoun that correctly completes each sentence.*

1. National memorials are places that honor important events.

   They can be found all over our country.

2. The Wright Brothers National Memorial is in North Carolina.

   It is a popular place to visit.

3. Orville Wright flew the first airplane.

   He flew the plane for twelve seconds.

4. Sue visited the Lincoln Boyhood National Memorial in Indiana.

   She learned that Abraham Lincoln's mother is buried there.

5. Visitors can see the log cabin and barn that sit on the grounds.

   They can also see a living history demonstration that shows what life was like then.

6. The Franklin Delano Roosevelt Memorial honors our 32nd president.

   It has four outdoor rooms that trace the history of FDR's four terms in office.

Remember

A **subject pronoun** is used as the subject of a sentence. A pronoun must agree with its antecedent in number.

C *Here is an entry from Marsha's journal. Write a subject pronoun from the box to complete each sentence. You will use one pronoun more than once.*

I	you	he	she	it	we	they

Today, Uncle Jacob and I visited the Lewis and Clark National Historical Park. __We__ (1) *thought the park was really interesting.*

Meriwether Lewis and William Clark were American explorers. __They__ (2) *traveled across the United States in 1804 and 1805. Their expedition included a young Native American woman named Sacagawea.* __She__ (3) *helped guide the expedition.*

In the afternoon, Uncle Jacob and __I__ (4) *hiked a two-mile trail through the park. There was something really special about this hike.* __It__ (5) *followed the same path that Lewis and Clark took!*

Uncle Jacob said historical sites teach you about history firsthand. __He__ (6) *is right about that!*

Did __you__ (7) *know that the park is in two different states?* __They__ (8) *are Washington and Oregon.*

WRITE

Additional Resources at grammarworkshop.com

Sometimes you might repeat the same nouns too many times in your sentences.

> Keiki went to Philadelphia. Keiki hoped to hear the Liberty Bell, but Keiki was disappointed. The Liberty Bell hasn't rung for more than 160 years.

You can use subject pronouns to replace some of the nouns. That way, your writing will sound smoother and less repetitive. Be sure each pronoun agrees with its antecedent.

> Keiki went to Philadelphia. **She** hoped to hear the Liberty Bell, but **she** was disappointed. **It** hasn't rung for more than 160 years.

Liberty Bell

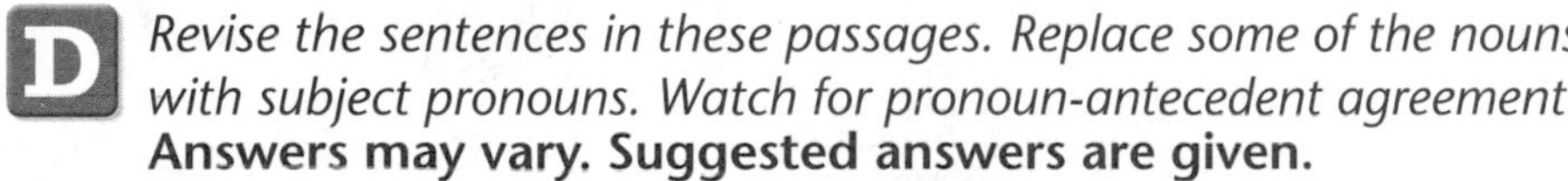
D *Revise the sentences in these passages. Replace some of the nouns with subject pronouns. Watch for pronoun-antecedent agreement.*
Answers may vary. Suggested answers are given.

1. Darla visited the Benjamin Franklin National Memorial in Philadelphia. Darla was amazed by the statue of Benjamin Franklin. The statue is 20 feet tall and weighs 30 tons. Franklin helped build our country. Franklin was a statesman and a writer. Franklin was also a scientist and inventor.

Darla visited the Benjamin Franklin National Memorial in Philadelphia. She was amazed by the statue of Benjamin Franklin. It is 20 feet tall and weighs 30 tons. Franklin helped build our country. He was a statesman and a writer. He was also a scientist and inventor.

2. The Benjamin Franklin National Memorial holds many of Franklin's possessions. The Benjamin Franklin National Memorial also displays Franklin's early writings. Darla saw a Franklin stove there. Darla also saw the lightning rod that Franklin invented. The lightning rod saved many buildings from fire.

The Benjamin Franklin National Memorial holds many of Franklin's possessions. It also displays Franklin's early writings. Darla saw a Franklin stove there. She also saw the lightning rod that Franklin invented. It saved many buildings from fire.

Lesson 36: Pronoun-Verb Agreement

LEARN

- In every sentence, the verb must agree with the subject.
  - When the subject pronoun is *he, she,* or *it,* add *-s* or *-es* to the present tense of most action verbs. If the verb ends in *y,* change the *y* to *i* before adding *-es.*
    He hurries to the campsite.
    She pitches the tent.
    It protects the campers from wind and rain.
  - When the subject pronoun is *I, we, you,* or *they,* do not add *-s* or *-es* to the verb.
    I pack everything in my bag.
    We camp all the time.
    You start a campfire.
    They go for a swim.

PRACTICE

A *Write the verb in parentheses that correctly completes each sentence.*

1. I ____paddle____ across the lake with Mom. (paddle, paddles)
2. She ____fishes____ from the canoe. (fish, fishes)
3. We ____catch____ two fish after a while. (catch, catches)
4. You ____wave____ to Dan at the tent. (wave, waves)
5. He ____rushes____ to the dock. (rush, rushes)
6. I ____race____ back to camp. (race, races)
7. We ____prepare____ a campfire for Mom. (prepare, prepares)
8. She ____cleans____ the fish with Dan. (clean, cleans)
9. They ____fry____ it over the fire. (fry, fries)
10. It ____tastes____ delicious! (taste, tastes)

B *Write the present tense of the verb in parentheses to correctly complete each sentence.*

1. We ___unroll___ our sleeping bags at sundown. (unroll)
2. You ___hear___ mosquitoes in the tent. (hear)
3. They ___buzz___ loudly in Dan's ears. (buzz)
4. He ___scratches___ his arms and legs. (scratch)
5. I ___itch___ all over, too. (itch)
6. He ___brings___ the flashlight out to Mom. (bring)
7. She ___switches___ the flashlight on. (switch)
8. It ___shines___ for three seconds, and then it goes out. (shine)
9. We ___see___ lightning in the sky. (see)
10. It ___flashes___ brightly just before the raindrops start. (flash)
11. We ___scurry___ into our sleeping bags. (scurry)
12. They ___feel___ slightly damp! (feel)
13. I ___try___ to get comfortable, but I'm lying on a rock. (try)
14. It ___pushes___ into my back all night. (push)
15. I ___hope___ we have better luck tomorrow. (hope)

Remember A present-tense verb must agree with the subject pronoun.

C *Charles wrote this essay about camping. He made seven mistakes in pronoun-verb agreement. Use the proofreading marks in the box to correct the errors.*

Proofreading Marks

^	Add
⊙	Period
ℓ	Take out
≡	Capital letter
/	Small letter

I like camping for many reasons. When you camp, you rely on your own skills to solve problems. Here are some examples. How do you find your way if you get lost in the woods? You ~~uses~~ use a compass and a map. What do you do if your tent looks unsteady? You ~~pitches~~ pitch it again and do a better job this time.

Camping also gives you a chance to relax. When my family camps, we leave our digital devices behind. I ~~enjoys~~ enjoy the silence, and so does my Mom. She ~~try~~ tries to write every day. I always ~~carries~~ carry a few books and spend time reading.

Camping is just plain fun, too. We ~~sings~~ sing songs and tell stories around the campfire. Mom watches for unusual birds. They ~~flies~~ fly around our camp sometimes. Other kinds of animals come close, too.

It's true that camping isn't always comfortable. Even so, it makes you feel great!

Did you correct seven verbs that did not agree with the pronouns?

Write Your Own

Additional Resources at grammarworkshop.com

WRITE

D *Look at the picture. Then write a sentence to tell what the person or thing named in parentheses is doing. Use a subject pronoun and a present-tense verb in each of your sentences. The first one is done for you.*

Answers will vary. Sample answers are given.

1. (the baby ducks) *They swim after their mother.*

2. (the squirrel) **It climbs up a tree.**

3. (the girl) **She tries to catch fish.**

4. (the woman and the boy) **They paddle a boat.**

5. (the man) **He draws a picture of the ducks.**

CCSS Language 1f. (See pp. T6–7.)

Proofreading Checklist ☑

- ❑ ***Did you use subject pronouns for the subjects of your sentences?***
- ❑ ***Did you use present-tense verbs?***
- ❑ ***Did you check that your subjects and verbs agree?***

Lesson 37: Object Pronouns

LEARN

- An **object pronoun** follows an action verb. It may also follow a word such as *to, in, at, of, with, during,* or *through.*

  I visited **the Washington Monument**.
  I visited **it**.

  Kim joined **my family and me** during our visit.
  Kim joined **us** during our visit.

  I had dinner with **my grandparents** afterwards.
  I had dinner with **them** afterwards.

- These are the object pronouns. Notice that the pronoun *you* can be singular or plural.

Singular	me	you	him	her	it
Plural	us	you	them		

Washington Monument

PRACTICE

A *Write the object pronoun in each sentence.*

1. My grandparents took me to Washington, D.C. ____me____
2. A tour guide showed us the sights. ____us____
3. "First, I will take you to the National Mall," the guide said. ____you____
4. My grandmother asked her about the Washington Monument. ____her____
5. Workers finished work on it in 1885. ____it____
6. The bus had taken me past many tall buildings. ____me____
7. The Washington Monument is the tallest of them all. ____them____
8. A glass elevator whisked us to the top of the monument. ____us____

PRACTICE A *continued*

9. "The guide will show you the Capitol next," Grandma said. ___you___
10. "We will see it soon," I answered. ___it___

B *Read each sentence. Replace the word or words in* ***boldface*** *with an object pronoun.*

1. Our nation's lawmakers meet in **the Capitol**. ___it___
2. Some of **the lawmakers** were at work in the building. ___them___
3. The Statue of Freedom stands on top of **the dome**. ___it___
4. I followed **my grandfather** into the Rotunda. ___him___
5. The huge round room impressed **my grandparents and me**. ___us___
6. Thousands of people visit **the room** each day. ___it___
7. I asked **my grandmother** about the large paintings in the Rotunda. ___her___
8. One of **the paintings** shows the first reading of the Declaration of Independence. ___them___
9. My grandmother pointed to the **statues of great Americans**. ___them___
10. We looked closely at **one statue**. ___it___
11. The person's face was familiar to **my grandmother and me**. ___us___
12. Since 1986, the Rotunda has been home to this statue of **Dr. Martin Luther King, Jr**. ___him___

Remember

An **object pronoun** follows an action verb. It also follows a word such as *to, in, at, of, with, during,* or *through.*

C *Here is a description of a visit to the White House. Write an object pronoun from the box to complete each sentence. You will use some pronouns more than once.*

me	you	him	her	it	us	them

"More than a million people come to the White House every year," our guide told **us** (1) at the start of the tour. It seemed to **us** (2) that most of **them** (3) were in our tour group!

"I can only show **you** (4) 5 of the 132 rooms in the White House," the tour guide explained. "All of **them** (5) are on the first floor."

The most interesting room to **us *or* me** (6) was the dining room. There are enough tables and chairs in **it** (7) for 140 dinner guests!

The president works downstairs in the West Wing, but we didn't see **him** (8). What about the first lady? We didn't see **her** (9) either.

The living area in the White House is upstairs, but the tour guide couldn't take **us** (10) there. The only way I'll see that part of the White House is if the country elects **me** (11) president someday!

WRITE

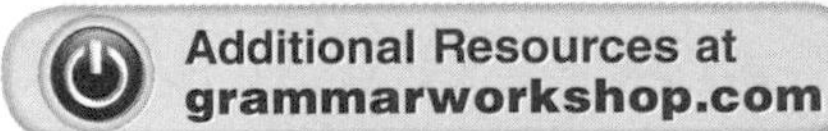

Your writing will sound dull if you use the same nouns over and over again.

The Lincoln Memorial honors Abraham Lincoln.
It has a 19-foot statue of Abraham Lincoln inside.

When the overused nouns come after action verbs or after words such as *of* or *to*, you can replace them with object pronouns. Using object pronouns correctly will make your writing clearer and smoother.

The Lincoln Memorial honors Abraham Lincoln.
It has a 19-foot statue of **him** inside.

Lincoln Memorial

D *Revise the second sentence of each pair. Replace an overused noun in the second sentence with an object pronoun.*
Answers may vary. Suggested answers are given.

1. Take a close look at a penny. The front of the penny shows Lincoln's face, and the back of the penny shows the Lincoln Memorial.

Take a close look at a penny. The front of it shows Lincoln's face, and the back of it shows the Lincoln Memorial.

2. The Lincoln Memorial stands at the end of the National Mall. Many people think the Lincoln Memorial is the most beautiful monument in Washington, D.C.

The Lincoln Memorial stands at the end of the National Mall. Many people think it is the most beautiful monument in Washington, D.C.

3. Lincoln's famous words are carved on the monument. You can read Lincoln's famous words as you walk through the monument.

Lincoln's famous words are carved on the monument. You can read them as you walk through it.

4. Lincoln looks sad to some visitors. Other visitors look at Lincoln and say he is smiling slightly.

Lincoln looks sad to some visitors. Other visitors look at him and say he is smiling slightly.

Lesson 38: **Using *I* and *Me***

LEARN

- **Be careful when you use the pronouns *I* and *me* in sentences. The pronoun *I* is a subject pronoun. *I* is used only as the subject of a sentence.**

  I watch the stars with Adam and Rosa.

The pronoun *me* is an object pronoun. *Me* is used after an action verb or after a word such as *at, for, of, to,* or *with.*

  Rosa lends **me** a telescope.
  Adam names some stars for **me**.

- **When you speak about yourself and another person, always name the other person first. Then follow the rules above for when to use *I* and *me*.**

  Rosa and I like astronomy.
  Brian shares a telescope with **Rosa and me**.
  At the park, **my friends and I** wait for the nighttime sky.

PRACTICE

A *Write the word or words in parentheses that correctly complete each sentence.*

1. Rosa invited **Adam and me** to a star-watching party. (Adam and I, Adam and me)
2. She showed **me** how to use a telescope. (I, me)
3. **I** found the Big Dipper. (I, Me)
4. Adam told **me** that there are 100 billion stars in our galaxy. (I, me)
5. **Rosa and I** didn't even know that our sun is a star. (Rosa and I, Me and Rosa)
6. Adam showed **Brian and me** the star Sirius. (Brian and me, me and Brian)
7. **Brian and I** were amazed by its brightness! (Brian and I, Brian and me)
8. Brian asked **me** why the stars seem to twinkle. (I, me)

PRACTICE A *continued*

9. Adam explained the reason to ___the others and me___. (the others and I, the others and me)

10. Now ___my friends and I___ are fascinated by the stars. (my friends and I, me and my friends)

B *Write **I** or **me** to correctly complete each sentence.*

1. My twin sister Tina and ___I___ have a telescope.
2. Uncle George bought it for Tina and ___me___ last week.
3. Mom helped ___me___ assemble it.
4. My sister and ___I___ waited for a clear night.
5. Dad told ___me___ that starlight takes millions of years to reach Earth.
6. Tina and ___I___ found that hard to believe.
7. Mom pointed out the Great Bear constellation to Tina and ___me___.
8. That group of stars didn't look like a bear to ___me___.
9. My family and ___I___ visited the planetarium yesterday.
10. The guide showed my parents and ___me___ a model of the solar system.
11. She told ___me___ that the stars shine day and night.
12. Another guide gave ___me___ a book about the stars.
13. Both my sister and ___I___ learned many facts about outer space.
14. Learning about the stars has also inspired ___me___.
15. ___I___ wrote a poem called "Starry Day" just yesterday.

The Great Bear (Ursa Major)

C *Ray wrote this thank-you note to his uncle. He made seven mistakes when using the pronouns **I** and **me**. Use the proofreading marks in the box to correct the errors.*

Remember

The pronoun *I* is used only as the subject of a sentence. The pronoun *me* is used after an action verb or a word such as *to, for, at,* or *with*.

Proofreading Marks	
^	Add
⊙	Period
ℓ/	Take out
≡	Capital letter
/	Small letter

Dear Uncle George,

Tina and ~~me~~ I want to thank you so much for the telescope! Mom helped ~~I~~ me set it up last night. You couldn't have gotten ~~me and Tina~~ Tina and me a better present! Fortunately, the nights are darker here than in most places. The whole family and ~~me~~ I can get a great view of the night sky!

Please come visit my family and ~~I~~ me soon! Tina and I will show you some stars and planets. Mom has already pointed out two planets, Venus and Mercury. With the telescope, ~~I and Tina~~ Tina and I hope to spot Jupiter soon.

Thanks again,

Ray

P.S. ~~Me and Tina~~ Tina and I also are using the sky chart that came with the telescope. It makes everything a lot easier!

Did you correct seven mistakes with *I* and *me*?

WRITE

Pairs of related sentences can sound choppy when you read them. Try combining the sentences into one sentence that expresses the same idea. You can combine the sentences below by joining the noun in the subject of the first sentence and the subject pronoun in the second sentence.

Tina invited Tim to our Planet Watch Party.
I invited Tim to our Planet Watch Party.
Tina **and** I invited Tim to our Planet Watch Party.

Sometimes you can combine related sentences by joining the noun that follows the action verb in the first sentence and the object pronoun in the second sentence.

Tim thanked Tina.
Tim thanked me.
Tim thanked Tina **and** me.

Combine each pair of sentences by joining a noun and a pronoun.

1. Dad showed Tim the planet Venus. I showed Tim the planet Venus.
Dad and I showed Tim the planet Venus.

2. Kari lent her binoculars to Luke. Kari lent her binoculars to me.
Kari lent her binoculars to Luke and me.

3. Venus looked so bright to Jessie. Venus looked so bright to me.
Venus looked so bright to Jessie and me.

4. Chris tried to find Jupiter. I tried to find Jupiter.
Chris and I tried to find Jupiter.

5. The planets fascinate my friends. The planets fascinate me.
The planets fascinate my friends and me.

Lesson 39: Possessive Pronouns

LEARN

- A possessive noun shows *who* or *what* has something. A **possessive pronoun** takes the place of a possessive noun.

  Heather's cat is a Siamese.
  Her cat is a Siamese.

- There are two kinds of possessive pronouns. One kind is used before a noun. The possessive pronouns that can be used before a noun are *my, your, his, her, its, our,* and *their.*

  My pet is a tabby cat.
  Your friend has three cats.
  Her cat won a ribbon.
  I love **their** beautiful coats.
  Its gray fur is so soft.
  The cat show was held in **our** town.

The other kind of possessive pronoun is used alone. The possessive pronouns that can stand alone are *mine, yours, his, hers, ours,* and *theirs.*

The Persian cat is **hers**.
The black kitten is **mine**.
His is black, too.
Theirs has white paws.
This one is **ours**.
Where is **yours**?

PRACTICE

A *Underline the possessive pronoun in each sentence. Then write **before a noun** or **used alone** to tell how it is used.*

1. The white cat is mine. ___used alone___
2. Siamese cats are known for their blue eyes. ___before a noun___
3. Your cat is a calico. ___before a noun___
4. Its coat has black, orange, and white patches. ___before a noun___
5. Is this cat carrier yours? ___used alone___
6. Tonya says the Manx cat is hers. ___used alone___
7. Where is its tail? ___before a noun___

PRACTICE A *continued*

8. Mr. Kubo brought <u>his</u> cat to the show. **before a noun**

9. The large Burmese cat is <u>his</u>. **used alone**

10. <u>Our</u> cat show will be a great success. **before a noun**

B *Write the possessive pronoun that correctly completes each sentence.*

1. **Her** tabby cat has a yellow coat with dark stripes. (Her, Hers)

2. **My** cat weighs 23 pounds. (My, Mine)

3. Tails help cats keep **their** balance. (their, theirs)

4. One of the winning cats is **hers**. (her, hers)

5. **Its** hair is short and curly. (It, Its)

6. The longhaired white cat is **ours**. (our, ours)

7. Which cat is **yours**? (your, yours)

8. **Your** Maine Coon cat is larger than most. (Your, Yours)

9. The 20-year-old cat is **mine**. (my, mine)

10. The final decision is **theirs**. (their, theirs)

11. I admire **its** independence and curiosity. (it, its)

12. Look at the painting of **our** cats. (our, ours)

C *Sue wrote this report about a cat show she went to. She made seven mistakes using possessive pronouns. Use the proofreading marks in the box to correct the mistakes.*

Remember

The possessive pronouns *my, your, his, her, its, our,* and *their* are used before a noun. The possessive pronouns *mine, yours, his, hers, ours,* and *theirs* stand alone.

I have a tabby cat named Ali and a Persian cat named Timtam. Last week, I entered Timtam in a cat show. Timtam is a large male whose fur is long and shiny. Ali is a female, and ~~hers~~ her fur has dark stripes. "~~Ours~~ Our two cats are beautiful, but Timtam is the more unusual of the two," I told ~~mine~~ my mother.

I carried Timtam to the show in a cat carrier. I had lined its sides with light blue silk to make Timtam look even better. At the show, my eyes widened, and ~~mine~~ my mouth fell open. I had never seen so many cats!

"Is this cat ~~your~~ yours?" a judge asked me. "Yes, Timtam is mine," I replied. The judges studied Timtam carefully. Then they moved on to the other cats.

Timtam won a blue ribbon! I laughed and said to Timtam, "This is ~~yours~~ your ribbon, but in a way, it's ~~my~~ mine, too. After all, we worked together to win it!"

Proofreading Marks

∧	Add
⊙	Period
ℓ	Take out
≡	Capital letter
/	Small letter

Did you correct seven possessive pronouns?

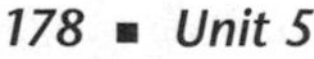

WRITE

D *Read each short description, and imagine the scene. Then write two sentences to tell more about what is happening. Use a possessive pronoun in each sentence. The first one is done for you.*

Answers will vary. Sample answers are given.

1. Two cats are asleep on a sofa.

The cats sleep in their favorite place.

Each cat enjoys its nap.

2. A girl is brushing the long hair of a cat.

The girl is slowly brushing her cat.

The cat loves its owner.

3. Two judges are awarding a ribbon to a prize-winning cat. The cat's owners are standing nearby.

The judges have made their decision.

The owners are proud of their cat.

4. A boy pulls a piece of string to play with a pet cat.

The boy has fun playing with his cat.

The cat enjoys their game.

5. A mother cat washes the small kittens.

The mother cat keeps her kittens clean.

The kittens stay close to their mother.

6. A cat watches while a woman opens a can.

The woman is getting ready to feed her cat.

The cat is waiting for its dinner.

CCSS Language 1f. (See pp. T6–7.)

Proofreading Checklist ☑

☐ ***Did you use the correct possessive pronoun in each sentence?***

Lesson 40: Relative Pronouns and Relative Adverbs

LEARN

- **In a complex sentence, the second idea is related to the first idea. Sometimes the second idea is introduced by a relative pronoun. The relative pronoun relates the two ideas, linking the second idea to a noun in the first idea.**
  - Abbey is the girl **who** is on our swim team.
  - She is the person **that** brought the team to victory.
  - The swim cap **which** (or **that**) she lost has red and white stripes.
  - This is the team **whose** coach was honored.
  - He is the coach **whom** we met last year.

When talking about people, use *who, whom,* or *that.* When talking about things, use *that* or *which.* To show who something belongs or relates to, use *whose.*

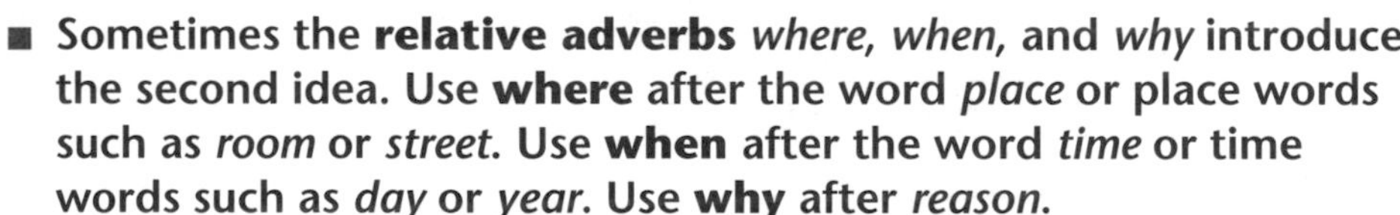

- **Sometimes the relative adverbs *where, when,* and *why* introduce the second idea. Use where after the word *place* or place words such as *room* or *street.* Use when after the word *time* or time words such as *day* or *year.* Use why after *reason.***
  - This is the pool **where** the team practices.
  - There was a time **when** we practiced outdoors.
  - There is no reason **why** we can't try again.

PRACTICE

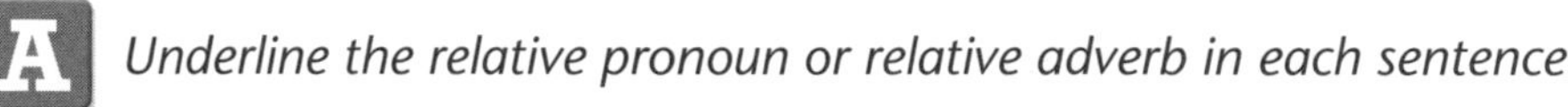

A *Underline the relative pronoun or relative adverb in each sentence.*

1. The swim meet which takes place at our school is always the most thrilling!
2. The swimming events are the only ones that take place indoors.
3. I found the lane where my relay partner was warming up.

 CCSS Language 1a. (See pp. T6–7.)

PRACTICE A *continued*

4. Angela is the girl with whom I swim in the relay race.

5. There is a good reason why the other team arrived so late.

6. The first race starts at 1 P.M. when everyone is on her mark.

7. The judge who explains the rules was one of the coaches last year.

8. The team that gets the most points will go to the state championships.

9. The team whose mascot is a dolphin won the most medals.

10. We will get our medals tomorrow when we have our team dinner.

B *Write the relative pronoun or relative adverb in parentheses that correctly completes each sentence.*

1. Olympic athletes are the people ___**whom**___ I look up to the most. (which, whom)

2. Kim is the girl ___**whose**___ parents were both Olympic swimmers. (who, whose)

3. She trains at the sports arena ___**which**___ has an Olympic size swimming pool. (which, who)

4. Roberto is the young man ___**who**___ beat the state record for the 50-meter butterfly. (which, who)

5. The butterfly is a stroke ___**that**___ may seem difficult at first. (that, whom)

6. The lake near my house is ___**where**___ Roberto learned to swim. (when, where)

7. Roberto joined the Men's U.S. Olympic team the year ___**when**___ it won six gold medals. (when, why)

8. His dream of becoming an Olympic champion is the reason ___**why**___ he practices so much. (where, why)

CCSS Language 1a. (See pp. T6–7.)

C *Here is a description of a baseball game played at a sports festival. Write a relative pronoun or relative adverb from the box to complete each sentence.*

who	when	whose	why
that	where	which	whom

Remember

Use the relative pronouns *who, whom,* or *that* when talking about people. Use *that* or *which* when talking about things. Use *whose* to show who something belongs to. Use the relative adverbs *where* after place words, *when* after time words, and *why* after the word *reason.*

For the first game of the season, the Jonestown Lions played the Smithfield Tigers. The Tigers were the team **who *or* that** won the district championship last year. Its players are the best in the league.

The game started and the Lions were the first to bat. Lucas is the team's star batter **whose** arms are so strong he can knock the ball out of the park. On the first pitch, he hit the ball long and hard. As he slid into home, the umpire called, "Out!"

Lucas asked him for the reason **why** he had made that call. The umpire said the left fielder had caught the ball the moment **when** Lucas began his slide into home. Lucas could not believe it.

In disbelief, Lucas went back to the dugout **where** his team was sitting. It was a call **which *or* that** no one would forget. It was still a close game **which *or* that** ended with the Lions' first win over the Tigers!

CCSS Language 1a. (See pp. T6–7.)

WRITE

You can combine two related sentences with a relative pronoun or relative adverb. When you combine sentences in this way, you avoid repeating words.

The Red Rockets is a soccer team. The soccer team participated in the South Shore tournament.
The Red Rockets is the soccer team **that** participated in the South Shore tournament.

My dad drove me to the soccer field. My team was getting ready for the game there.
My dad drove me to the soccer field **where** my team was getting ready for the game.

D *Read each pair of sentences. Use the relative pronoun or relative adverb in parentheses to combine the sentences. Write the new sentence on the line.*

1. We spotted the player. We admire her the most. (whom) ____________

We spotted the player whom we admire the most.

2. Rachel is the new player. She joined our team last weekend. (who) ____________

Rachel is the new player who joined our team last weekend.

3. Mr. Arnold is the coach. His job is to improve our soccer skills. (whose) ____________

Mr. Arnold is the coach whose job is to improve our soccer skills.

4. Dribbling is a skill. It requires a lot of practice. (that) ____________

Dribbling is a skill that requires a lot of practice.

5. No one knows the reason. The referee cancelled the game. (why) ____________

No one knows the reason why the referee cancelled the game.

6. Frosty's is the ice cream shop. My team goes there after every game. (where) ____________

Frosty's is the ice cream shop where my team goes after every game.

CCSS Language 1a. (See pp. T6–7.)

Lesson 41: Contractions with Pronouns

LEARN

- A **contraction** is made by joining two words together. An apostrophe (’) takes the place of any letters that are left out.

Many contractions are formed by joining a pronoun and a verb.

Pronoun and Verb	Contraction	Pronoun and Verb	Contraction
I am	**I’m**	I have	**I’ve**
she is	**she’s**	she has	**she’s**
it is	**it’s**	it has	**it’s**
you are	**you’re**	you have	**you’ve**
they are	**they’re**	they have	**they’ve**
I will	**I’ll**	I had	**I’d**
you will	**you’ll**	you had	**you’d**
we will	**we’ll**	we had	**we’d**
they will	**they’ll**	they had	**they’d**

- Be especially careful when you use the contractions *he’s, she’s,* and *it’s*. The contractions for *he, she,* and *it* and the verbs *is* and *has* are the same.

It is time to go home.
It’s time to go home.

I think **he is** the best writer.
I think **he’s** the best writer.

It has been a busy day.
It’s been a busy day.

We know that **he has** won the prize.
We know that **he’s** won the prize.

PRACTICE

A *Write the contraction for each pair of words.*

1. I am ___I’m___

2. you will ___you’ll___

3. he is ___he’s___

4. we are ___we’re___

5. they had ___they’d___

6. I have ___I’ve___

PRACTICE A *continued*

7. they are they're
8. she has she's
9. we had we'd
10. it has it's

B *Read each sentence. Replace the pronoun and verb in* ***boldface*** *with a contraction.*

1. **I am** Becky's friend. I'm
2. **You are** Becky's friend, too. You're
3. **She is** at the National Spelling Bee in Washington, D.C. She's
4. **We will** meet her at the airport when she returns. We'll
5. **She has** never been to Washington, D.C. She's
6. **You have** visited many times. You've
7. **You will** have plenty to talk about. You'll
8. **It is** the day of Becky's flight. It's
9. **We had** better hurry, or we will be late. We'd
10. I wish **I had** checked the schedule earlier. I'd
11. I hope **she will** arrive late. she'll
12. **It has** taken us an hour to get to the airport. It's
13. **They are** Becky's mom and dad. They're
14. I think **he is** Becky's brother. he's
15. I see that **we are** not late after all. we're

Remember

An apostrophe (') takes the place of the letter or letters that are left out of a contraction.

C *A group of students collected these sayings and bits of advice from their friends and family members. While listing the sayings, they made eight mistakes when using contractions. Use the proofreading marks in the box to correct the errors.*

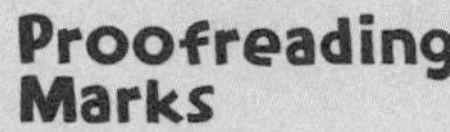

Proofreading Marks

^	Add
⊙	Period
℘/	Take out
≡	Capital letter
/	Small letter

- It's called common sense, but ~~its~~ it's always very rare.
- If you don't believe in something, ~~youll~~ you'll fall for anything.
- ~~Hed~~ He'd tried to have it both ways and ended up with neither.
- Fish don't get caught if ~~theyve~~ they've kept their mouths shut.
- We'll have to break some eggs to make an omelet.
- ~~Id~~ I'd rather wear out than rust.
- If you nurse your troubles, ~~theyll~~ they'll only grow larger.
- It's better to give than to receive.
- ~~Your'e~~ You're going to catch more flies with honey than with vinegar.
- Teach people to fish, and ~~theyr'e~~ they're fed for a lifetime.

Did you correct eight contractions?

Write Your Own

WRITE

D *Imagine that you are writing an ad for a new laundry detergent called Supersuds. Write some sentences that might appear in your ad. In each sentence, include the contraction in parentheses. The first one is done for you.*

Answers will vary. Suggested answers are given.

1. (it's) *It's the best laundry detergent ever!*

2. (she's) **My mom says she's never going to use any other detergent.**

3. (we've) **We've never seen clothes so clean.**

4. (I've) **I've been amazed by its cleaning power.**

5. (they've) **My friends say they've never seen such clean clothes.**

6. (you'll) **You'll want to try it right away.**

7. (I'm) **I'm a big fan of Supersuds.**

8. (you're) **You're sure to love it as much as I do.**

Now imagine that you are a scientist writing a review of Supersuds for a newspaper. How might the sentences you write for the review be different from the sentences above? Discuss this question with your classmates.

Possible answer: The sentences would include more scientific information and facts about Supersuds.

CCSS Language 1f, 3c. (See pp. T6–7.)

Proofreading Checklist ☑

- ❑ ***Did you use a contraction in each sentence you wrote?***
- ❑ ***Did you spell each contraction correctly?***

Unit 5 Review
Lessons 35–41

Subject Pronouns (pp. 160–163) *Write the subject pronoun in each sentence.*

1. I have two friends who are unable to hear. I

2. They communicate with American Sign Language. They

3. It is also known as ASL. It

4. We speak this language together. We

Pronoun-Verb Agreement (pp. 164–167) *Underline the verb in parentheses that correctly completes each sentence.*

5. I (practice, practices) the ASL finger alphabet with Terry.

6. We (spell, spells) our names.

7. She (teach, teaches) me with the help of a chart.

8. It (show, shows) all the letters.

Object Pronouns (pp. 168–171) *Write the object pronoun in each sentence.*

9. Sign language helps us in many ways. us

10. It helps my friends talk to me. me

11. I can tell them jokes using ASL. them

12. We wouldn't communicate as well without it. it

Using *I* and *Me* (pp. 172–175) *Underline the word or words in parentheses that correctly complete each sentence.*

13. Jim and (I, me) know some Braille.

14. Grandma taught my cousin and (I, me) about this writing system.

15. Grandma showed her Braille writer to (me and Jim, Jim and me).

16. (Jim and I, Jim and me) like to use this machine sometimes.

Possessive Pronouns (pp. 176–179) *Write the possessive pronoun in each sentence.*

17. Louis Braille invented his famous alphabet in 1829. his

18. Blind readers use their fingers to read raised dots on paper. their

19. Each group of dots has its own meaning. its

20. Is this Braille book yours? yours

Relative Pronouns and Relative Adverbs (pp. 180–183) *Write the relative pronoun or relative adverb in parentheses that correctly completes each sentence.*

21. Mr. Niles is the school custodian whose job it is to post all Braille signs. (who, whose)

22. The new elevator at the school is the place where a Braille sign was just posted. (when, where)

23. Our teacher purchased a Braille labeler last year when the class started to learn about Braille. (when, why)

24. Helen Keller is a well-known person who raised money for the blind. (whom, who)

Contractions with Pronouns (pp. 184–187) *Read each sentence. Write a contraction for the pronoun and verb in* ***boldface****.*

25. They have put the chart of Braille letters on the wall. They've

26. He is touching the dots with his finger. He's

27. I think **it is** the letter *a*. it's

28. She has found the dots for the word *hello*. She's

Unit 5 Test

DIRECTIONS *Fill in the circle next to the sentence that shows the correct spelling and use of pronouns, verbs, adverbs, and contractions.*

1. ○ Me and my cousins visit Grandpa every summer.
   ○ We sees something new every time we go there.
   ○ He take us to the aquarium.
   ● We're amazed by the size of the huge tanks.

2. ○ Derek and me hurry to the penguin exhibit.
   ○ It's always been ours favorite.
   ● "The penguins missed you," Grandpa says.
   ○ "Your favorite visitors are here!" he tell the penguins.

3. ● My cousin Olivia calls to Derek and me.
   ○ Shes' in a hurry to see the walruses.
   ○ "Weve looked at penguins long enough," she says.
   ○ She want to see something else.

4. ○ We reads a sign about one walrus.
   ○ Look at the walrus who tusks are 39 inches long.
   ○ It weigh over a ton.
   ● It's able to float on a chunk of ice.

5. ○ Grandpa shows my cousins and I the octopus exhibit.
   ○ He'is as excited as we are.
   ○ I watches the biggest one for a long time.
   ● It moves its eight arms gracefully.

6. ○ "Well visit the sea otters next," Olivia says.
   ○ The otters are cleaning theirs fur.
   ○ We watches them for several minutes.
   ● Then it's time to move on.

7. ○ Me and the others walk through the jellyfish room.
   ○ We talks about their colors and movements.
   ● My cousins and I are fascinated by them.
   ○ They swims and drifts in their tank.

8. ○ We hurries outside to the dolphin area.
   ○ That is the place who we most want to visit.
   ○ They is up to their usual tricks.
   ● All of us love these amazing mammals.

DIRECTIONS *Read the paragraph, and look carefully at each underlined part. Fill in the circle next to the answer choice that shows the correct use and spelling of pronouns, verbs, and contractions. If the underlined part is already correct, fill in the circle for "Correct as is."*

The dolphins in the show at the aquarium are bottle-nosed dolphins. They're gray in color. Theirs stomachs (9) are a lighter gray, and their backs are a darker gray. One of the dolphins seems to smile at my cousin and me (10). Its not really smiling, but it's mouth (11) looks like a smile. All of a sudden, it leaps out of the water. It snatch (12) a fish from the trainer and swims away. What a show! Youre sure to have the time of your life (13) at the aquarium. My family and me did! (14)

9. ● They're gray in color. Their stomachs
   ○ Theyre gray in color. Their stomachs
   ○ Theyre gray in color. Theirs stomachs
   ○ Correct as is

10. ○ at me and my cousin
   ○ at my cousin and I
   ○ at I and my cousin
   ● Correct as is

11. ● It's not really smiling, but its mouth
   ○ It's not really smiling, but it's mouth
   ○ Its not really smiling, but its mouth
   ○ Correct as is

12. ○ it leap out of the water. It snatch
   ● it leaps out of the water. It snatches
   ○ it leap out of the water. It snatches
   ○ Correct as is

13. ○ Youre sure to have the time of yours life
   ○ You're sure to have the time of yours life
   ● You're sure to have the time of your life
   ○ Correct as is

14. ○ Me and my family did
   ○ I and my family did
   ● My family and I did
   ○ Correct as is

Lesson 42: Writing Sentences Correctly

LEARN

- **When you write, you must show where each sentence begins and ends.**

Begin every sentence with a capital letter, and end every sentence with a punctuation mark. The end punctuation you use depends on the kind of sentence you write.

Scientist installing part of an earthquake warning system

- **End a declarative sentence with a period (.).**
  About a million earthquakes occur each year.
- **End an interrogative sentence with a question mark (?).**
  Are there really that many?
- **End an exclamatory sentence with an exclamation mark (!).**
  What a huge number that is!
- **End an imperative sentence with a period (.).**
  Read this article about earthquakes.

- **When you rewrite a run-on sentence as two separate sentences, be sure to use capital letters and end punctuation marks correctly.**

RUN-ON	Can earthquakes be predicted scientists are working on a warning system.
CORRECTED SENTENCE	Can earthquakes be predicted? Scientists are working on a warning system.

PRACTICE

A *Read each item. Write **correct** or **incorrect** to tell whether the sentence or sentences are written correctly.*

1. Most earthquakes occur under the sea. How lucky that is! ____correct____

2. Why do you say that ____incorrect____

CCSS Language 1f, 2a, 3b. (See pp. T6–7.)

PRACTICE A *continued*

3. most underwater earthquakes are never even noticed **incorrect**

4. Large underwater earthquakes can cause tsunamis
The results can be very dangerous **incorrect**

5. What is a *tsunami*? It's a Japanese word for a huge wave. **correct**

6. all earthquakes occur along fault lines in the earth's crust **incorrect**

7. Have you ever felt an earthquake usually the ground
shakes gently. **incorrect**

8. Large earthquakes make loud, rumbling noises. **correct**

9. most earthquakes last less than a minute **incorrect**

10. Smaller aftershocks can rattle for days afterward. **correct**

B

Write these sentences correctly. Use capital letters and the correct end punctuation marks. Write each run-on sentence as two sentences.

1. scientists use the Richter scale to measure the strength of earthquakes
Scientists use the Richter scale to measure the strength of earthquakes.

2. look at this chart of measurements the scale goes from 0 to 10
Look at this chart of measurements. The scale goes from 0 to 10.

3. earthquakes below 5 usually don't cause much damage
Earthquakes below 5 usually don't cause much damage.

4. do you see the 9.5 on the chart
Do you see the 9.5 on the chart?

5. that is the measurement for the biggest earthquake ever the earthquake occurred in Chile in 1960 **That is the measurement for the biggest earthquake ever.**
The earthquake occurred in Chile in 1960.

C *Melissa wrote this report about the San Francisco earthquake. Four sentences in the report are missing capital letters. Eight sentences are missing end marks. Find the mistakes, and use the proofreading marks in the box to correct them.*

Remember

Begin every sentence with a capital letter. Use the correct end punctuation for each of the four kinds of sentences.

On April 18, 1906, the sun had just risen most people in San Francisco were asleep. Some were getting ready for work.

Suddenly a loud roar filled the air. The ground was shaking, and buildings and power lines were falling. What was happening A huge earthquake was tearing the city apart.

Gas poured out of broken gas lines. Fires broke out everywhere How disastrous they would be Why weren't the fires put out The water lines had broken, too.

After three days, the fires were finally out the shaking had stopped, too. Over 25,000 buildings had fallen. about 490 city blocks had been destroyed.

What lessons did people learn from this disaster? They learned to build stronger buildings they decided to use more flexible pipes, too. What a difference these changes would make in the future

Proofreading Marks

^	Add
⊙	Period
ℓ	Take out
≡	Capital letter
/	Small letter

Did you correct four mistakes in capitalization and eight mistakes in end punctuation?

San Francisco, 1906

CCSS Language 1f, 2a, 3b. (See pp. T6–7.)

Revising Sentences

WRITE

D *Read each explanation below about earthquake safety. Then write a statement, command, exclamation, or question you might say to respond to each explanation. The word in parentheses tells you what kind of sentence to write. The first one is done for you.*

Answers will vary. Sample answers are given.

1. Earthquakes can be dangerous. Fortunately, there are some important steps you can take to reduce the danger. (question)

What steps can I take to reduce the danger?

2. Identify the "danger zones" in your house. These include areas with windows, tall furniture, and heavy objects. These things are dangerous during an earthquake. (exclamation)

Wow, I didn't think household things could be dangerous!

3. You should be aware of safe spots, such as a sturdy desk or table, in a room. They provide cover from falling objects. (question)

Is a chair a safe spot?

4. If you are outside, move away from tall buildings and power lines. If possible, go to an open space or park. (command)

Tell me where else I might go.

5. Most people will never experience a serious earthquake. Still, it's a good idea to be prepared. (statement)

I will tell my family about how to prepare for an earthquake.

CCSS Language 1f, 2a, 3a, 3b. (See pp. T6–7.)

Lesson 43: Capitalizing Proper Nouns

LEARN

A **proper noun** names a specific person, place, or thing. Each important word in a proper noun begins with a capital letter.

- The names of people, pets, and special groups always begin with a capital letter.
  Darren **S**mith　　**S**parky　　**L**ittle **L**eague
- The names of special places begin with a capital letter.
  Elm **S**treet　　**O**verton **P**ark　　**C**anada
  Detroit　　**N**ew **M**exico　　**M**ills **E**lementary **S**chool
- The names of days, months, and holidays begin with a capital letter.
  Tuesday　　**N**ovember　　**E**lection **D**ay
- Family titles that refer to specific people begin with a capital letter.
  Grandma　　**U**ncle **D**ave　　**A**unt **S**ue
- Titles of respect that are used with names begin with a capital letter.
  Mr. **L**una　　**M**s. **E**lkins　　**M**ayor **Q**uinn　　**P**resident **R**oosevelt

PRACTICE

A *In each sentence, underline the noun or nouns that should begin with a capital letter. A sentence may have one, two, or three proper nouns.*

1. The last monday in may is memorial day.
2. People from maine to california honor those who gave their lives for our country.
3. The holiday began in 1866 in waterloo, new york.
4. At that time, it was called decoration day.
5. Different states celebrated this holiday in april, may, and june.
6. In 1971, memorial day became a legal holiday throughout the united states.
7. This year, dennis and I marched with the cub scouts in a parade.

CCSS Language 2a. (See pp. T6–7.)

8. The parade began at lakehurst elementary school.

9. It ended on main street.

10. Ms. hernandez led the band, and mayor dixon gave a speech.

B *Rewrite each sentence. Capitalize each proper noun correctly.*

1. The fourteenth day of june is called flag day.
The fourteenth day of June is called Flag Day.

2. On that day in 1777, our country's leaders met in philadelphia and adopted the first flag. **On that day in 1777, our country's leaders met in Philadelphia and adopted the first flag.**

3. In 1885, a teacher named bernard cigrand suggested a holiday called flag birthday. **In 1885, a teacher named Bernard Cigrand suggested a holiday called Flag Birthday.**

4. President harry truman made flag day an official holiday in 1949.
President Harry Truman made Flag Day an official holiday in 1949.

5. We celebrate a different national holiday in july.
We celebrate a different national holiday in July.

6. The holiday is called independence day.
The holiday is called Independence Day.

7. Our country declared its freedom from great britain on july 4, 1776.
Our country declared its freedom from Great Britain on July 4, 1776.

C *Mitchell wrote this report about Labor Day. He forgot to capitalize seven proper nouns, and he capitalized one common noun by mistake. Use the proofreading marks in the box to correct the errors.*

Remember

A **proper noun** names a specific person, place, or thing. Begin each important word in a proper noun with a capital letter.

Proofreading Marks

^	Add
⊙	Period
⸚	Take out
≡	Capital letter
/	Small letter

Many holidays honor famous leaders such as abraham Lincoln and Martin Luther King, Jr. The first monday in September, however, honors ordinary working people.

How did this Holiday begin? Two hard-working men get the credit. One was a carpenter in New York. The other was a machine operator in Paterson, new Jersey. Both men wanted everyone to appreciate how hard some people work. In september 1882, they organized a big parade for workers in New York city.

The idea of honoring workers caught on. In 1887, Oregon was the first state to make Labor Day a holiday. In 1894, president Grover Cleveland made it a national holiday. Other countries have similar holidays. In Australia, people celebrate Eight Hour Day. It honors the successful struggle for a shorter working day. In most of the world, a workers' holiday is celebrated on the first day in may.

Did you correct eight mistakes in capitalization?

 CCSS Language 2a. (See pp. T6–7.)

WRITE

D *Think about the holidays listed below. Write a few sentences to explain why we celebrate each holiday. Tell how you might celebrate the holiday at school or at home. Use proper nouns in your sentences.*

Answers will vary.

1. Martin Luther King, Jr., Day ______

2. President's Day ______

3. Thanksgiving ______

4. New Year's Eve ______

CCSS Language 1f, 2a; Writing 2, 4. (See pp. T6–7.)

Proofreading Checklist ☑

- ❑ *Did you use proper nouns in your sentences?*
- ❑ *Did you begin each important word in a proper noun with a capital letter?*

Lesson 44: Abbreviations

LEARN

- An **abbreviation** is a short way of writing a word. Many abbreviations begin with a capital letter and end with a period. Here are some of them.

Titles of Respect

Ms. Margaret Wong **Mr.** Alberto Mador **Dr.** Susan Lewis

Addresses

St. (Street) **Ave.** (Avenue) **Rd.** (Road)
Blvd. (Boulevard) **Rte.** (Route) **P.O.** (Post Office)

Months and Days of the Week

May, June, and *July* do not have abbreviations.

Jan. Feb. Mar. Apr. Aug. Sept. Oct. Nov. Dec.
Sun. Mon. Tues. Wed. Thurs. Fri. Sat.

- An **initial** is used in place of a name. It is written as a capital letter followed by a period.

Kim Ann Chin **John Edward** Murphy
Kim A. Chin **J. E.** Murphy

- State names that are used with ZIP codes have special two-letter abbreviations. Both letters are capitalized, and no period is used.

AL (Alabama) **CA** (California)

PRACTICE

A *Write each name or abbreviation correctly.*

1. Jan 11 Jan. 11
2. dr ellen rossi Dr. Ellen Rossi
3. 201 Milton ave. 201 Milton Ave.
4. Feb 21, 2013 Feb. 21, 2013
5. rte. 202 Rte. 202
6. Elm st Elm St.
7. mon Mon.
8. mr L M Kent Mr. L. M. Kent
9. Oakland, ca Oakland, CA
10. PO. Box 112 P.O. Box 112

CCSS Language 2a. (See pp. T6–7.)

B *Read each item below. Follow the directions in parentheses to change it. Use capital letters and periods correctly.*

1.	Joan Richards	**J. Richards** (Change the first name to an initial.)
2.	863 Clayton Avenue	**863 Clayton Ave.** (Use an abbreviation.)
3.	27 Red Rock Boulevard	**27 Red Rock Blvd.** (Use an abbreviation.)
4.	Saturday, March 5	**Sat., Mar. 5** (Use two abbreviations.)
5.	Ms. June Marie Garcia	**Ms. J. M. Garcia** (Change the first and middle names to initials.)
6.	Mobile, Alabama 36601	**Mobile, AL 36601** (Use an abbreviation.)
7.	Post Office Box 1413	**P.O. Box 1413** (Use an abbreviation.)
8.	Closed: Saturday, Sunday, and Monday	**Closed: Sat., Sun., and Mon.** (Use three abbreviations.)
9.	192 Village Road	**192 Village Rd.** (Use an abbreviation.)
10.	Doctor Makara Bel Singh	**Dr. M. B. Singh** (Use an abbreviation and two initials.)

Remember

Most abbreviations begin with a capital letter and end with a period.

C *Look at the items below. In each one, some of the abbreviations are written incorrectly. In two of the items, the initials are also written incorrectly. Altogether, there are eleven errors. Use the proofreading marks in the box to correct the errors.*

Proofreading Marks

^	Add
⊙	Period
ℓ	Take out
≡	Capital letter
/	Small letter

1.

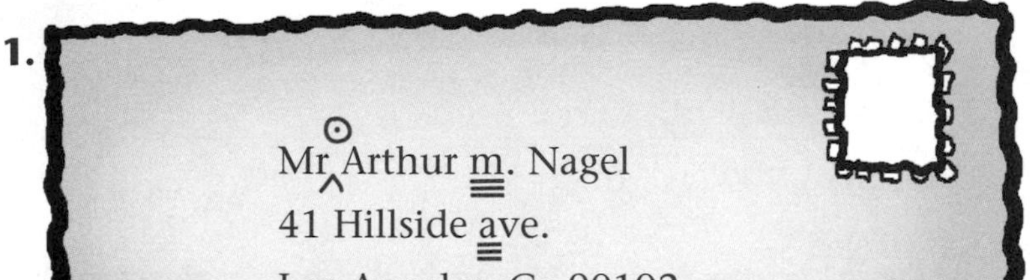

2.

3.

4.

Welcome to the Ellen S King Library

Library Hours: Mon — Thurs. 9–5

fri. — Sat. 9–4

Closed Sun.

5.

Date Apr 14

For Sally

Josh called.

Message Don't forget to bring your rock collection to school on tues.

Did you correct a total of eleven mistakes?

CCSS Language 2a. (See pp. T6–7.)

WRITE

D *Imagine that a cousin named Jackie is visiting you. You took each telephone message described below for her. Fill in the message pad with the missing information. Use abbreviations whenever possible. Part of the first one is done for you.*
Answers may vary. Sample answers are given.

1. Doctor Clement's office called on August 24 to ask if Jackie can change her dental appointment from August 31 to September 1 at 10 o'clock.

Date Aug. 24

For Jackie

Dr. Clement's office called.

Message **Can you change your appointment from Aug. 31 to Sept. 1 at 10 o'clock?**

2. Jackie's friend Anna called on August 25. She wants to know if Jackie can come to a book club meeting this Thursday at 4:30 at the Gomez's house at 240 Kent Road.

Date **Aug. 25**

For **Jackie**

Anna called.

Message **Can you come to a book club meeting this Thurs. at 4:30? It's at the Gomez's house at 240 Kent Rd.**

Proofreading Checklist ☑

- ❑ *Did you begin each abbreviation with a capital letter?*
- ❑ *Did you end each abbreviation with a period?*

Lesson 45: Titles

LEARN

- Titles of books, magazines, and newspapers are set off by italics in printed material. When you write by hand, underline these titles.

PRINTED	*Middletown News* **(newspaper)**
HANDWRITTEN	Middletown News
PRINTED	*James and the Giant Peach* **(book)**
HANDWRITTEN	James and the Giant Peach

- Titles of songs and most poems are set off by quotation marks.

"Home on the Range" **(song)** "The Farmer in the Dell" **(song)**
"Casey at the Bat" **(poem)** "What Is Pink?" **(poem)**

- Notice that the first word and each important word in the titles begin with a capital letter. Words such as *a, an, at, and, by, for, in, of, on, the, to,* and *with* are not capitalized unless they are the first or last word in the title.

PRACTICE

A *Write each title correctly.*

1. elmsford journal (newspaper) — Elmsford Journal
2. highlights for children (magazine) — Highlights for Children
3. the sound of music (song) — "The Sound of Music"
4. my side of the mountain (book) — My Side of the Mountain
5. paul revere's ride (poem) — "Paul Revere's Ride"
6. a bicycle built for two (song) — "A Bicycle Built for Two"
7. who has seen the wind? (poem) — "Who Has Seen the Wind?"
8. national geographic for kids (magazine) — National Geographic for Kids

CCSS Language 2a. (See pp. T6–7.)

PRACTICE **A** *continued*

9. the adventures of Tom Sawyer (book) <u>The Adventures of Tom Sawyer</u>

10. hudson valley news (newspaper) <u>Hudson Valley News</u>

B *Write the title in each sentence on the line. Capitalize each title. Also underline or add quotation marks to set off the title.*

1. I just read this month's sports illustrated for kids.

   <u>**Sports Illustrated for Kids**</u>

2. oodles of noodles is a funny poem.

   "Oodles of Noodles"

3. We sang I've been working on the railroad in music class.

   "I've Been Working on the Railroad"

4. A mouse acts bravely in the book mrs. frisby and the rats of NIMH.

   <u>**Mrs. Frisby and the Rats of NIMH**</u>

5. If you like funny books about school, read amber brown is not a crayon.

   <u>**Amber Brown Is Not a Crayon**</u>

6. your big backyard is a magazine for very young readers.

   <u>**Your Big Backyard**</u>

7. There was an old man with a beard is a short and funny poem.

   "There Was an Old Man with a Beard"

8. The magazine stone soup publishes stories by children.

   <u>**Stone Soup**</u>

9. The fans sang happy days are here again at the end of the game.

   "Happy Days Are Here Again"

C *Alexander wrote this review of the school talent show. He made seven mistakes when writing titles. Use the proofreading marks in the box to correct the errors.*

Remember

Capitalize the first word and each important word in a title. Do not capitalize words such as *a, an, at, and, by, for, in, of, on, the, to,* and *with* unless they begin or end the title.

Proofreading Marks

^	Add
⊙	Period
ℓ/	Take out
≡	Capital letter
/	Small letter

Did you ever wonder if the students in our school are talented? Last night's talent show proved that we are.

Dylan got the show off to a great start! He played "on the Sunny Side of the Street" on the trumpet. Terry played "Sandpipers on the beach" on the flute. The sad, beautiful sound of her instrument filled the auditorium. Finally, Roxanne's fiddle version of "Turkey In the Straw" had us tapping our feet.

A few students read aloud. Jacob had memorized the poem "Stopping by Woods on a Snowy Evening" by Robert Frost. Maya read a funny passage from her favorite book, Alice's Adventures in Wonderland.

The singers were great, too. Patrick sang "Give My Regards To Broadway." Gina also did a great job. She sang "my Favorite Things" while playing a guitar.

All in all, it was a great show. I don't think anyone can say that our students lack talent.

Look Back **Did you correct seven mistakes in the titles?**

 CCSS Language 2a. (See pp. T6–7.)

WRITE

D *Read each description of a make-believe book, song, or poem. Then make up a title for it. Write your title on the line. The first one is done for you.*

Answers will vary. Sample answers are given.

1. a poem about a boy who likes to climb trees with his cat

"Up in the Branches"

2. a song about paddling a canoe on a river

"Paddling on the Big River"

3. a magazine for children who like to collect stamps and coins

Stamps and Coins for Kids

4. a book about two identical twins who play tricks on their classmates

Double Trouble

5. a poem about the start of a new school year

"What Will Happen in the Year Ahead?"

6. a magazine for people who want to help and protect endangered animals

Wildlife Watch

7. a song about a big family get-together in the summer

"The Big, Big Picnic"

8. a book about an immigrant family coming to the United States in 1900

They Came to America

9. a poem about a snowstorm that drops two feet of snow on your neighborhood

"Today Is a Snow Day!"

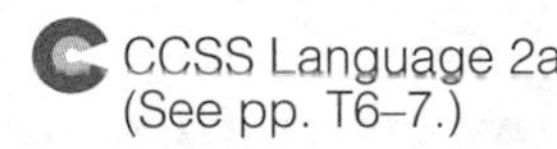

Proofreading Checklist ☑

- ❑ *Did you begin the first word in each title with a capital letter?*
- ❑ *Did you begin each important word in a title with a capital letter?*

Lesson 46: **Commas in a Series**

LEARN

A comma separates words or ideas in a sentence and tells the reader when to pause.

Sometimes a sentence has a series, or list, of three or more items. Use a comma to separate the items in a series.

Our **teachers, parents, and classmates** planned a field day.

The event took place on a **beautiful, warm, sunny** Saturday.

I brought **sunglasses, a hat, and some sunscreen**.

To get to the park, many people **walked, biked, or drove**.

Do not use a comma after the last word in the series.

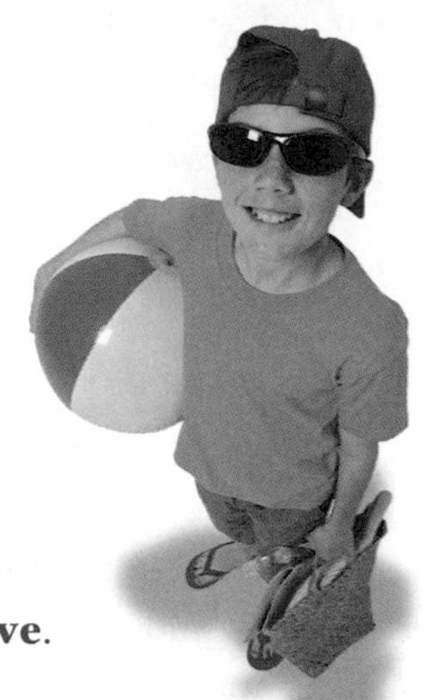

PRACTICE

A *In each sentence, the items in a series are in* ***boldface****. Add commas to separate the items.*

1. Parents organized **races, contests, and activities**.
2. People played **softball, volleyball, and basketball**.
3. I **pitched, batted, and scored** in the softball game.
4. **Friends, relatives, and pets** sat nearby and watched us play.
5. **Jess, Mario, and Kate** hit home runs.
6. For lunch, my Dad grilled the **hamburgers, hot dogs, and ribs**.
7. I put **lettuce, tomato, and ketchup** on my hamburger.
8. The ribs tasted **hot, spicy, and delicious**.
9. Everyone **gnawed, nibbled, munched, and crunched** corn on the cob.
10. For dessert, we ate **big, ripe, juicy** peaches.

B *Underline the items in a series in each sentence. Then add commas to separate the items.*

1. At the field day, the fishing contest was for parents, teachers, and students.
2. Blue, red, and yellow ribbons had been prepared for the winners.
3. I had brought my rod, tackle, and bait.
4. I hummed, whistled, and waited for a bite.
5. I caught a small, wet, wiggly trout right away.
6. It had a blue, green, and silver back.
7. Next, I hooked two sunfish, a catfish, and a crab.
8. I threw them back, and they flopped, splashed, and swam toward the rock.
9. My rod suddenly twitched, jerked, and pulled.
10. I had hooked a big, strong, lively bass!
11. I tugged, strained, and reeled it in.
12. Parents, students, and the judge gathered around.
13. No one else had caught such a big, healthy, beautiful bass.
14. I didn't want to carry, clean, and cook it.
15. Everyone cheered, clapped, and shouted when I let it go.

C *Paula saw this list of rules at the park. The list contains twelve mistakes in the use of commas in a series. Some commas were left out, and some appear where they don't belong. Use the proofreading marks in the box to correct the errors.*

Remember
Use a comma to separate three or more items in a series.

Proofreading Marks

^	Add
⊙	Period
ℓ	Take out
≡	Capital letter
/	Small letter

PARK RULES

- The trees shrubs and wildflowers in this park are protected. Visitors should not cut, damage or remove any plant.
- The hunting trapping or harming of animals is forbidden. Fishing in the pond and streams is permitted.
- Walking jogging, and bicycling are permitted, on park trails.
- Horseback riding is permitted on marked trails. Visitors should not lead, ride or walk a horse in other areas of the park.
- No one is permitted to sell, food, drinks, or other items in the park.
- Park fireplaces stoves and grills may be used in picnic areas. No one is permitted to light build, or maintain a fire in other areas of the park.

Did you correct twelve mistakes in the use of commas in a series?

Combining Sentences

WRITE

Additional Resources at grammarworkshop.com

Sometimes you can use a series to combine short, choppy sentences to make your writing smoother. The underlined words in each sentence below tell what games the children played. You can put the words in a series to make one smooth sentence.

The young children played tag.
They played hopscotch.
They played dodgeball.

The young children played tag, hopscotch, **and** dodgeball.

You can also put groups of words in a series.

The parents grilled hamburgers.
They made fruit salad.
The parents poured water for everyone.

The parents grilled hamburgers, made fruit salad, **and** poured water for everyone.

D *Rewrite the underlined sentences in this journal entry on the lines below. Combine each group of underlined sentences into one sentence by using a series.*

I wasn't looking forward to the class trip to the park. Now I'm glad I went. The trip was fun. It was interesting. The trip was educational.

I liked the nature walk best. Along the way, I saw a red-tailed hawk. I saw a Baltimore oriole. I saw a scarlet tanager. I was also surprised by how many different trees grow in the park. Chestnut trees grow in the park. Walnut trees grow there. Pecan trees grow in the park, too.

Back at the picnic tables, we had some more fun. Everyone gathered around Ms. Grady, our teacher. Ms. Grady handed out songbooks. She played the guitar. She led a sing-along. What a great way to end the day!

The trip was fun, interesting, and educational.

Along the way, I saw a red-tailed hawk, a Baltimore oriole, and a scarlet tanager.

Chestnut trees, walnut trees, and pecan trees grow in the park.

Ms. Grady handed out songbooks, played the guitar, and led a sing-along.

Lesson 47: More Commas

LEARN

Here are some more uses for commas.

- Use a comma to set off an introductory word such as *yes, no,* or *well* from the rest of a sentence.
  Yes, I have some silly riddles to tell.
  No, not everyone likes them.
  Well, I think they're funny.

- Use a comma or commas to set off the name of a person being spoken to.
  - If the name is at the beginning of the sentence, place a comma after the name.
    Todd, what gets wet the more you dry?

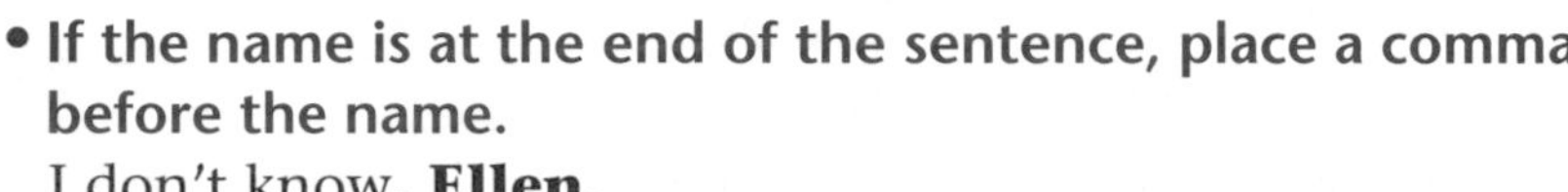

  - If the name is at the end of the sentence, place a comma before the name.
    I don't know**, Ellen.**
  - If the name is in the middle of the sentence, place commas before and after the name.
    The answer**, Todd,** is a bath towel!

PRACTICE

A *Read each sentence. Write* **introductory word** *or* **name of person spoken to** *in order to tell what words are set off by the comma or commas.*

1. Michelle, do you know what gets bigger the more you take away from it? **name of person spoken to**
2. No, I can't imagine what it could be. **introductory word**
3. The answer, Michelle, is a hole in the ground. **name of person spoken to**
4. What crosses the country without moving, Tino? **name of person spoken to**
5. Jodi, is this another silly riddle? **name of person spoken to**
6. Yes, and the answer is a superhighway. **introductory word**

PRACTICE **A** *continued*

7. Avi, what breaks whenever you say it? — **name of person spoken to**

8. Hmm, I have no idea. — **introductory word**

9. I think, Brenda, that the answer is "silence." — **name of person spoken to**

10. That is the correct answer, Tom! — **name of person spoken to**

B *In each sentence, add commas where they are needed. The first one is done for you.*

1. Do you know a place,Bob,where you can always find happiness?
2. Well,let me think about that.
3. Ray,is the answer "the dictionary"?
4. Yes,you got it!
5. What coat is always wet when you put it on,Nancy?
6. Hmm,I think it's a coat of paint.
7. What is lighter than a feather,Sandy,but harder to hold?
8. Hmm,could it be "a thought"?
9. No,the answer is "your breath"!
10. Okay,I have one for you.
11. Pam,what's the difference between the North Pole and the South Pole?
12. It's all the difference in the world,Ben!
13. You've heard,Terri,that two's company and three's a crowd.
14. Well,do you know what four and five are?
15. Yes,I know that four and five are nine!

C *Leanne left out nine commas in the script that she wrote for the class comedy show. Find the mistakes, and use the proofreading marks in the box to correct the errors.*

Remember

Use a comma after introductory words such as *yes* and *no*. Also, use a comma to set off the name of a person being spoken to.

Proofreading Marks

^	Add
⊙	Period
ℓ/	Take out
≡	Capital letter
/	Small letter

Leanne	Akira, I hear things are looking up for your mom at work.
Akira	Yes, that's true. She just got a job as an astronomer.
Jamie	Hmm, I thought she was a weather forecaster on TV, Akira.
Akira	No, not anymore, Jamie. The weather here never agreed with her!
Jamie	Guys, my poor dad finds things really dull at his job.
Leanne	What kind of work does he do, Jamie?
Jamie	Oh, he's a knife sharpener.
Leanne	My dad is a jeweler. He sells watches all day.
Akira	That's funny, Leanne. My uncle watches cells all day. He works in a biology laboratory.
Jamie	I hear, Akira, that you want to be a pilot someday.
Akira	Yes, it's the type of job in which you can go really far! What about you, Jamie?
Jamie	Well, I'm thinking about becoming a roofer. That way, I can go straight to the top!

Did you add nine missing commas?

WRITE

D *On the lines below, write your own funny script that shows a conversation between you and one or two friends. You can use jokes you know or a funny conversation you have heard for ideas. In your script, use introductory words and the names of people being spoken to. Use the script on page 214 as a model.* **Answers will vary.**

1. ______________ ______________________________

____

____

2. ______________ ______________________________

____

____

3. ______________ ______________________________

____

____

4. ______________ ______________________________

____

____

5. ______________ ______________________________

____

____

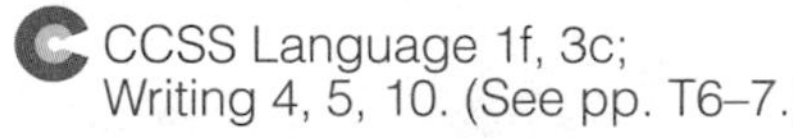
CCSS Language 1f, 3c; Writing 4, 5, 10. (See pp. T6–7.)

Proofreading Checklist ☑

- ❑ *Did you use commas after introductory words such as* ***yes***, ***no***, *and* ***well***?
- ❑ *Did you use commas to set off the names of people being spoken to?*

Lesson 48: Parts of a Letter

LEARN

- A **friendly letter** is written to someone you know well. In a friendly letter, the **greeting** and **closing** begin with a capital letter and end with a comma. Commas are also used in the **heading** to separate the city and state and to separate the day and year.

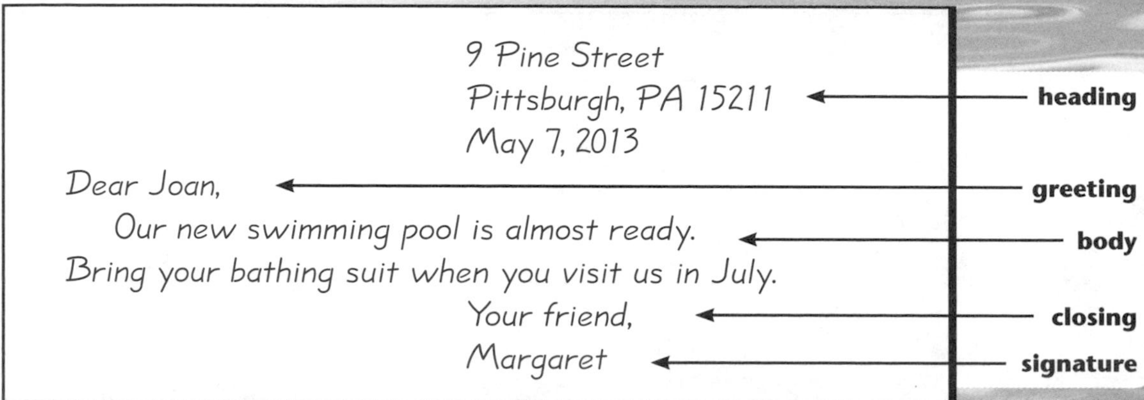

9 Pine Street
Pittsburgh, PA 15211
May 7, 2013

Dear Joan,

Our new swimming pool is almost ready. Bring your bathing suit when you visit us in July.

Your friend,
Margaret

- A **business letter** is usually written to someone you don't know. In a business letter, include an **inside address** that gives the name and address of the person you are writing to. Use a **colon (:)** after the **greeting**. You will also need to sign and print your name.

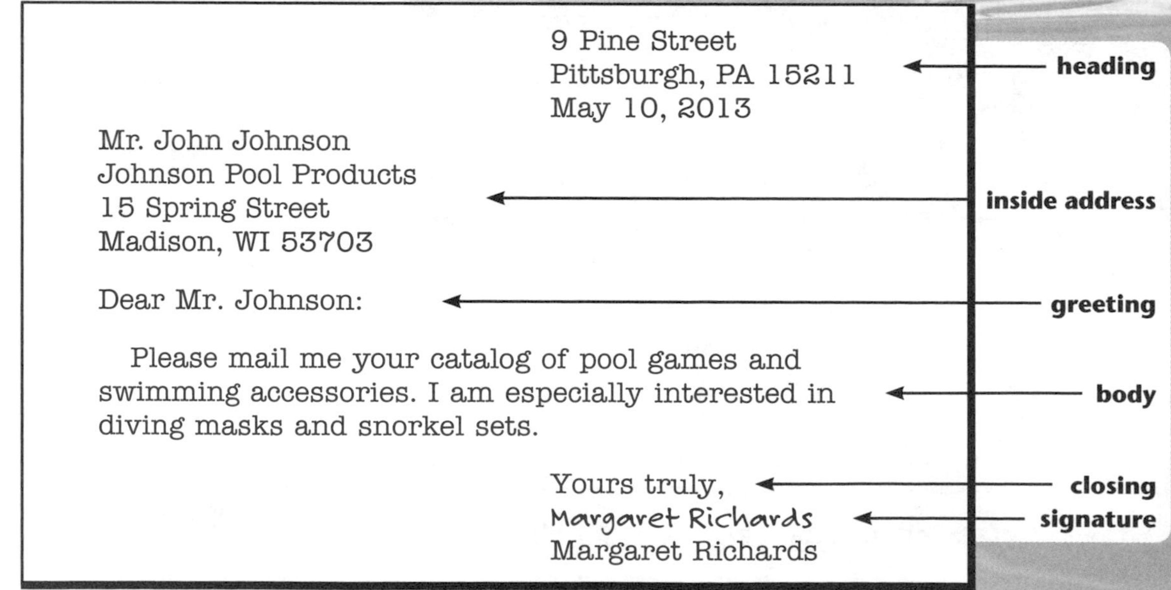

9 Pine Street
Pittsburgh, PA 15211
May 10, 2013

Mr. John Johnson
Johnson Pool Products
15 Spring Street
Madison, WI 53703

Dear Mr. Johnson:

Please mail me your catalog of pool games and swimming accessories. I am especially interested in diving masks and snorkel sets.

Yours truly,
Margaret Richards
Margaret Richards

CCSS Language 2a. (See pp. T6–7.)

PRACTICE

A *Write each letter part correctly.*

1. June, 17 2013 — June 17, 2013
2. Akron OH, 44319 — Akron, OH 44319
3. dear kenny — Dear Kenny,
4. your Friend — Your friend,
5. dear Ms. Cahill — Dear Ms. Cahill:
6. 21 fox lane — 21 Fox Lane

B *Complete the letter with the missing letter part. Write the letter part correctly.*

Gillette NJ 07933	184 ridge Road
your friend	dear margaret

184 Ridge Road
Gillette, NJ 07933
June 15, 2013

Dear Margaret,

I'm sorry to hear about the leak in your new pool. I hope the pool company can fix it soon. I know the whole family is looking forward to using it this summer.

I can't wait to see you in July. We have so much to catch up on.

Your friend,
Joan

C *Margaret wrote this letter. In all, she made six mistakes in the use of capitalization and punctuation. Use the proofreading marks in the box to correct the errors.*

Remember
Use a comma after the greeting in a friendly letter. Use a colon after the greeting in a business letter.

Proofreading Marks

^	Add
⊙	Period
ℓ/	Take out
≡	Capital letter
/	Small letter

9 Pine Street
Pittsburgh, pa 15211
June 28 2013

Ms. Tonya Ruiz
Community Park Recreation Center
111 Kensington Avenue
Pittsburgh PA 15211

Dear Ms. Ruiz

I heard that you will be offering swimming lessons for children under the age of 12 this summer. I am very interested in your swimming program. Please send me a schedule for these lessons.

sincerely Yours,
Margaret Richards
Margaret Richards

Did you correct six mistakes in capitalization and punctuation?

  CCSS Language 2a. (See pp. T6–7.)

WRITE

D *Write a friendly letter or a business letter. If you write a friendly letter, tell a friend or relative what you like most about school this year. If you write a business letter, make a suggestion to the principal of your school for a program or activity that your school might offer.*
Answers will vary.

CCSS Language 1f, 2a; Writing 4, 10. (See pp. T6–7.)

Proofreading Checklist ✓

- ❑ *Did you use commas and capital letters correctly in your letter?*
- ❑ *Did you use a comma after the greeting if you wrote a friendly letter?*
- ❑ *Did you use a colon after the greeting if you wrote a business letter?*

Lesson 49: Quotations

LEARN

- A **quotation** is a speaker's or writer's exact words. Follow these rules when writing quotations.
  - Use quotation marks in *dialogue* or to set off a speaker's or writer's exact words. Always capitalize the first word of a quotation.

    Nancy said, **"L**ittle inventions make life easier."
  - When a quotation comes at the end of a sentence, use a comma before the quotation to separate it from the words that name the speaker or writer. Put the end mark inside the quotation marks.

    Cy exclaimed**,** "How clever some inventors are**!**"
  - When a quotation that is a statement or command comes at the beginning of a sentence, put a comma inside the closing quotation marks.

    "Harvey Kennedy invented shoelaces**,"** Nancy said.
    "Try living without them**,"** she added.
  - If the quotation is a question or an exclamation, put the question mark or the exclamation mark inside the closing quotation marks.

    "Who invented the toothpaste tube**?"** Liam asked.
    "What a great invention that was**!"** I exclaimed.

- Do not use quotation marks when you do not use a speaker's or writer's exact words.

  Nancy said, "Let's look up the inventor's name."
  Nancy said that we should look up the inventor's name.

PRACTICE

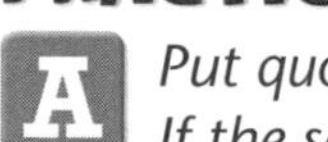

Put quotation marks around each speaker's or writer's exact words. If the sentence does not give the exact words, do not add quotation marks.

1. Terry claimed that the best inventions are very simple.
2. Liam said, "Look at this picture of Benjamin Franklin."

CCSS Language 2a, 2b. (See pp. T6–7.)

PRACTICE A *continued*

3. "He invented the lightning rod!" Liam shouted.

4. "How did he get the idea for it?" Amy asked.

5. Liam said that Franklin wanted to protect buildings from lightning.

6. Mei said, "Here's a picture of the first paper clip."

7. I asked, "When was it invented?"

8. "It was invented in 1899 in Norway," Mei replied.

9. Nancy added that paper clips, tape, and ballpoint pens were all great inventions.

10. "Where would we be without them?" she asked.

B *Rewrite each sentence that is incorrectly written. Use quotation marks, capital letters, and punctuation marks correctly. If a sentence is correct as is, write* ***correct****.*

1. The traffic light was invented in 1923 Liam said. ________________

   "The traffic light was invented in 1923," Liam said.

2. Who invented it asked Mei. ________________

   "Who invented it?" asked Mei.

3. Liam replied that the inventor was Garrett Morgan. ________________

   correct

4. Nancy said here's an 1883 picture of the first zipper. ________________

   Nancy said, "Here's an 1883 picture of the first zipper."

5. Terry asked how did it get its name? ________________

   Terry asked, "How did it get its name?"

6. Nancy explained that the invention made a *z-z-zip* sound. ________________

   correct

C *Read the conversation below. In it, there are nine mistakes in the use of capital letters, commas, quotation marks, and end marks. Use the proofreading marks in the box to correct the errors.*

Remember

Use quotation marks around the exact words of a speaker.

Proofreading Marks

^	Add
⊙	Period
✓	Take out
≡	Capital letter
/	Small letter

Terry asked "Are all inventors geniuses?"

Amy responded, "no, I don't think so." She added that some inventors just see a need for a new product and work hard to fill it.

"Other inventors have a sudden, bright idea," Mei added.

"According to this book, some important inventions were accidents" Nancy exclaimed.

Cy remarked, I once had a good idea for making adjustable training wheels for my bike"

Terry asked, "Did you do anything with your idea?

"No, I wasn't sure how to go about it" Cy replied.

Nancy said, "I'd like to be an inventor someday."

Mei said, "there's no time like the present."

"What do you mean" asked Nancy.

"I mean we could form our own club for young inventors," Mei responded.

Did you correct nine mistakes in punctuation and capitalization?

CCSS Language 2a, 2b. (See pp. T6–7.)

Additional Resources at grammarworkshop.com

WRITE

D *Imagine you are one of the students in the conversations below. Join each conversation by asking a question, making a statement, giving a command, or uttering an exclamation. Use quotation marks to set off your words.*

Answers will vary. Sample answers are given.

Conversation 1

"I have a great idea for an invention," Terry said.

"It's an electric sweater," she added.

"How would it work?" asked Cy.

"A battery would warm up the wires in the sleeves," Terry replied.

"I don't think that's very practical!" Liam exclaimed.

"How could it be washed safely?" I asked.

Conversation 2

"Inventors need to patent their inventions," said Mr. Rossi, a local inventor.

"What's a patent?" Liam asked.

"It protects an inventor's ideas," Mei explained.

"It also makes it possible for an inventor to earn money from an invention," Mr. Rossi added.

"Please tell us more about patents," I said.

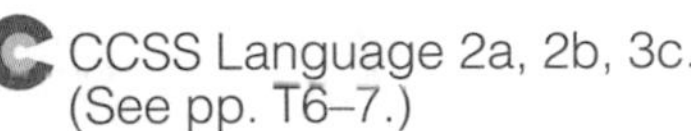

CCSS Language 2a, 2b, 3c.
(See pp. T6–7.)

Proofreading Checklist ☑

- ❑ *Did you set off your words with quotation marks?*
- ❑ *Did you use capital letters, commas, quotation marks, and end marks correctly?*

Lesson 50: Words Often Misspelled

LEARN

- **Homophones** are words that sound the same but have different spellings and meanings. Some homophones are possessive pronouns, such as *their*, and others are contractions, such as *they're*. Think about the meaning of the word to help you choose the correct spelling.

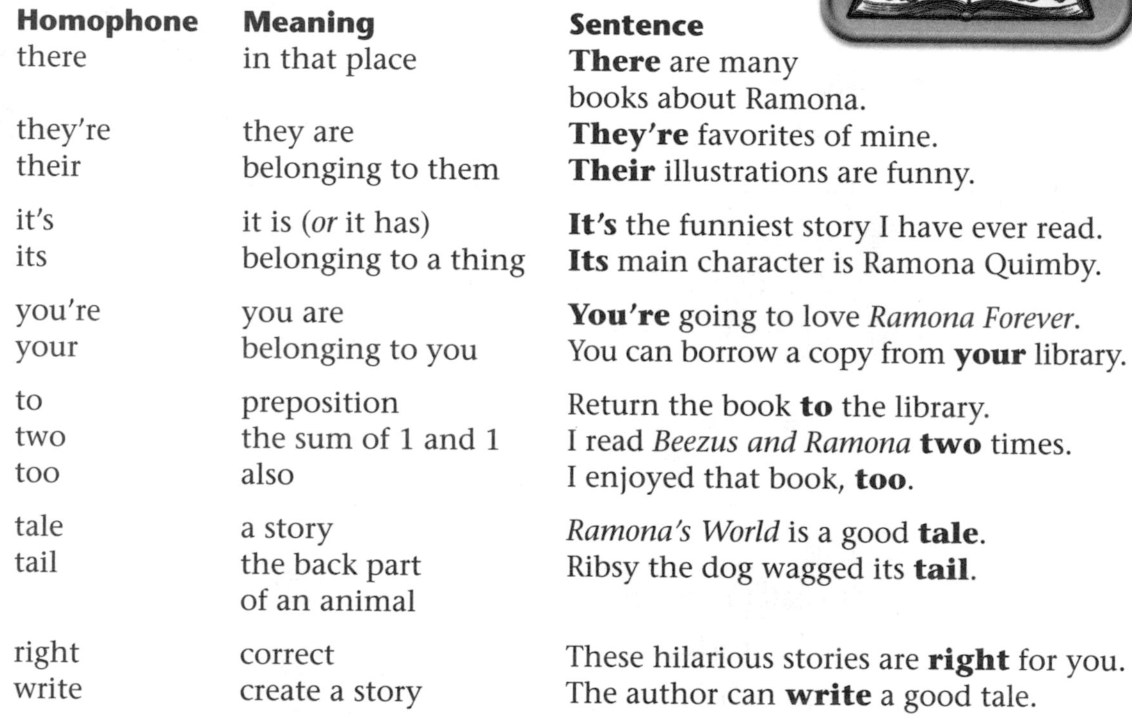

Homophone	Meaning	Sentence
there	in that place	**There** are many books about Ramona.
they're	they are	**They're** favorites of mine.
their	belonging to them	**Their** illustrations are funny.
it's	it is (*or* it has)	**It's** the funniest story I have ever read.
its	belonging to a thing	**Its** main character is Ramona Quimby.
you're	you are	**You're** going to love *Ramona Forever*.
your	belonging to you	You can borrow a copy from **your** library.
to	preposition	Return the book **to** the library.
two	the sum of 1 and 1	I read *Beezus and Ramona* **two** times.
too	also	I enjoyed that book, **too**.
tale	a story	*Ramona's World* is a good **tale**.
tail	the back part of an animal	Ribsy the dog wagged its **tail**.
right	correct	These hilarious stories are **right** for you.
write	create a story	The author can **write** a good tale.

- **When unsure which spelling is correct, use a dictionary.**

PRACTICE

A *Write the meaning of each homophone. Then write **contraction** if the homophone is a contraction. Write **possessive pronoun** if it is a possessive pronoun. If it is neither, write **neither**. The first one is done for you.*

1. their ___belonging to them___ ___possessive pronoun___
2. they're ___**they are**___ ___**contraction**___
3. there ___**in that place**___ ___**neither**___

CCSS Language 1g, 2d. (See pp. T6–7.)

PRACTICE **A** *continued*

4. its	belonging to a thing	possessive pronoun
5. right	correct	neither
6. you're	you are	contraction
7. tail	the back of an animal	neither
8. too	also	neither

B *Write the homophone in parentheses that correctly completes each sentence.*

1. Will you bring your copy of *Ramona's World* ___to___ school? (to, too)

2. ___It's___ a popular book among young readers. (Its, It's)

3. Beverly Cleary is ___its___ author. (its, it's)

4. She grew up in Oregon, and her stories are set ___there___. (their, there)

5. I have read ___two___ of her books. (two, too)

6. You are ___right___ about her books. (right, write)

7. It may even make you want to ___write___ your own Ramona adventure. (right, write)

8. You might enjoy a book called *Henry and Ribsy,* ___too___. (to, too)

9. It is a ___tale___ about Henry Huggins and his dog Ribsy. (tale, tail)

10. ___Their___ neighborhood was once a quiet place. (There, Their)

11. ___It's___ up to Henry and Ribsy to change that! (Its, It's)

12. ___You're___ sure to love Beverly Cleary's books. (Your, You're)

CCSS Language 1g, 2d. (See pp. T6–7.)

C *Maria wrote this book report. She made six mistakes when using homophones. Use the proofreading marks in the box to correct the errors.*

Remember

When using homophones, pay attention to the way they are used. For example, *they're, it's,* and *you're* are contractions, while *their, its,* and *your* are possessive pronouns that show ownership.

<u>Ramona's World</u> by Beverly Cleary is a very funny book. ~~Its~~ It's a story about the kind of everyday events all of us can recognize. ~~There~~ They're told in such a humorous way that they cause everyone ~~too~~ to laugh.

When the book begins, it is the first day of school. Ramona is looking forward to an exciting year, but there are a few problems, ~~two~~ too. Ramona's teacher likes her first essay, but it's filled with misspelled words. When the teacher begins to ~~right~~ write the mistakes on the board, Ramona is horrified.

On the bright side, Ramona and Daisy Kidd become friends. One day, they're playing in an upstairs crawl space. Its floor is only a layer of plaster, and Ramona's legs break through the attic. Is she hurt? Are you curious? Read the book. ~~Your~~ You're sure to enjoy it.

Proofreading Marks

^	Add
⊙	Period
℘	Take out
≡	Capital letter
/	Small letter

Did you correct six spelling mistakes?

CCSS Language 1g, 2d. (See pp. T6–7.)

WRITE

D *Write a short book report about a book you've enjoyed recently. Be sure to give the title and author of the book. Then give your opinion about the book. Tell why you think your classmates might enjoy the book, too. Use some of the homophones below in your report.*

it's	its	you're	your	they're
there	their	to	too	two
right	write	tail	tale	

Answers may vary. A sample answer is given.

One of my favorite adventure stories is a tale about animals by Beverly Cleary. It is titled *The Mouse and the Motorcycle.* In the story, a little mouse and a boy live in a hotel. The two meet and have several adventures. The book is filled with action that will keep you turning pages. The best part is that it's very funny, too! I recommend this book to everyone because it's a tale that anyone can enjoy. It's not every day that a boy becomes friends with a mouse. Ralph, the mouse, loves to ride his motorcycle. When he does, his tail waves in the wind. He has to make sure he goes in the right direction. Once the vacuum almost sucked Ralph up! Beverly Cleary has written three books about Ralph. So if you like this one, there are more!

CCSS Language 1g, 2d; Writing 1, 4, 10. (See pp. T6–7.)

Proofreading Checklist ☑

- ❑ *Did you use some of the homophones in your report?*
- ❑ *Did you spell each homophone correctly?*

Lesson 51: Words Often Confused

LEARN

- When two words sound alike or are similar in spelling, the two words can be confused. For example, the word *advice* is often confused with the word *advise*. To avoid confusion, learn the meaning and spelling of each word. *Advice* is helpful information you give to someone. When you *advise* someone, you give him or her a helpful suggestion.

  Our teacher gave us **advice** on ways to prepare for test day.
  He said, "I **advise** you all to stop studying tonight and to sleep well."

- If you are unsure of which word to use, you can use a dictionary.

PRACTICE

A *Match each word in Column A to its meaning in Column B. Write the letter of the correct meaning on the line. If you are unsure of the meaning, check a dictionary.*

	A	B
d	**1.** desert	**a.** the star that Earth revolves around
l	**2.** proof	**b.** more distant
j	**3.** all ready	**c.** to show that something is true
f	**4.** further	**d.** dry, sandy land
a	**5.** sun	**e.** a male child
i	**6.** by	**f.** in addition to something
c	**7.** prove	**g.** by this time
h	**8.** dessert	**h.** a sweet food served at the end of a meal
b	**9.** farther	**i.** preposition that tells who/what did the action
g	**10.** already	**j.** completely ready

CCSS Language 1g, 2d. (See pp. T6–7.)

PRACTICE A *continued*

__k__ **11.** buy

__e__ **12.** son

k. to get something by paying for it with money

l. evidence

B

Write the word in parentheses that correctly completes each sentence.

1. Today, we had to write our favorite ____**dessert**____ recipes. (desert, dessert)

2. My favorite recipe for lemon cookies was given to me ____**by**____ my great grandmother. (buy, by)

3. The first step in my recipe is to ____**buy**____ all the ingredients. (buy, by)

4. When mixing the batter, I would ____**advise**____ everyone to use a wooden spoon. (advice, advise)

5. If you want to go a step ____**further**____, try making a lemon frosting. (farther, further)

6. Today, a guest chef and his ____**son**____ came to our school. (sun, son)

7. They gave our class ____**advice**____ on how to bake bread. (advice, advise)

8. They said that the ____**proof**____ of a good baker is "in the pudding." (prove, proof)

9. It was ____**already**____ time for lunch when the chef took fresh baked bread out of the oven. (all ready, already)

10. I took a loaf of bread home to ____**prove**____ to my family that I am now a real baker! (proof, prove)

C *Raj wrote this journal entry about his art class. He made six mistakes when writing words that are often confused. Find the mistakes, and use the proofreading marks in the box to correct the errors.*

Remember
Use the word with the intended meaning. Spell the word carefully.

Today in art class, our teacher, Ms. Nova, described a scene and asked us to paint it. Before we started, we each got a piece of paper and some paints. When we were ~~already~~ all ready, she started to read the description.

Ms. Nova talked about cactuses, sand, and tumbleweed. That's when I knew she was describing a ~~dessert~~ desert. I quickly picked up my pencil and started drawing. Then I used watercolors to fill in my drawing. I had a few green cactus plants in front. ~~Further~~ Farther away were sandy, brown hills. Beyond this, I could think of nothing ~~farther~~ further to draw! That's when I asked Ms. Nova for ~~advise~~ advice. She told me to close my eyes and imagine the picture again. When I opened my eyes, I knew just what to add. I drew a bright, orange ~~son~~ sun, a scaly iguana, and a flying eagle that soared through the air. I was so happy with my colorful desert scene that I couldn't wait to take it home!

Proofreading Marks

^	Add
⊙	Period
ℓ/	Take out
≡	Capital letter
/	Small letter

Did you use the correct meaning of six words that are often confused?

CCSS Language 1g, 2d. (See pp. T6–7.)

WRITE

Write sentences about how to make or do something. Use the word in parentheses in each sentence.
Answers will vary. Sample answers are given.

1. (already) **Perhaps your family has already learned that sometimes, the goods you purchase can be damaged.**
2. (advice) **Experts offer all sorts of good advice about what to do to get your money back if this should happen to you.**
3. (sun) **However, if an item is damaged because it was left out in the hot sun or in the pouring rain, it usually cannot be returned.**
4. (proof) **You will need a proof of purchase, like a sales slip, if you want to return a product that is defective.**
5. (buy) **It is always a good idea to keep the receipts of the things that you buy, in case something is damaged and you have to return it.**
6. (further) **A further step involves carefully repacking the product, if possible, in the original carton.**
7. (all ready) **Once you have taken these steps, you are all ready to return the product.**
8. (prove) **As long as you can prove that the product was defective when you bought it, the seller should refund your money or replace the damaged goods.**

CCSS Language 1g, 2d; Writing 2. (See pp. T6–7.)

Proofreading Checklist ☑

❑ *Did you use each word in parentheses correctly?*

Unit 6 Review
Lessons 42–51

Writing Sentences Correctly (pp. 192–195) *Write each sentence correctly. Write each run-on sentence as two sentences.*

1. what sorts of things do you collect

What sorts of things do you collect?

2. we have many cards we trade them sometimes

We have many cards. We trade them sometimes.

3. what a great collection you have

What a great collection you have!

Capitalizing Proper Nouns (pp. 196–199) *Read each sentence. Write each proper noun correctly.*

4. My aunt lives near golden gate park. Golden Gate Park

5. We visited her on the fourth of july. Fourth of July

6. I gave aunt betty a small figurine of a cat. Aunt Betty

Abbreviations (pp. 200–203) *Write each name or abbreviation correctly.*

7. dr Vivian Hayes Dr. Vivian Hayes

8. thurs Thurs.

9. mr Donald a Banks Mr. Donald A. Banks

10. p o Box 124 P. O. Box 124

Titles (pp. 204–207) *Write each title correctly.*

11. the mouse and the motorcycle (book) The Mouse and the Motorcycle

12. a day at the beach (poem) "A Day at the Beach"

13. sports illustrated for kids (magazine) Sports Illustrated for Kids

Commas (pp. 208–215) *In each sentence, add commas where they are needed.*

14. My mother, father, and brother all collect things.

15. Mom, do you collect old maps?

Parts of a Letter (pp. 216–219) *Write each letter part correctly.*

16. dear Charlie	**Dear Charlie,**
17. sincerely yours	**Sincerely yours,**
18. Baltimore MD 21202	**Baltimore, MD 21202**
19. dear Mayor Hanks	**Dear Mayor Hanks:**

Quotations (pp. 220–223) *Add commas and quotation marks where necessary to show each speaker's words.*

20. Claire said, "Everyone in my family collects something except me."

21. Mimi asked, "How many miniature horses do you have on your dresser?"

22. "I guess I have a collection after all!" Claire laughed.

Words Often Misspelled (pp. 224–227) *Underline the homophone in parentheses that correctly completes each sentence.*

23. (Their, There) will be a doll auction this weekend.

24. Mia's cousin likes to attend doll auctions, (to, too).

25. (Your, You're) favorite hobby is collecting art.

26. (Its, It's) a family tradition to go to auctions every spring break.

Words Often Confused (pp. 228–231) *Underline the word in parentheses that correctly completes each sentence.*

27. A furniture collector can (prove, proof) that Fran's chair is worth a lot of money.

28. At the auction, her chair is (farther, further) down the aisle.

29. To get (advise, advice) on collecting comics, Mike spoke to an expert.

30. The annual auction was (already, all ready) closed to the public.

Unit 6 Test

DIRECTIONS *Fill in the circle next to the sentence that shows the correct use of commas, capital letters, end marks, spelling, and quotation marks.*

1. ○ This summer, I went to day Camp.
○ I went from july 15 to august 12.
● Dad drove to the Jackson Recreation Center, too.
○ He took Hyland road to Oak avenue.

2. ○ What did I like most about camp.
● Well, the counselors gave really good advice.
○ We played basketball soccer, and tennis.
○ We wrote practiced and performed our own plays.

3. ○ The camp director was Ed I Fox.
○ What a great camp director he is?
○ "Let's have another great day! he told us every morning.
● He kept everyone safe, happy, and busy.

4. ○ Ms. Tonya Gray wants prove that we are good swimmers.
● "Anyone can learn to swim," she said.
○ She took us to the pool at hillsdale Park, too.
○ We also took day trips to the zoo the museum, and a baseball game.

5. ● We had a sing-along every Friday.
○ Mr Fox played "You Are My Sunshine" on his guitar.
○ I sang "I'm Sitting On Top Of The World" for everyone.
○ "You sing well", they told me.

6. ○ Would you be surprised to hear that we read each day.
○ Ms. Nieves said "Reading will help you be ready for school."
○ "You can also read just for the fun of it" she added.
● We traded books every Wednesday.

7. ○ Some campers also go to south valley school.
○ I will look for them this fall
○ "We didn't know you last year." they told me.
● "We will now be friends at school," I replied.

8. ○ Robert, do you want to go to camp next summer.
○ Yes I'd love to!
● Friends, counselors, and teachers made camp special.
○ I want to spend July and August at green valley park!

DIRECTIONS *Read the letter, and look carefully at each underlined part. Fill in the circle next to the answer choice that shows the correct use of commas, capital letters, end marks, and quotation marks. If the underlined part is already correct, fill in the circle for "Correct as is."*

199 Crestview Avenue
Little York, IN 47139
September 14 2013 (9)

dear mr Fox (10)

I'm back in school from Monday to friday, and Summer is over. (11) Still, I think about day camp at Green Valley Park. What a great experience it was!

I told my friend Ed about camp. Now he says, "next year, I'll go with you". (12) I know he'll love the lessons, activities, and trips (13). Thank you for everything.

yours truly (14)
Robert Walker

9. ○ September, 14 2013
● September 14, 2013
○ september 14, 2013
○ Correct as is

10. ○ dear Mr Fox
○ Dear Mr. Fox
● Dear Mr. Fox,
○ Correct as is

11. ○ friday, and summer is over.
● Friday, and summer is over.
○ Friday. And Summer is over
○ Correct as is

12. ● "Next year, I'll go with you."
○ "Next year, I'll go with you".
○ "next year, I'll go with you."
○ Correct as is

13. ○ lessons activities and trips
○ lessons, activities and trips,
○ lessons, activities, and trips,
● Correct as is

14. ○ Yours truly
○ Yours Truly
● Yours truly,
○ Correct as is

INDEX

A

B

C

T

U

V

W

Y